RELIGION
and
WOMEN

McGill Studies in the History of Religions,
A Series Devoted to International Scholarship
Katherine K. Young, Editor

RELIGION
and
WOMEN

edited by
ARVIND SHARMA

introduction by
KATHERINE K. YOUNG

State University of New York Press

Published by
State University of New York Press, Albany

© 1994 State University of New York

All rights reserved

Printed in the United States of America

For information, address State University of New York Press, State
University Plaza, Albany, N.Y., 12246

Production by E. Moore
Marketing by Theresa A. Swierzowski

Library of Congress Cataloging-in-Publication Data

Religion and women / edited by Arvind Sharma ; introduction by
   Katherine K. Young.
      p.   cm. — (McGill studies in the history of religions)
   Includes bibliographical references and index.
      ISBN 0-7914-1689-5 (alk. paper). — ISBN 0-7914-1690-9 (pbk. :
alk. paper)
      1. Women and religion.   I. Sharma, Arvind.   II. Series.
BL458.R45   1993
291.1'78344—dc20   92-40320
                                                              CIP

10 9 8 7 6 5 4 3 2 1

For
Donna Runnalls
McGill's first woman Dean
and
Dean of the Faculty of Religious Studies

The knowledge that men can acquire of women is wretchedly imperfect and superficial and will always be so until women themselves have told all that they have to tell.

—John Stuart Mill (1806–1873)

CONTENTS

CONTENTS

Arvind Sharma

PREFACE

The publication of *Women in World Religions* (SUNY Press 1987)
represented an innovation. In that book seven women scholars
wrote about the position of women in seven different religions of the
world. The book was so well received that we decided to imitate
ourselves. The present volume extends the phenomenological
standpoint, with its sensitivity to the adherents' point of view, to
include a treatment by women scholars of the position of women
in Native American, African, Shinto, Jaina, Zoroastrian, Sikh, and
Baha'i faiths. It thus constitutes a companion volume to the previous work and we hope will be welcomed as such.

As the authors demonstrate so clearly in the individual chapters
and Katherine Young so visibly in her general Introduction, when it
is the question of the texture of women's experience in the religious
traditions of the world, to think of religions as different is a matter
of relative indifference, for the major themes of women's experience
often cut across them.

Katherine K. Young

INTRODUCTION

In this book, the discussion of women and religion by women scholars begun in *Women in World Religions* (SUNY 1987) is extended to more religions. That book focused on religions in societies that had undergone state formation, defined by anthropologists as large-scale or complex societies. I categorized them as (1) ethnic religions, based on a communal identity—that is, birth into a "people" defined by the ancestors, territory, and language, (2) universal/ reform religions, based on an associational identity formed by voluntary allegiance to a leader or by conversion to the founded religion, characterized by a reformed mode of life, experience, and universal salvation, and (3) nature religions, based on cosmic identity—that is, the experience of the harmony or unity of nature, the individual, and cosmos as salvific.

More religions of large-scale societies of the universal/reform type are examined in the present volume. Ketayun H. Gould examines the position of women in Zoroastrianism (originating in Iran between the fifteenth and the sixth century B.C.E.). Nalini Balbir surveys the history of women in the Śvetāmbara and Digambara sects of Jainism (starting in India about the sixth century B.C.E.). Rajkumari Shanker offers pioneering research on women in Sikhism (beginning in India in the fifteenth century C.E.). And Susan S. Maneck narrates the story of women's position in Baha'i (developing in Iran in the nineteenth century C.E.). All these religions are still living traditions; while some were more prominent in former times—Zoroastrianism, for example, was once the state religion of the Achaemenid and Sasanian dynasties of Persia—today their numbers are small (though they belong to large-scale societies) when compared to those of religions surveyed in the first volume such as Hinduism, Buddhism, Islam, and Christianity. To broaden the perspective, the present volume has included the religious orientation of a number of small-scale societies—those of hunters and gatherers and horticulturalists—from North America and Africa. Accordingly, Kathleen M. Dugan looks at women and feminine symbolism in Native American religions and Rosalind I. J. Hackett offers an overview of women in African traditional religions. Since a focus of the present volume is on changes in feminine symbolism and women's religious roles, it is important to examine the transition from small-scale to large-scale societies. In this context, Michiko Yusa's study of feminine imagery and women's ritual roles in early Shinto is particularly helpful, as is Hackett's discussion of African religions. The chapters presented here make possible three levels of generalization: *intersynchronic* (between the class of small- and large-scale religions), *intrasynchronic* (among the large-scale religions themselves), and *diachronic* (within a given religion).

Several general patterns emerge from the rich materials gathered in this volume.[1] (1) Where feminine symbolism is common in small-scale societies, as in some hunting and gathering groups and many horticultural communities, women have higher religious status—more official ritual roles and leadership positions—and higher economic and social status. The presence of feminine symbolism is not, however, universal: there is no supreme mother goddess in all small-scale societies. (2) A decrease or marginalization of feminine symbolism often occurs with a social change from matrilineality to patrilineality; an economic change from simple horticulture to plow agriculture and trade; or a political change from small-scale societies to large-scale ones involving state formation. (3) Abuses of power are very common in the transition to large-scale societies. (4) These abuses inspire reforms. General reforms and ones specifically to improve women's lives lead to an increase in feminine symbolism, ritual roles for women, and laws to safeguard their interests. (5) These reforms, however, are historically limited in duration; reform is followed by decline in times of stress. (6) When a religion has reform as part of its foundational identity, however, it is easier to institute new reforms by calling for renewal of the fundamental vision. This often happens in the modern period. But since the modern period brings in its wake new stresses, these reforms too are of limited duration in some countries.

FEMININE SYMBOLISM IN SMALL-SCALE SOCIETIES

It has been difficult to recover feminine symbolism in small-scale societies.[2] Early ethnographers neglected oral traditions, on the one hand, and larger ideological patterns, on the other, both of which reveal much about feminine symbolism and women's religious practices. Almost always men, and often Jesuits, they were oblivious to women's religion. But even if they had wanted to learn about the women's world, they would have been prevented from doing so because of the separate spheres of men and women as well as economic and ritual specialization along gender lines. Their lack of interest in female spirits and rituals was matched by native women's traditional secrecy regarding their own religious practices. While the few female ethnologists could have had access to women's spheres and secrets, they generally modeled their questions on those of their male colleagues. Today ethnography is rapidly changing as aboriginal women and female scholars document women's lives, describe traditional women's religion, and relate their observations to comparative studies. Both male and female scholars are also taking another look at the archaeological record and reexamining previous ethnographies with questions of feminine symbolism and women's lives in mind. This has led to some major scholarly debates on the historical record.

The study of North American Indian religions is benefiting from the new interest in feminine symbolism and women's religious roles. One focus of this is the mistress of animals. A mistress of animals has been associated with the renewal of the supply of game in many hunting and gathering societies. From paleolithic times, humans have contemplated the death of the animals killed in the hunt; in cave paintings they have portrayed sacred acts for the animals' appeasement, restitution, return, and multiplication. In this volume, Kathleen Dugan notes that the Sioux of North America speak of White Buffalo Calf Woman who "mysteriously appears in a time when the people are beset by hunger and without clear direction . . . ; she is associated with the generation of new sources of life." Because female figures are linked directly to regeneration and rebirth, they are linked indirectly to death, which makes rebirth necessary. Accordingly, the symbolism of the mistress of animals comes to embrace the continuity of life, death, and rebirth.

The presence of feminine symbolism in hunting and gathering societies is correlated with an egalitarian ethos. These societies have separate spheres and gender roles for men and women who are considered different but complementary and equal. Men hunt; women gather food and take care of children. Women's menstrual blood is powerful; a menstruating woman, for instance, can jeopardize the safety and effectiveness of hunters and shamans. Consequently, taboos restrict women's participation in these activities, though exceptions are sometimes made for nonreproductive women or role reversals when survival is at stake. Women also have important religious roles. Some are medicine women with a great knowledge of herbs; others are shamans with extraordinary powers who can move about in the various realms of existence, communicate with the spirits, and instruct the community. In this volume, Dugan describes their visionary quests.

Central to the discussion of feminine symbolism in native North American religions is the concept of Mother Earth. Dugan suggests, for instance, that the earth was an important feminine symbol in native North American religions. So does Jordan Paper. He observes that prehistoric images of vulvae in North American caves are similar to paleolithic ones in European caves and concludes that the cave is the vagina of the earth, the "life-giving female cosmic creator . . . the mother of all life."[3] The symbol of the vulvae, continues Paper, also appears in Ojibwe writing. In the sacred symbolism of the Sacred Pipe ritual, at least fifteen hundred years old, smoke offerings made to the directions of the cosmos include offerings to the nadir of the earth, the primary female numinous being of procreation and nurture. The earth is addressed as "Mother" or "Grandmother," as are various spirits:

> In native religious traditions from North to South America, Earth is understood as a numinous being of procreation and nurture. The details of this general understanding vary from culture to culture, subculture to subculture, but the essentials agree. From the Earth Mother's surface grow the plants essential to life and health, from clefts in her body emerge the game animals which share their life with the people, from her veins issue the life-giving fluid of water, from her cycles and those of her celestial and nighttime aspect, from Grandmother Moon, come the rhythms of women's bodies.Within Earth's narrow, dark, warm, moist crevices humans encounter her essence. Earth is the epitome of motherhood. Women mirror Earth.[4]

The feminine as earth, says Paper, is often coupled with the masculine as sun in creation stories. In some accounts, moon is the grandmother, earth the mother. According to him, North American

Indians see animals such as the bear and buffalo as manifestations of the earth. Black bears are prominent in myths not only because of their value as food but also because of their similarity to humans in diet, skeleton, ability to stand upright, and intelligence. They are identified with the earth because they hibernate within it during the winter and because the female emerges in spring from its caves with her new cubs. The female bear is a life-giving and healing spirit. Similarly, in their myth about the origin of buffalo, the Lakota describe how the buffalo were found in a hole in the ground and were driven up on the earth to become food for the people. Because of this, the spirits of the buffalo and the earth are the same.

Sam D. Gill, however, disputes this symbol of Mother Earth as an archaic and pervasive feature of native North American religions.[5] First, he finds no basis for considering Native American religions as a single tradition. He has studied the religions of many native tribes and has found a variety of female figures in myths and rituals; some are "associated with the earth, others with the sky, the sea, plants, or animals."[6]

Secondly, he finds that traditional myths and rituals do not speak of Mother Earth as a major goddess, though this image appears in later sources. He traces the latter to a commonly quoted statement attributed to Tecumseh, the Shawnee leader in 1810: "The earth is my mother and on her bosom I will repose." (Elsewhere it is reported as "the sun is my father, and the earth is my mother; she gives me nourishment, and I repose upon her bosom."[7]) This statement, which was simply about the fact that Tecumseh wanted to sit on the ground during negotiations and not in the strange chair of the white man, became part of the Tecumseh legend and entered nineteenth-century American fiction and history books. By contrast, the earliest records of Shawnee religion as reported in early ethnographies, such as Trowbridge's *Shawnese Traditions* (1824) and Morgan's *The Indian Journals* (1859–1862), show that they believe in a male supreme creator associated with celestial realms, not a goddess of the earth. By the 1930s, however, the Shawnee had come to identify their major deity who creates and oversees the world as "Our Grandmother," though she was a celestial, not an earth, creator deity.

Gill does admit that there may have been some feminine spiritual entities associated with the earth as "Earth Person," but they were by no means a major, supreme, creator figure. He then examines other references that contributed to popular literature by looking at a story of imagining America that began back in 1575. At this time, Europeans personified America as a female Indian queen—

an Amazonian with bow and arrow—in graphic and decorative
arts. By the colonial period, she was younger and less ferocious, virtually a Greek goddess; now the daughter of Britannia, the Indian
princess symbolized American liberty and held the American flag.
Gill argues that the story of the Indian princess Pocahontas was also
a tale with well-known folk motifs turned into popular fiction and
eventually into history. The story of Pocahontas first saving a white
man (Captain John Smith) and then marrying another (John Rolfe)
symbolized the union of European and native peoples. But it was
also premised on the idea that Pocahontas gave up her Indian ways;
the story thus symbolized the sacrifice or death of native cultures
and the acquisition of Christianity and "civilization." Already by
1933, Archibald MacLeish had transformed Pocahontas into the
counterpart of Ceres, Demeter, and Gaea; she was now a "fertility
goddess, an earth mother, a mother of a new race in America" who
was sacrificed:

> The statement attributed to Tecumseh and the story of Poca-
> hontas are two aspects of the same American story: the story
> of the sacrifice of the Indian in the triumph of civilization
> over savagism. This powerful story reveals the sentiments of
> Americans and their need to conceive the earth as female and
> as Indian. There is a homology between the conception of the
> earth as the mother on whose bosom (a term peculiarly prom-
> inent in all of these stories) Tecumseh and the Indians would
> prefer to rest, the sequence of images of America as female
> Indian, and the stories of Pocahontas who, in laying her
> bosom upon the head of John Smith, entered into marriage
> with Europeans and their cultivating ways. Pocahontas, the
> Indian princess, the earth mother, is mother to us all and sac-
> rificial victim to American respectability. The seeds are thus
> sown. The conception of Mother Earth in North America has
> taken place.[8]

Gill notes that the statement attributed to Tecumseh was not only
quoted by E. B. Tylor in his influential work *Primitive Culture*,
(1873), but also that Tylor used it as the lynch pin of a major theory
about the origin of religion. "The idea of the Earth as a mother is
more simple and obvious," said Tylor, "and no doubt for that reason
more common in the world, than the idea of Heaven as a father."[9]

The statement attributed to Tecumseh and the story of Pocahontas are only part of Gill's reconstruction of the history of the

earth goddess in North America. He also examines a similar history of the statement "shall I tear my mother's bosom" (about the destruction of the earth created by ploughing her fields and cutting down her forests) attributed to a Wanapum man, Smohalla, who had led a millenarian style protest, with Christian elements, against the white settlers. The change from a metaphor of the earth as feminine to a goddess was first popularized in James Mooney's monograph "The Ghost Dance Religion and Sioux Outbreak of 1890." Now Gill argues that we need corroboration for these accounts about a supreme deity who is Mother Earth from native oral traditions and rituals, but that this is not forthcoming.

More importantly, how do we account for the fact that the imagery of a mother goddess as female creator enters into native religions at this time? This occurred, Gill suggests, because of the American policy to transform native hunters into cultivators. To do this, the Indian tradition of holding the land in common had to be changed into the desire for individual property. In the northwest, native peoples rejected this demand for change. They appealed to a supreme creator who made the earth and then its people from it. From this creation account came explanations for a number of things. Natives were darker than whites because they were made from the earth. And they were more moral because as hunters, gatherers, and fishers they neither cut into the land with sharp plows nor cut down her forests. The creator told the prophets that oppressors would be killed or transformed, and that natives must maintain their protection of the land. Based on this religious authority, legal demands for inherited native rights to the land were made.[10] From the mid 1850s, native leaders spoke of the earth metaphorically: Indian culture depends on the land as a child on its mother. Gill concludes:

> Ambient imagery of non-native origin is appropriated and put to meaningful use of tribal traditions, even incorporated into oral traditions. . . . Statements about the earth that were metaphorical and political, though contained within a basically religious perspective, were consistently misinterpreted as theological. In time (not such a very long time, really), these misinterpretations were appropriated by Native Americans who transformed metaphor into divinity.[11]

This divinity was none other than Mother Earth, the supreme creator.

Gill also examines the "world-parent" cosmogony—that is, the story of how Father Sky and Mother Earth begot the world—among the horticultural tribes of the American southwest. Once again, he shows through his careful scrutiny of existing scholarship that the locus classicus of this myth, the Zuni account of creation, is really the fictional creation of Frank Hamilton Cushing. Cushing was a controversial nineteenth-century ethnologist who created a literary and imaginative synthesis out of his knowledge of Zuni culture and claimed that it was common throughout North America. These ideas were borrowed, in turn, by H. K. Haeberlin who wrote a popular monograph on the tribes of the southwest. Gill demonstrates that many tribal female figures—a mistress of the animals, a goddess of vegetation, a personification of rain, a moon goddess, and occasionally even an earth mother (though not a progenitor of creation with the sun)—have been formed into a major goddess, Mother Earth, at the hands of scholars. This was done by associating the earth, womb, water, and fertility with stories about the impregnation of a woman by the sun and accounts of the return of the dead to the underworld. When this earth goddess was associated with the sun god, the claim was made that the myth of the world-parents is characteristic of horticultural societies in general. After examining similar claims of a world-parent cosmology attributed to the Luiseno tribe of California, Gill concludes that this too is the creative rendering of a highly influential scholar, in this case, Alfred L. Kroeber. He conveniently ignored the tenuous connections to the earth and the fact that in the Luiseno myth the couple are a brother and sister, the act of begetting is by incestuous and primal rape, and the resulting order has the male dominate over the female.

This discussion of native North American religions serves as warning to be attentive to the sources; story and history, as Gill observes, are often interdependent. Stories, furthermore, may originate in different communities, be based on quite different concepts of authority (historical or ahistorical), and maintain meanings that are distinct though they significantly overlap, as did those of the European-Americans and the Native Americans. In addition, Gill reminds us of the role played by a mother goddess in theories about the origin and nature of religion. We have already encountered Tylor's contribution to the theory of an original earth mother. Because Tylor thought that the idea of earth mother was more "simple" than that of the sun god, he viewed the native Indians as primitive. (In reality, he probably worked back from the idea of the natives as primitive to the idea of the earth goddess as original.) Tylor's ideas influenced Hubert Bancroft, who also drew on Bachofen's ideas of motherright for his 1882 book *The Native Races*. And both Tylor and Bancroft influenced many historians of religions including Andrew Lang, Albrecht Dieterich, Hartley Burr Alexander, James Frazer, Frederick Heiler, Joachim Wach, Gerardus van der Leeuw, E.O. James, Raffaele Pettazzoni, and Mircea Eliade.

Let us take the example of Eliade. Eliade, says Gill, thought that the earth goddess was known to paleolithic peoples and is common even today with hunters and gatherers, though she is by no means the only deity. In his *Patterns of Comparative Religion* (1958), he bases his discussion of the original *Tellus Mater* on the Smohalla quotation cited by Mooney, suggesting that it reveals "relics of the old worship of the Earth-Mother" and that these words "come to us from very distant ages. The emotion that we feel when we hear them is our response to what they evoke with their wonderful freshness and spontaneity—the primordial image of the Earth-Mother. It is an image that we find everywhere in the world, in countless forms and varieties."[12] After establishing the ubiquitous Mother Earth, Eliade proceeds to quote from Frazer and Cushing. Gill suggests that Eliade has selected his data for structural consistencies, both his phenomenology of the earth and his idea of the cosmogonic "centre." And he notes that Eliade, like his predecessors, combines various feminine figures into one structure or deity through a chain of associations that merge all "myths dealing with Life and Death, with Creation and generation, with sexuality and voluntary sacrifice."[13] Eliade's ideas are then used by Åke Hultkrantz in his book *The Religions of the American Indians* (1979) and in his essay "The Religion of the Goddess in North America" (1983).

Gill concludes that this mother goddess must exist in the minds of these scholars before their examination of the data. They then select information to fit their preconception. This too is a story in the making. Gill's point is not to argue that there are no feminine figures or goddesses in native North American religions, but that there is no *one* goddess, much less a supreme goddess, called Mother Earth. Suspicious about how other evidence may have been ignored, he looks briefly at Hultkrantz's evidence for the earth goddess of the paleolithic hunters of Europe and northern Asia. Hultkrantz identifies some feminine figurines in ivory, bone, and stone as birth goddesses, even though their identification as deities, much less their meaning, has been very controversial. He identifies them, in turn, with the mistress of animals of today's Siberian hunters. Gill suggests that this gives Hultkrantz the great synthesis needed to gather all feminine figures into one great deity through time, though she may subsequently take other transformations. All native North American figures, for example, are identified with her from the Sioux's White Buffalo Calf Woman to the Shawnee's "Our Grandmother," to the Iroquois' corn goddesses, the Hopi's Spider Woman, and the Navajo's Changing Woman. It is no wonder, concludes Gill, that today the Hopi are doing sand paintings of Father Sky and Mother Earth.

Despite his debunking of the concept of the original and ubiquitous Mother Earth—which he charitably calls the making of a story—Gill leaves the door open to the possibility that goddesses associated with the earth and vegetation become common in horticultural religions. These goddesses, however, are multiple; they are often one among many figures and vary from group to group. Because they arise in certain historical conditions, moreover, they are historically contingent, not primordial and archetypal.

It does seem to be the case that goddesses are prevalent in horticultural societies. The Hopi, says Dugan, speak of Spider Woman who breathes life into the first man and first woman. The Seneca refer to Sky Woman who is pregnant and falls to earth; she subsequently gives birth to a daughter who then gives birth to sacred twins and they, then, give birth to all the beings of creation.

Feminine figures are also associated with vegetation. Dugan speaks of the importance of vegetation, especially corn, to southern horticulturalists in North America. With the development of horticulture, she observes, the deeply feminine aspects of native American religion emerged and took a sharper definition.[14] The Abanaki, for instance:

> Speak of First Woman who came to live with a spirit being called Kloskurbeh and a disciple. She offers them her power and love, and she and the disciple have many children. However, a famine interrupts their peace, and in the suffering that is created, First Woman begs her husband to slay her. Then she instructs him to have her body dragged through a field until all her flesh is gone. He was to bring her bones to the center of the field and let them alone for several months. When that time was over, they were to return and gather the food produced by this act. All that is accomplished is done by the power of this sacred woman and by her sacrifice. The food is the tangible sign of her love and concern, and they are reminded that they are to eat it with thankfulness and in

peaceful harmony, for thus will the love of the first mother be fulfilled.

The story of the sacrifice of a first woman to create food is extremely common among horticulturalists the world over. Other North American myths say that the origin of food (corn, squash, and beans) is a gift from a sacred woman or that corn gives rise to First Woman and First Man, and then to Changing Woman as with the Navaho.

It has been suggested that women, who collected edible plants in hunting and gathering societies, were responsible for their domestication. The discovery of this technique, with its revolutionary implications for human life, may have inspired stories of the origin of plants from a divine woman. Of course, it is also possible that older motifs of a mistress of the animals who discovers or regenerates the food supply may have inspired these accounts; plants were simply substituted for animals. Be that as it may, women in horticultural societies have had an important economic role as gardeners. Matrilocal residence (dwelling with the wife's female kin) and matrilineal succession (inheriting through the female line), common in horticultural societies, have also contributed to woman's status and power.

William Divale,[15] who combines methods of social anthropology and historical research, explains this as follows. Matrilocality was an accommodation to constant warfare.[16] When competition over land occurred because of a change in the means of production, population explosion, or migration of other groups into their territory, groups faced the choice of whether to flee or fight. Those who chose the former were relegated to marginal lands and a more harsh existence, if not extinction; those who chose the latter often prospered. Because land conflicts occurred over centuries, societies developed social structures and residence patterns to maximize their military effectiveness to gain and maintain territorial control. It was important for warriors to bond together, rather than to kin, for protection of the group. To weaken the bonds with their natal families, they had to move to other villages for marriage. And to weaken the bonds with their wives and children, they had to live in a "men's house" or spend considerable time there. Such societies were matrilocal. Over time, with the development of private property and inheritance, matrilocality developed into matrilineality. These types of residence and lineage permitted the bonding of female kin and contributed to their status in horticultural societies.

George R. Mead defines this arrangement as a matricentric family:

> A woman in occupying the structural position of wife/mother is usually the *de facto* leader of the family group, and when, the man occupying the structural position of father/husband, although the *de jure* head of the household group, is marginal to the complex of internal relationships of the group. By marginal is meant that the man associates relatively infrequently, or in a much reduced level of interaction, with the other members of the group, and is on the fringe of the effective ties which bind the group together. In other words, the paternal dyad is extremely weak, although still present, while the maternal dyad is the main cohesive force for the family group.[17]

Economic, domestic, and lineage power have sometimes been expressed politically. Iroquois women tended gardens and managed households. And they had matrilineal descent:

> Iroquoian female power was part of a centuries-old tradition . . . in which women were officially proclaimed the progenitors of the people and the owners of the land and the soil. . . . During the early Colonial period, the Iroquois could be described as matrifocal at the village level and patrifocal at the level of League and intervillage affairs. Before the establishment of the League and the tribal units that united to form the League, the Iroquois could perhaps be described as matriarchal, if this term is redefined to mean female economic and ritual centrality and not female rule.[18]

Iroquois women, moreover, could nominate and depose chiefs.[19] Along with these worldly powers, Iroquois women have had divine powers and important ritual roles.

With these aspects of horticultural societies in mind, let us think about feminine symbolism in African religions. Although scholarship on African traditional religions has focused on masculine symbolism, there is evidence of feminine symbolism in African pantheons when scholars decide to look for it. "Contrary to the pantheons constructed by most studies of African traditional religions," says Rosalind Hackett in the present volume:

> It is exciting to discover that there exist a number of female creator gods. The Uzo (or Ijo), a matrilineal people of the Ni-

ger Delta region of Nigeria, for instance, speak of God in strictly female terms. They have four principal names for the Supreme Being, namely Temearu ... "she who is the moulder of all," Ayeba ... "the foundress of the universe", Woyingi ... "Our Mother," and Oginarau, "she who dwells in the heavens." There are also references in a ritual context to Ayo, which also means "mother" and to Pere Bau, meaning "the sovereign queen."

In Africa, societies with feminine symbolism and women's rituals are often horticultural; these are located from southern Zaire to Angola in the southwest and to the coasts below the Zambesi River in the southeast. As is true of other horticultural societies, the ones in Africa exist at a subsistence level and have little political organization beyond the village level. Here too gender roles are carefully defined; women care for children and tend gardens; men focus on hunting, herding, and war.[20] These societies are often matrilocal or matrilineal. Women may be religious specialists in distinct spheres; ultimately, there is ritual complementarity, "transcending everyday hierarchical social relationships" (Hackett).

This discussion of native American Indian religions and African religions shows that there is evidence of more feminine figures in small-scale societies now that scholars have begun to examine the evidence. But as Gill's study has shown, it is important to look at the ethnographic record and to examine carefully one's own views about goddesses and the theories of religion and gender related to them. This is necessary so that one does not find goddesses where they did not exist traditionally, nor elevate them to supremacy when they did not have this position. Despite these concerns, a correlation is found between feminine religious symbolism and a comparatively high status, compared to complex societies, for women, related to religious, economic, and social roles considered vital for the horticultural community.

While feminine symbolism is common in small-scale, especially horticultural religions, it is by no means universal. Peggy Reeves Sanday, for instance, finds that gender symbolism in creation stories is related to the mode of production. Masculine origin symbolism predominates when large animals are hunted, feminine origin symbolism when small game is hunted, and couple or dual sex symbolism when both small and large game are hunted.[21] Dugan, when speaking of North American hunting and gathering tribes, observes that North American Indian tribes that hunt large buffalo have predominantly masculine images of faunal life and the sky, though they also recognize the earth, the moon, and the mistress of animals as feminine sacred symbols. Other groups have a master of animals instead of a mistress of animals. Here we are reminded of the many male deities mentioned by Gill: the great male spirit who is the creator of all and dwells in the sky, corn fathers, and male begetters, such as two brothers in the Mohave account of creation. Often the female figures are subsidiary to these male deities. And in the ritual sphere, the institutionalized aspect of religion often belongs to men; the informal, private, and domestic ones to women. Hackett warns us that much more research is needed to reconstruct the women's religious world in Africa "not just in contradistinction to, but also in interaction with, men's religious lives."

WHEN FEMININE SYMBOLISM IN SMALL-SCALE SOCIETIES DISAPPEARS

The story of the decline of feminine symbolism is sometimes described in moral terms. This is now au courant in certain feminist circles. In the beginning was the goddess, matricentric society, and a time of peace. Then men usurped power, violently displaced women, erased memory of the goddess, and ushered in a history of tyranny. This gynocentric version of the Western myth of the fall— here it is men instead of women who introduce evil and end the golden age in the garden—calls the process the "male-takeover" or the "patriarchal revolution."[22] But is there evidence for this idea of a paradise that was destroyed by men? And was the reason for changes to male symbolism and male dominance in certain sectors simply men's abuse of power over women?

Small-scale societies with feminine symbolism were not always peaceful. Many horticultural societies throughout the world, in fact, had endemic warfare.[23] Moreover, the issue of a male "takeover" is not simply a question of immoral use of power and victimization of women. On the contrary, horticultural societies had created a number of problems for men. Matrilocality and matrilineality, in that they privileged women for continuity of residence and lineage, contributed to the erosion of concepts of equality so common in hunting and gathering societies. In some arenas, women were perceived as superior in horticultural societies. Endemic warfare, which was necessary to secure lands for survival or well-being, made men extremely vulnerable and highlighted the comparative security of the women who were protected. Men's arduous initiation rites for the formation of warrior identity also highlighted how women attained their feminine identity naturally and easily through menarche. Both male risk of life through initiatory raids and subsequent warfare caused men to envy women.

Myths of matriarchy were common in many of these horticultural societies.[24] Women may not have ruled (in fact, no one did in these very decentralized societies; chiefs, if they did exist, had little authority). But women were perceived by men, and with good reason, to be comparatively powerful because of their household power, their lineage rights, their natural power to give birth, their spiritual power to regenerate life, and their ability to make the crops grow. Men projected their envy and fear onto women; central to the myths of matriarchy was the fall of women from this position of power because of some wrongdoing or incapacity and the need for men to takeover.

From this brief exposition, we understand why there was a subsequent change in social structure. The fact that men were marginalized from family life in these societies and had no intergenerational continuity in the same place may have led them to desire household and lineage continuity, hence a change to patrilocality and patrilineality. The move toward real male dominance over women, to reverse what was perceived as women's dominance, was supported by development of surplus crops and herds, trade, specialization, and booty from raids. With distribution of resources through male alliances, the invention of iron plows, control of new resources through trade, and more complex patterns of political organization, the power of some men over other men and over all women became entrenched and endemic warfare began to subside. In short, when community survival and well-being were at stake in horticultural societies, men risked their lives and submitted themselves to family marginalization in order to be good protectors and providers, for everyone, including women and children. From men's perspective, there were legitimate reasons why they wanted to change society and its symbolism. These reasons are not accounted for in the feminist reconstruction that speaks of a takeover by *immoral* men. Acknowledging some legitimate reasons for the new social changes does not mean, however, that the methods—including, in some societies, threat of rape to keep women in line—or the outcome of real male dominance, rather than restoration of equality, should not be judged for going too far.

The historical record does not always give the reasons why a change occurred. It does, however, testify to the change. Sometimes these changes occurred during state formation. At other times they occurred under the impact of colonialism, which often introduced state formation or fundamentally altered the nature of the indigenous state. To illustrate the former, let us examine a change in the Shinto religion of ancient Japan, which accompanied state formation.[25]

A Chinese reference in the *History of the Kingdom of Wei* mentions the queen Himiko (Pimiko) who ruled Yamatai (Wa), one of the Japanese islands. From the account, which describes how over one hundred male and female attendants followed her to the grave when she died, it is obvious that there had been state formation. The structure, however, was fragile. The old matrilineal pattern of the former horticultural society had continued in the tradition of female ruler. But after Himiko's death, there were attempts by men to change this to male rule. We are told, for instance, that a man established himself on the throne. The people, however, revolted; the king was assassinated and a relative of Himiko's was made queen. For some time power went back and forth between queens and kings. Jingū, for instance, ruled independently after the death of her husband. Not only was she a queen; she was also a shamaness, for she would become possessed by the sea goddess Amaterasu and give oracles. Finally, male rule was established.

Robert Ellwood[26] reconstructs ancient Japanese history from clues in the *Kojiki* and *Nihonshoki*. He thinks that changes of royal imagery, spiritual authority, and religious symbolism reflect historical changes. The royal lineage, for instance, no longer went through the female line but rather the male line. Intimacy between gods and humans declined; household shrines were needed to make the deities present within the family and female shamans to communicate with them.[27] The symbolism of the goddess Amaterasu went through a series of changes. First she became identified with the sun, and vertical or transcendent symbolism, rather than the sea, and lateral symbolism. Then Amaterasu, as the female spirit of the sea, married Yamato no Ōkunidama, the male spirit of the land. They coexisted as a female and male kami, representing heaven and earth. Later Amaterasu was banished first to a village and then to Ise on a remote peninsula. At this time, Yamato became the male supreme god. Priests and the authority of dreams replaced priestesses and the authority of shamanism and oracles.

Ellwood thinks that the Sujin/Suinin narratives, which allude to these events, reflect the emergence of a new dynasty in the late third and early fourth centuries C.E. This development may have been related to an invasion from Korea. The ruler's name, Mimaki, resembles the name of the southern tip of Korea called Mimana. The account of the mythic figure Jimmu Tenno points to an incoming prince. And a new archaeological style (Kofun or great tomb) indicates a new cultural wave. The transition was not smooth; the narratives mention confusion, epidemics, vagabondage, and rebellions. Ellwood concludes that the suppression of goddesses and priestesses of the old regime amounts to a "patriarchal revolution." More specifically, he suggests that the *Kojiki* and *Nihonshoki*, the sources of the aforementioned accounts, were compiled during a period (seventh and eighth century c.e.) when several women succeeded to the throne for lack of a male emperor. Amaterasu may have been rediscovered at this time. In the present volume, Yusa draws our attention to parallelism among the accounts of Himiko, the empress Jingū, and the queens who ruled at the time of the compilation of the texts. But according to Ellwood, even though a few queens ruled after the "patriarchal revolution," they were mere matriarchal tokens and figureheads, just as Amaterasu was in heaven; society had lost its real *female* magic, mystery, and personality. From this period, priestesses were chosen from the unmarried daughters of the emperor to officiate at Amaterasu's shrine in Ise. Because Ise was far from the capital, feminine religious leadership was marginalized.

A similar process occurred in Africa. The Asante, for example, had one of the great African kingdoms. Although the kingdom was headed by a king and male chiefs, features of their society indicated a former matrilocal and matrilineal phase. When Asante society was first described by westerners, it still had matrilineality at the village level; each chief had a senior woman who assisted him; the office of the king was inherited through the female line; both priests and priestesses officiated at all major rituals; and a sky god and earth goddess were the two major deities.[28]

The process of state formation is happening even now in Africa. Long before this actually happens, economic, religious, and political changes may be signaled by a change in symbolism. African myths themselves provide clues to the decline of feminine symbolism.[29] Here are some examples provided by Hackett. (1) Eka Abassi, which means the mother of God, was once the primordial deity of the Ibibio. She was the mother of all created things, the source of life. The myths suggest a subsequent period when she was both the mother of Obumo, the thunder god and his consort. Today, however, she is either a *deus otiosus* who cannot be mentioned or a mundane agent of fertility mandated by Abasi Ibom, now the male, supreme being, to deliver unborn babies. It is "a jealously guarded secret," notes Hackett, "that, in earlier times, it was woman, not man, who was the dominant sex . . . and source of creation." (2) Similarly, the Ewe people of the republic of Benin (formerly Dahomey) have myths that tell how the goddess Mawu created the earth but then withdrew because of trouble with men. There are no temples or worship for her. Some myths call her mother or elder but others associate her with the male god Lisa (her consort, twin, or only son). It is likely, therefore, that the early phase of the religion focused on her; the next phase associated her with male figures; and the last phase virtually displaced her by male gods. (3) Such stories are found in neighboring regions. In the Central Republic of Benin and Togo, observes Hackett, the female deity Nana buku was associated with creation; more recently, she has been paired with the male god Osha identified with Lisa. (4) In some regions of Yorubaland, a goddess ruled over both the gods and the good things of the earth at the time of creation. In other areas, a supreme pair of creators—Orisanla (or Obatala) and his wife Odudua—replaced this goddess; they, in turn, were replaced by the male god Olodumare (Olorun) and the earth goddess Onile. And, according to a secret doctrine of the Ogboni sect, the god Olodumare has now displaced the goddess Onile because he is superior to her. (5) The decline of a female creator can also be detected in the myths of the Akan of Ghana. Some stories describe how the moon goddess gave birth to the universe. But others, which associate her with the female aspect of a bisexual deity or identify her with the male deity Nyame, suggest a process of displacement. The fact that the queen of the Akan state is still ritually identified with the moon and the headwomen of the clans have her statue put on their graves—because of her power over death and rebirth symbolized by the waning and waxing moon—suggests the former supremacy of the moon goddess. (6) The goddess Idemili of the Nnobi Igbo was domesticated and transformed into the wife of the once weaker god Aho. Her cult decreased in popularity; the patriarchal ancestral cult increased in popularity.

The preceding examples suggest that an older, usually horticultural, stratum of many African cultures had a female creator. She was displaced in various ways either directly by a supreme male god or indirectly by being paired first with a male figure and eventually replaced by a supreme male deity. As a result, the archaic female creator eventually became a *deus otiosus* or a mundane fertility figure, though occasionally her significance was maintained in the rituals of royal women. Reasons for the displacement of the goddess are sometimes given in mythology. The goddess herself withdraws because of trouble with men; a god steals her superior creative and mystical powers and becomes the supreme deity; or a god takes over because she cannot keep secrets,[30] because she is unwilling to wage war, or because she destroyed paradise and introduced death.

Hackett observes that despite the great cultural diversity of the African continent, male deities now predominate. There is also an increase in male secret societies accompanied by men's ambiguity or hostility to women as "purveyors of evil and misfortune, witchcraft, polluters." This observation of more male symbolism and ritual leadership is confirmed by Marion Kilson who finds in her study of thirteen African societies mainly male supreme beings and deities in the pantheon, male ancestors in national cults, and male priests in central communal rituals. Female figures appear generally as the wives and mothers of gods. And queens, female mediums, and priests' wives are found only in lesser ritual roles.[31]

Changes to feminine symbolism happen when small-scale societies turn to plow cultivation and trade; the new mode of production makes possible permanent settlements, food surpluses, craft differentiation, and eventually state formation. State formation is also inspired by contact with neighboring states, religions such as Islam and Christianity, and international contacts. As in other parts of the world, so in Africa men do the more strenuous plow cultivation and travel, and replace matrilocal and matrilineal structures by patrilocal and patrilineal ones. With these changes, women often lose economic and social status.[32] Men view menstruation more negatively.[33] Myths describe how a woman's primordial offense led to the origin of menses, taboos, and confinement in a hut during her "impure" period. Such myths are reflected in social practice. On the death of their husbands, women are subject to lengthy rituals, seclusion, and physical ordeals in order to eliminate pollution, in effect a kind of punishment. They are also relegated to subordinate roles in public rituals. Ibibio women, for instance, once had responsibility for the burial of their dead warriors; by moving sacred boughs over the body of a deceased warrior, they extracted his virility for the community. Today this important ritual has disappeared.

Despite the new masculine symbolism and male dominance, a degree of female power and status remains. (1) In life-cycle rituals, in a submerged line of descent, or in personal rituals of status transformation, women exercise their spiritual qualities. (2) They also gain temporary power and overcome traditional male hierarchy through possession, divination, healing, and mystical knowledge. Greenbaum argues:

> Power . . . lies at the core of possession ideology. The essential trait . . . is *heteronomy:* personal powerlessness to define the authentic self. . . . Possession is therefore common and institutionalized . . . in hierarchical societies . . . ; possession trance is not merely a protest against imposed identity and oppressive power: it also ironically affirms these realities on an ultimate level, or the transcendental spirit that "possesses" one also submerges the impotent self.[34]

The Gã of Ghana may be a case in point. Hackett says "the priesthood is a kinship-ascribed male status chiefly concerned with representing humans to the gods; mediumship is an achieved female status concerned with communicating the messages of gods and humans to one another." (Of course, despite its origin in a reaction against subordination, female religious power and authority through possession are still powerful and authoritative. They attract both men and women.)

(3) Sometimes political power continues to be passed through the female line; this helps preserve some status for women. The sanctity of Lovedu, the rain queen of the Transvaal, observes Hackett, is preserved by various royal institutions and royal matrilineality; her feminine qualities of reconciliation, reciprocity, and diplomacy are highly regarded. These qualities also characterize the district heads called "mothers," even though some are now men, who mediate between the queen and her people. This helps to maintain the high status of women in an otherwise patrilineal society. (4) That traditional African societies have had distinct male and female spheres helps women to preserve power. Says Hackett, "women frequently act collectively within their own sphere, either through voluntary associations or through institutions that parallel those of men." (5) Women continue, moreover, to do much of the agricultural labor and trade; they dominate the retail food trade, for example, in West Africa. This may cause problems with men. Among the Nupe, for instance, women occupy a strong economic position as itinerant traders; because men are often indebted to or dependent on them, they fear women's secrecy, supernatural powers, knowledge, and refusal to become pregnant for professional reasons. Consequently, they often view women as witches. By contrast, women

think their secrecy is necessary for marital and social harmony. (6) Moreover, says Hackett, women who retain control of their property in marriage have economic power and more autonomy.

Though women manage to retain some power, their position has declined overall. Hackett says: some scholars attribute the decline to "a general bias towards male superiority, others to unequal access to resources, while some would point to the various cultural restrictions that may keep women subordinate, such as long puberty and mourning rites involving seclusion, menstrual and childbirth taboos, and male secret societies, which are culturally legitimated ways of suppressing women."

Finally, Hackett points to the role of colonialism in bringing about a decline in feminine symbolism and women's position in Africa: "It is generally agreed that colonialism weakened the position of African women both politically and economically, with the importation of Western culture, bureaucratic structures and military technology. It served to heighten gender stratification, adding European sexism to the patriarchal elements in indigenous cultures."

Colonialism, of course, has also been given as the reason for the decline in feminine symbolism and the position of women in North American Indian religions. According to Paper, the prevalence of feminine symbolism and the status of women in North America declined dramatically with conquest by Europeans who imposed a religion and culture with more male symbolism, exclusively male ritual roles, and real male economic dominance. The main features of this dramatic change are as follows. Because of criticism and even criminalization of their religion, natives turned this assessment negatively upon themselves and transformed it. The vocative "Grandfathers and Grandmothers" was replaced by just "Grandfathers," the concept of a male god as supreme creator was developed, and female spirits were now viewed as evil. When native religion was made illegal, all native ritual went underground, but women's fasting, puberty rituals, full moon ceremonies, and menstrual rites went even more underground, and remained unknown to ethnographers though they have continued to the present. Women's healing power, moreover, came to be viewed as sorcery.[35] Paper thinks that the feminine aspects of the tradition have disappeared because of Christian influence promoting the idea of a supreme masculine deity.

Mead has observed that capitalism, which accompanied Christianity, contributed to these changes. It broke down descent groups and caused a shift from the extended family toward the nuclear family. In matrilineal societies this strengthened the position of the father as against the mother's brother, since a man will have more loyalty to his own biological children than to his sister's.[36] Ultimately it contributed to the change from matrilocality and matrilineality to patrilocality and patrilineality. Paper points out, for example, that the change from extended to nuclear families and from matrilineality to patrilineality occurred with the European subjugation of the Creek, Cherokee, and Choctaw in America. This was accompanied by a change from hunting and fishing to agriculture (because of depletion of game and confinement on reservations). The more successful native farmers accumulated property and wealth, which created hierarchy and tension within the lineage causing it to break down. This disturbance in the traditional economy and values eventually undermined the old order.[37]

Paper's observation and explanation of the decline of an archaic female deity does not tally with Gill's observation that contact of native hunting societies with settlers of European origin often led to a transformation of a native male creator god to a female one through the European desire to see native culture as the sacrificed goddess and the Indian desire to see native culture as the protected goddess. This is not an anomaly. It is common when there is cultural contact that the dominant culture will facilitate its subjugation of a people by absorbing temporarily the latter's deities; this may be symbolized by a marriage between foreign and native deities. Such was the case during a critical stage of state formation in ancient Japan when the god Yamato no Ōkunidama married the goddess Amaterasu. It was also the case in a number of the Africa cases surveyed. A variant on this theme occurred during the rise of Islam when society was in transition from matrilineal to patrilineal social structure, from tribal society to statehood, and from a pantheon that included some female deities to a supreme male god (Allāh). A brief interim experiment incorporated the several goddesses as the daughters (rather than the wives) of Allāh.[38] Thus, it should not surprise us to find a legend about a European man marrying an Indian princess who comes to be imaged as a goddess. The North American context is more complicated, however, because there can be no real myth of a divine marriage since Christianity is monotheistic and since there was no real native supreme goddess until one was invented by those outside and inside native religion. Eventually, the Christian male god triumphed, that is, until native religions began to reawaken toward the end of the twentieth century.

Before leaving this topic of the decline of feminine symbolism and the position of women, it is important to mention that sometimes history repeats itself with minor variations. Take, for example, the case of Amaterasu (as described by Yusa). Although her importance had been eclipsed for some centuries, it seemed she was making a comeback when she was used as a symbol to unify Japan in the twelfth century C.E. by the first shogun of the Kamakura period, who sought divine legitimation of his rule and made her the protectress of the country. The popularity of Amaterasu grew progressively during the Muromachi period when priests from Ise spread the idea throughout the countryside, during the Tokugawa period when Ise became a popular place of pilgrimage, and during the Meiji period when the government used Amaterasu as a symbol to unify Japan into a modern nation. But once Amaterasu gained supreme status again and Japan was unified, she was changed by the Meiji from a goddess to a god. Her "true" sex was rediscovered only with the advent of modern scholarship. Along with the rise in the status of Amaterasu culminating in a sex change, a progressive worsening in the status of women occurred; they were subjected to many pollution taboos from the fourteenth century. Yusa attributes these ideas of ritual uncleanliness based on negative views of women to Indian Buddhism and Chinese Neoconfucianism. From the preceding discussion, however, we know that the process of unification and state-formation is usually correlated with high stress and with a gradual loss of women's status. Even though in this case the symbolism changed only at the end of the process thereby disguising what was happening to women's status, in point of fact the overall process is similar to our other examples.

ABUSE OF POWER AND RELIGIOUS REFORM IN LARGE-SCALE SOCIETIES

State formation ushered in real male dominance. After some time reforms were necessary to eliminate abuses of power and hierarchy in general and male power over women in particular. The next group of religions to be surveyed here—Zoroastrianism, Jainism, Sikhism, and Baha'i—have their formation in such a context of reform that also addressed women's issues. As I described in *Women in World Religions*, reform or universal religions:

Began with a reform that was so major that it was perceived in time as a new religion. The shift from ethnic identity to universal identity meant that doctrine and experience crystallized around a charismatic leader who initiated change to restore or fulfil an original order or to categorically transcend the social and cosmic order altogether. When the new group was formed, its identity was based initially on association rather than birth, and access to the soteriology was individual, though it often came to be mediated by the group. Hence *experience* was focal, despite the fact that it was eventually ritualized. Because of women's participation in the initial reform and the universal dimensions of the new view, women not only belonged to the group but had direct access to the soteriology through their individual or group experiences. The corollary of the above is that the family had secondary importance compared to the group, though its value was by no means underestimated and marriage was sometimes sacramentalized.[39]

Zoroastrianism, which originated in Russia or somewhere east of Iran (perhaps Bactria or Chorasmia), is a case in point. The initial reforms are attributed to the prophet Zarathustra who lived prior to the sixth century B.C.E.[40] perhaps as early as 1400–1200. At this time, the use of bronze and the horse-drawn chariot had developed. This had led to a new economy based more on fighting and raiding than the traditional occupation of herding cattle. A priest, a composer of hymns, and a learned person, Zarathustra witnessed the violence of the Indo-European war-bands that pillaged villages for cattle[41] and desired order, peace, and justice. A way to bring this about was revealed to him by a supreme god called Mazdāh, also known as Ahura or Mazdāh Ahura.[42] The resulting reform was a spiritualization and moralization of the old Indo-European religion.[43] In subsequent texts called the younger Avesta—mainly ritual texts that have synthesized aspects of both Zoroaster's reform and the former Indo-European religion—the word *daēva* (Sanskrit *deva*), which once meant deity, now means demon. These texts have an apocalyptic view of world history: a combat between the good ones (righteous worshipers of Ahura Mazdāh, as the supreme god is now called) and the evil ones (unrighteous worshipers of *daēvas* led by Angra Mainyu, the personification of evil). It is foretold that the good will eventually win when the future savior Astvatereta arrives. The cult is based on initiation with the sacred cord, exposure of the dead to carcass-eating birds, fire rituals, and the pressing of the nonintoxicating *haoma* substitute. This religion of eastern Iran was partially adopted by the Achaemenid dynasty (558–330 B.C.E.), which originated in western Iran. The Achaemenids now called the supreme god Ahuramazdā and moved toward monotheism, identifying the deity with the supreme god of other groups (Marduk, Yahweh) and looking on other deities as *daivas* (Avestan *daēvas*), or those unworthy of worship. They replaced exposure of the dead by burial and introduced more syncretism throughout their large empire.

Another line of development is reflected in the Pahlavi texts of the Sasanian dynasty (226–651 C.E.), committed to writing in the ninth century. At this time, the continuation of the religion of the younger Avesta (considered orthodox Zoroastrianism) became the state religion, though it too was subject to changes: the supreme god, again virtually monotheistic, is called Ohrmazd and his antagonist Ahriman.

According to Ketayun Gould, with Zoroastrianism came more feminine symbolism. Although Ahura Mazdā is a male supreme deity often called "father," he first created six beneficent divinities— the Ameša Spentas or bounteous immortals—three of whom were females to help him fight Angra Mainyu. Other female divinities called *yazatas*, some of whom once belonged to the Indo-European pantheon, were incorporated over time into the pantheon to protect earth, water, and plants. In the list of the names of former men and women who are worthy of veneration, the wife of Vishtaspa (Zoroaster's patron) is mentioned among the first hearers and teachers of the doctrine.[44] Like men, women were eligible for salvation. According to Gould's summary of the sources for Zoroastrianism, women were included in the main religious activities. They were formally initiated into the religion with the investiture of sacred shirt and girdle. They were educated in religious schools. They participated in all rituals and acted as priests in minor ones. Women's (and men's) role was to banish evil. Publicly spreading the message of Zoroastrianism, they functioned as teachers. Since morality was the means to salvation, moreover, it made the pursuit of salvation attractive to ordinary women who viewed their roles as wives and mothers. Marriage and procreation were sacred duties: husband and wife were viewed in their complementary roles as master and mistress of the household. Although marriage was generally arranged, a relationship based on mutual affection was encouraged. "The begetting of children for the propagation of the race and the spreading of the faith," says Gould, was "a religious function—to further the kingdom of Ahura Mazdā and cripple the power of Angra Mainyu." As in India, sons were preferred and necessary for the death ritual. But because the religion was based in the home, importance was given to women's activities. In fact, housework was said to sweep away dirt and decay, the weapons of Angra Mainyu, and was viewed as prayer.

Zoroastrian women had social, economic, and legal rights. There was no seclusion or veiling; women frequented social and religious events with men. They owned and managed property in their own right and could legally manage the affairs of their husbands. It is noteworthy that they could seek redress for mistreatment by a husband in a court of law and be the legal guardian of a son disinherited by his father. Finally, they could give evidence in court and be judges.

Jainism is also a universal or reform religion. The rise of the first states in the middle Gangetic plain of northern India, from about the eighth to the sixth century B.C.E., was accompanied by abuses in power and by breakdown in kinship and family structures.[45] (In the Brāhmaṇas, texts written at this time, evidence of misogyny appears.[46]) Because of this, the sixth century B.C.E. in India was marked by political, social, and religious ferment. Jainism, Buddhism, and Upaniṣadic Hinduism arose, in part, as reforms of Vedic religion, which was rooted in Indo-European traditions. The Jains followed the teacher Mahāvīra, also known as the Jina or victor, who lived in the same area of northern India (now Bihar) and at the same time as the Buddha. In Jainism, the concept of *saṅgha* provided an alternative to lineage identity, defined by blood relations, for it was an associational community that different people could join. Because both men and women and those of different social classes belonged to it, it had the semblance of a universal religion. But the religion had the semblance of universalism in another sense: salvation, at least according to some sects, could be attained by anyone through preparation as a lay person and final realization as a monastic either in this life or another.

Closely related to concepts of community and universal salvation, then, was the notion of equality. Just at a time in India when women were losing status by being regarded less as the complement of men in marriage (the view of the *Rgveda*) and more as their uneducated, impure, subordinates (the view of the Brāhmaṇas), there was an attempt to stem this decline by Jainism and other new religious movements of the day. There is no supreme deity in Jainism (rather, Jainism is pluralist, for it recognizes several ontological entities such as souls, matter, space, movement, rest, and time); this prevents the problem of viewing the ultimate as a particular sex. For Jains, the purpose of human life is to eliminate karma by asceticism in order to recover the essential nature of the soul.

A similar pattern of reform is found in the Indian religion of Sikhism, which developed in the fifteenth century C.E. This period was one of caste rigidity, excessive ritualism, and confinement of women in the home. A group formed around the figure of Guru Nānak. It worshiped one supreme deity known as Sat Kartār (the true creator) or Sat Nām (the true name) who has different epithets and names drawn from Islam and Hinduism: Pitā, Pritam, Khasam, Mālik, Sāhib, Rab, Rahim, Rām, Govinda, and Hari. According to Shanker in the present volume, God is a male figure, though frequently described as both the mother and father of all living beings. But Sikhs also speak of his ineffable (*nirankār*) nature beyond all form. Drawing from Hindu Bhakti and Islamic Sufism, Sikhs attempted to reform aspects of Indian society under ten gurus beginning with Nānak (the name Sikh means disciple). Their association was the *dharamsāla* or abode of faith. Disciples were to congregate and chant the hymns composed by gurus and collected in the *Ādi Granth*. Sikhism simplified rituals and customs. It eliminated image worship, stressed monotheism, and discouraged caste hierarchy by promoting the equality of Sikhs.

Many Sikh reforms related directly to the lives of women. Salvation for women as well as men was promoted. Indeed, women now had easy access to salvation, since asceticism was rejected by Sikhism and the householder orientation was made normative for everyone. By increasing the status of the domestic realm, Sikhism indirectly increased the status of women. Stories about the lives of the gurus (the Janam Sākhīs) and the guides to Sikh life (the Rāhat Maryādā) included criticisms of infanticide, purdah, child marriage, polygamy, nonremarriage, and suttee. The Sikhs also set standards for good marriages; while the family assists in finding a prospective mate, the criteria should be virtue, temperament, and age, not social status, wealth, and dowry. Women could study the scriptures, be initiated, participate in all religious ceremonies, and lead the religious service.

Our last example of this pattern of reform is Baha'i, a religion whose followers worship a supreme deity (because of the nature of the languages, the deity is male in Arabic, but without sexual designation in Persian). It grew out of Islam in Iran in the early nineteenth century. Baha'i claims to be a reform of previous practices and an embodiment of modernity with its ideas of universal education, sexual equality, and world government. In an atmosphere of female segregation and purdah, the prophet Baha'u'llah (1817–1892) promoted the equality of men and women in Tehran. Women were even allowed to perform obligatory prayers and fasts during menses.

Intuition, love, and service were to replace force and war. Maneck describes how the ideal of sexual equality was embodied in the nineteenth-century figure of Tahirih. The daughter of a prominent, clerical family of Quazvin, she was a well-educated poet and translator. When she embraced the movement, she began to appear in gatherings of believers without a veil. Jailed for sparking controversy, Tahirih eventually was strangled to death when Muslims tried to quell the movement. At the moment of her death, she said, "You can kill me as soon as you like, but you cannot stop the emancipation of women."

WHEN REFORMS DO NOT SUCCEED

Despite the important change introduced by the reform religions, the gains for women were not always sustained. Sometimes the decline occurred almost immediately; at other times, it took place some centuries later. Let us consider the case of Zoroastrianism. Despite reforms, Zoroastrianism had patriarchal features. Some were retained from its Indo-European past; husbands, for instance, remained head of the household and of all family worship. Some features were developed in the course of its history, especially in periods when conservatism prevailed. At such times, thinks Gould, ambivalence toward women—present to some degree in all patriarchal religions—was given religious and social validation undermining the initial vision with its new possibilities for women.

The first conservative trend began with the Parthians (141 B.C.E.-224 C.E.) who ruled between the Achaemenid and the Sasanian dynasties. In the *Vendidad*, written at that time, a concern with combating evil appears, because some of the tradition had been lost on account of the havoc caused by Alexander the Great and the Macedonians.[47] Evil or impurity was to be combatted with purity. The concern with purity affected women in particular, because menstrual blood was considered a polluting substance.

The second conservative trend occurred under the Sasanians who made Zoroastrianism the state religion; "women were . . . held to belong to their nearest male relatives—father, husband, brother or son; and the Mazkakite claim to their being common property may have sprung originally from a desire among poor people to free daughters or sisters who had been taken (probably often enough by force) into the huge households of women maintained by kings and nobles."[48]

The third conservative trend arose when Islam triumphed in Iran, making Zoroastrianism a minority religion and subjecting the community once again to considerable stress: stories of rape and abduction of Zoroastrian women at the hands of conquerors were common in the literature of the period. Because of the Islamic hegemony, Zoroastrian women were forced into seclusion and purdah. Gould points out: "The stress of survival has often been correlated with the rise in male patterns of dominance towards women—an easy target since females are the most powerless members of a victimized group."

The fourth major trend followed the migration of Zoroastrians to India in the tenth century C.E. in order to escape persecution by Muslims. Because under Muslim rule in Persia they already had come to practice customs such as child marriage, polygamy, purdah, and seclusion of women in the household, they easily integrated into high caste Indian culture. The establishment of temple worship, says Gould, created a "powerful elite of chief priests who wielded considerable power—hereditary offices that were an exclusive male domain."

A similar kind of decline is seen in Jainism. Whereas the Buddha had decisively declared that women were capable of salvation, Mahāvīra, the early leader of the Jain community, made no such direct statement, as least as reported in later texts. He was, moreover, a nude ascetic. This posed certain problems for the subsequent community: did all mendicants have to be "sky clad" (nude) in imitation of the founder or was there an option of wearing "white" [clothes] (śvetāmbara)? If the requirement was nudity, then this posed special problems for women ascetics—both safety in a society that placed a premium on chastity and privacy during menstruation.

The conflict erupted between 300 B.C.E. and 200 C.E., another period of social and political strife in India. At this time, women's status in Hindu society had further declined; women and low caste Śūdras were often equated as those who serve.[49] The bhakti movement was countering this trend, however, by reemphasizing universalism, equality, and the exemplary spirituality of women.[50]

Jainism was a microcosm of these trends. In the present volume, Balbir notes that Kundakunda (second century C.E.) was the first to argue against the salvation of women "by establishing a direct connection between the fact that a woman cannot go naked and the affirmation of nudity as a sine qua non condition for the attainment of emancipation." This was expressed in a distinctly Jain idiom:

The genital organs of the woman, her navel, armpits, and the area between her breasts, are said [in the scriptures] to be breeding grounds of subtle forms of life. How can there be [full] renunciation for a woman? Their minds are not pure and by nature they are not firm in mind or in body. They have monthly menstruation. Therefore, for women there is no meditation free from fear. (Jaini trans.)[51]

Kundakunda concluded that a woman cannot attain liberation. His position began a long debate in the Jain tradition. Let us examine Jaini's reconstruction of it. The Digambaras argued, for example, that women are inherently inferior to men (hīnatvāt). They do not have excellence of knowledge, and their bodies arise because of "wrong view." Menstruation, moreover, occurs because of sexual passion, analogous to a wet dream; it begets shame and the need for clothes. Hence, the Digambaras argued that a woman can only be an advanced laywoman even though she may be called a nun out of respect. Ultimately a woman must be reborn as a man to attain enlightenment.

The opposite case was argued first by the Yāpanīya sect and then by the Śvetāmbara sect. The latter said that neither perception nor scripture prove that women are incapable of salvation, that a right view can always supplant a wrong view, and that lack of participation in public debates and inability to conjure up occult powers for this task are not necessary for liberation. The Śvetāmbara had more difficulty refuting the Digambaras when the matter was women's inferior status within the Śvetāmbara monastic order itself. Like the Buddhists, the Śvetāmbaras insisted on special monastic rules for women. In the Chedasūtra, notes Balbir, in this volume, these rules describe how nuns must honor monks; they also describe how nuns cannot wander alone, cannot be alone with a superior, and must follow special regulations regarding alms, places to stay, and implements to use. Even for Śvetāmbara ascetics, a woman is a symbol of attachment and a threat to the monastic vow of chastity.

In theory, education was available to both monks and nuns; inscriptions from Tamil Nadu between the ninth and eleventh century, which mention schools run by nuns and some laywomen, indicate that this was sometimes the case. But there were few scholar-nuns judging from the colophons of the texts, which give the name and identity of the author. Similarly, no nuns attained the preeminent titles of Ācārya and Sūri, perhaps because it was male dignitaries who conferred them. Just below the Ācārya, who was the head of the monks and nuns, however, was the *Pramukha*, a woman who supervises the nuns. Although there were few female leaders, the Śvetāmbaras did attempt to rebut the Digambaras by citing some exemplary women. They also noted that the same criticisms could be leveled at men that the Digambaras leveled at women. And they reaffirmed the status of the householder by saying that each of the Jinas, individuals who had conquered their passions and achieved liberation, had to pass through this stage, a claim their opponents rejected.

To complete this discussion of women in Jainism, we must look at the position of the Jain laywoman. Many texts have been written about the Jain lay code of conduct (*śīla*). The ideal conduct for a woman is exemplified by the figures of Sītā and Draupadī, accepted by Jains as well as Hindus. As in Hinduism, the ideal laywoman is chaste; she has perfect loyalty to her husband (*pativrata*). Because of the dietary rules of Jainism—vegetarian food eaten at particular times—the Jain laywoman's status is associated with food in general and her offering of food to monastics in particular. The well-being and status of the Jain family, moreover, are associated with the woman's performance of vows (*vratas*).

With the development of Shaktism and Tantra in Hinduism, feminine symbolism increased throughout India from the sixth century C.E. Similarly, in Jainism, female attendants (*yakṣiṇīs*) of the Jinas became goddesses connected with fertility and worldly affairs. From medieval times, laywomen worshiped at the shrines of the Jinas and the benevolent Jain goddesses for the well-being of their families.

Although there was more feminine symbolism, this did not change the patrilineal structure of society. It did, however, enhance women's religious role in maintaining the family. Bhakti Hinduism went so far as to say that women could attain salvation as householders. In the Jain tradition, though, laywomen could not attain salvation in this life.

This example of Jainism shows that reforms leading to the establishment of a new religion may dramatically improve the status of women, but that there may be considerable slippage over time. In this case, one sect, the Śvetāmbara, advocated salvation for women, the other, the Digambara, rejected it. The Śvetāmbara may be classified as legitimating nominal male dominance, which was probably the legacy of the early community since it was based on a number of reforms; the Digambara, as legitimating real male dominance.

A similar kind of decline is seen in Sikhism. Despite many reforms and claims to egalitarianism, the *Gurū Granth*, the Sikh scripture, says Shanker, has come to include a number of views that are not so liberal. As in the larger Hindu tradition, the feminine may be associated with the "secular, powerless, profane, and imperfect." Segregation of women, purdah, polygamy, female infanticide, and suttee are found. Twenty-two wives of ruler Ranjit Singh (1780–1839 C.E.) performed suttee, for instance, at the time of his death. The Hindu ideal of a woman's purity, chastity, devotion, loyalty, and service to her husband (*pativrata*) remain common in Sikhism. Misogynist statements also appear; in this context, Shanker cites the phrase "the egoist is like a woman foul of mind." No woman, moreover, is found among the gurus of Sikhism. The Sikh family is structured by patrilineality, though the home as the locus of the woman's power and motherhood is praised. Shanker thinks that traditional attitudes toward women were too strong to be uprooted: "the patriarchal system suited the purpose of the gurus . . . to uphold the male dominated, monotheistic religious system."

Our last example of decline reported by the authors of this volume is that of Baha'i. Despite early reforms, Maneck claims that divorce and bigamy remained male prerogatives, virginity the prerequisite of marriage, and inheritance for women half that for men. When migrants brought the religion to America in 1892, men attempted to take control of the administration of the community, interpreting the scriptural phrase "men of the House of Justice" to sanction this move. They also tried to confine women's activities to teaching. A major struggle for control of the Chicago Baha'i community led Abdu'l-Baha to dismantle all male administrative bodies when he visited the United States in 1912. Nonetheless, according to Maneck, there has been little change in gender roles; women remain responsible for the raising of children and men for earning income. Still, the emphasis on the education of women has led many women into the job market. This, according to Maneck, has introduced some Baha'i women to the syndrome of "supermom stress." Recently, Baha'is have been rediscovering the liberalism of their faith in the wake of the women's movement. But according to Maneck, "in many instances Baha'i conceptions of equality have distanced them from more radical forms of Western feminism. . . . Whether or not Baha'i women will fully utilize the potentialities of Baha'i scriptures and history, or whether they will be relegated to a 'separate but equal' sphere that perpetuates structures of male dominance remains to be seen."

In this section, we have examined religions that start as a general reform, either of the abuses of state formation or the lapse of former reforms. While they are initiated by men, they address concerns of women. All these religions support patrilocality and patrilineality. Where supreme deities exist, they are male although they have incorporated significant feminine symbolism. The founders, moreover, are men: Mahāvīra, Zoroaster, Nānak, Baha'u'llah, as are other guides in Jainism and Sikhism, and priests in Zoroastrianism.

These examples show that many reforms—which influenced women's lives—eroded, especially in cases of societal stress when there was a disturbance in the status quo of sufficient novelty, magnitude, and duration that balance could not be restored by existing mechanisms. Women's lack of economic or political power and organization in the past meant that men ultimately made decisions regarding women's lives. They ignored or took away the reforms for women when they encountered stressful situations. Gould argues that women need to deal with the politics of both religious and societal institutions to transcend these problems. For this, they must have a power base. Women scholars, moreover, must go beyond the description of women's religious experience and bring a critical perspective to their study.

Even when texts have some egalitarian ideals, says Gould, they should be scrutinized for negative feminine images and prescriptions. Scholars should test text with context to determine whether the ideals are found in practice and where the tradition went astray. Gould observes that despite initial reforms in gender roles, religions generally adapt to their social environ, lose their ability to transform society, and come to mirror society at large. Consequently, a feminist perspective is necessary to reveal how religion has had a darker side for women. At the same time, it must have cultural sensitivity to avoid chauvinism, which may inspire, in turn, a denial that problems have existed for women or an apologetic for the tradition.

When reform religions enter the modern period, they have often returned to their egalitarian and universal roots since these themes are central to definitions of modernity. They have initially felt more comfortable with modern reform because these ideas were at the heart of their own tradition. Yusa observes that in 1872, the Meiji government abolished pollution taboos, though they completely disappeared only after World War II. She links the reassertion of egalitarianism in some of the modern Japanese sects to recovery of the ancient Shinto ethos as a way of displacing foreign religions and reasserting Japanese identity with its more positive view of women. A woman, Nakayama Miki (1798–1887), founded the Tenrikyō sect based on Shinto. Through possession she communicated with the kami spirits and was told to preach the equality of everyone and to end the taboos leveled against women. (Of course modern ideas of equality and democracy were also entering Japan and may have inspired these changes.) Similarly, Gould observes that with the eighteenth-century move of the Zoroastrians or Parsis, as they had come to be known in India, to urban centers, the community again encouraged education, including the education of women.

The initial impact of modernity on religions has often led to a renewal of the reform spirit. But modernization has also brought stress. Because of a low fertility rate and intermarriage, the Parsi community, for example, has been facing extinction. Formerly, Parsi women who married outsiders lost all status as Parsis, though men did not and their wives could convert. Now with the Bombay Prevention of Excommunication Act of 1949, the rights of Parsi women have been restored. Still the problem of demographic decline and extinction looms on the horizon.

In many reform religions, a subsequent phase of modernity has led to a crisis of identity and a reassertion of conservative norms. Religions forget about the liberal or reform aspects of their history and reassert their conservative ones. This is the spirit of fundamentalism: religious tradition with a modern face. The tension between reform and tradition is evident in Shanker's description of the role of today's Sikh women in the political movement for a Sikh state. In the past, heroic women who defended Sikhism were honored by the tradition. This may have inspired the participation of Punjabi women in the Akali Dal movement since the 1980s. With mass organization, Sikh women have spontaneously lent their support to the movement, especially at moments of crisis. They have viewed their public action as a duty to family and community. Inspired by the example of women's participation in the Indian struggle for independence, they have promoted the Sikh demand for a separate state (Khalistan) by traveling to different villages to spread the message and by courting arrest with authorities during marches.

But even though feminine norms have been relaxed in a time of emergency and women have risked their lives, this has been done, thinks Shanker, only as an aid to men's concerns and has not been translated into a notion of women's liberation as occurred in the earlier Indian independence movement. On the contrary, it was the male Akali Dal leadership that institutionalized the women's movement as the Stree Akali Dal. Especially in the rural areas, women must still have the permission of husbands or fathers to be politically active outside the home. Those women who have been raped when working for the cause have been ostracized. Men's political goals have prevailed; women's opposition on any issue has been squashed, at least in rural areas. The Akali Dal itself has even tried to introduce a new Sikh law that would take away a few inheritance rights of women and legalize levirate. With such real male domination in mind, Shanker views the appropriation of this movement by leftists, feminists, and those involved in development with some skepticism. Even in North America, Sikhs from the Punjab have often rejected women's requests for equality. In this context, it is important to mention the Gora or White Sikhs, North American converts to Sikhism, who have pressed for greater equality between men and women:

> The Gora Sikhs interpret the Gurus' teachings on the equality of men and women not simply as testifying to their equality in the eyes of God and in their ability to accept the coded substances of the Guru but as mandating their equal place in every other aspect of Sikh religious life. Thus, the Gora Sikhs object to what they regard as the "subordination of women" in Sikh affairs and have pushed for an expanded role for women in the Sikh gurdwaras (e.g., as officiants and participants in Sikh services and as members of the management committees of the temple societies). And it is this same insistence on the equality of Sikh males and females that has led the Gora Sikhs to interpret the Khalsa *rahit* as requiring turbans for women as well as men. As with so many of the Gora Sikh efforts to push their brand of radical egalitarianism, the attempts to get Punjabi Sikh women in North America to don turbans and take a more public—and to Punjabi Sikhs a more "male"—role in gurdwara affairs have been remarkably unsuccessful. The net effect has been merely to reinforce the Punjabi Sikh impression of the Goras' alien nature and to increase the Gora Sikh frustration at the failure of the Punjabis to live up to what the North American converts take to be essentials of the Sikh religion.[52]

Not all followers of the religions surveyed here would agree with the assessment by the authors of this volume that reforms were not complete, leaving a residue of patriarchy, and that reforms over time were undermined. The issue of equality is a particularly delicate one for members of reform religions, since it is central to their religious identity. Many Baha'is, for example, may find Maneck's assessment extreme. Baha'is see their religion as relevant to the modern world. Equality in general and the equality of men and women in particular are an important agenda for them. Even if equality has yet to be achieved, they argue, it is an still an ideal, a goal; the fact that Baha'i has this vision is what is important. They also argue that because Baha'i has no clergy, it does not have the problem of allowing women to assume these positions of leadership.

But as in Islam, it would be naive to foreclose a discussion of women in a religious institution by merely asserting that a particular religion has no clergy. Although Islam possesses no clergy, it does possess the ulamā who perform similar functions. And it makes good sense to raise the question, "Are women represented among the ulamā?" Since one of the domains in which gender roles are played out in a tradition is that of positions of authority, the discussion of women's access to administrative positions is of some importance. It is relevant to a discussion of women in Islam, therefore, to inquire whether women may or whether they have played "administrative roles." And it is also relevant to Baha'i. The attempt not to allow women administrators in the Chicago Baha'i community, and the attempt by the women led by Corinne True to ensure that women had this right, may have been, in fact, an important event in the history of Baha'i in determining that administrators at all levels of the organization are voted into office by universal suffrage.

While some people may argue that there really has been no decline in the manner outlined here, I would argue that unless one takes a monolithic view of the situation and has an uncritical acceptance of the proclamation of equality in the tradition as not merely its starting point but also its defining feature, then it becomes clear that such a decline in the religions discussed here has indeed taken place. Other people may also think that the reason for decline is moral. It may be argued, for instance, that all religions tend to lose their original vision. On the contrary, my argument is that decline is related to social, economic, and political conditions in conditions of stress. While this pattern is not inevitable, it has been extremely common in history.

Why is this so? One reason is that men must shore up masculine identity, which appears derivative and marginal in the face of women's reproductive role. Negative menstrual taboos, for instance, may try to deny or try to minimalize women's intrinsic reproductive power by calling it polluting. Even in otherwise egalitarian hunting and gathering societies, menstrual taboos exist; menstruating women, for example, cannot go near hunting men, because their blood is powerful. It is possible that these taboos also shore up male identity by creating virtually exclusive spheres for them.

This observation is neither to underestimate the importance of male hunting to provide the community with protein nor to underestimate the relative advantage of male size and strength for this activity. Rather, it is to hypothesize that in hunting and gathering societies, as in all other societies, men perceive a need to create culturally distinct identities. This helps them to separate from their mothers in childhood and to form an identity that is different from that of women. The idea of exclusivity also helps them to establish culturally what women have naturally, thanks to their ability to gestate and lactate. The fact that men control arenas of culture or form secret societies to create identity does not undermine women's culture, which was lively in other spheres. There is no simple distinction of culture equals male; nature equals female.

From this study, we find that women have virtual equality with men when they have some of the following: a vital contribution to the mode of production, matrilocality or matrilineality, access to inheritance, some feminine symbolism and ritual roles, and distinct spheres or organizations. The presence of all these factors, however, means the subordination or marginalization of men, which in turn would likely create problems of identity for them and negative reaction to women. Societies that want to be egalitarian must work out a balance so that the identity, security, and creativity of both sexes is maintained.

It is my opinion that we still have much to learn not only about women's lives but also about those of men. We need to focus now not just on questions of power but also identity. This may give us new insights as to why reforms do not always last or what instigates stress in the first place. How to do this with sensitivity to the distinct problems of both sexes and a commitment to justness for both men and women is the balancing act of the future. The discussion is by no means over as the hot debate between liberal and fundamentalist branches of various religions and between different branches of feminism and the new men's movement makes so clear.

Nonetheless, when all is said and done, scholars and members of the religions discussed here think that these religions have made many positive contributions to the status of women. Jaini, for instance, remarks: "The inferior status of the nuns in the Śvetāmbara mendicant community notwithstanding, the numerical superiority [compared to the monks] they have enjoyed through the ages must have contributed tremendously in shaping the Jain community. Their impact is especially evident in their ability to promote the individual asceticism of the Jain laywomen who routinely undertake severe dietary restrictions and long periods of fasting and chastity."[53] Through the centuries, Jainism maintained an order of nuns. Today, notes Jaini, it is being revived and is especially popular for unmarried, affluent women of the Oswal community in Rajasthan.

Similarly, Shanker concludes that Sikh women have fared comparatively well given the subordinate status of women in the larger Indian society; Sikh women are "cherished in private and treated with respect in public." And despite their auxiliary role, rural Sikh women who have been politically mobilized in the Akali Dal movement have gained self-confidence, knowledge, experience, mobility, solidarity with other women, different role models, and a new collective consciousness of their ability to act in the political domain. Their heroism also contributes to the movement's lore, thereby establishing their role in history.

Most Baha'is are proud of the status of women in their religion. Says Maneck, "Baha'i men and women alike, are agreed on one principle: hierarchical systems that place men above women in a divinely ordained order have no sanction within the Baha'i scriptures. In this respect the Baha'i faith is unique among revealed religions." And Zoroastrians have long enjoyed a reputation in India and abroad of having an extremely liberal tradition with reference to women.

While beyond the scope of the present book, it is important to remember that the new religions of Japan—many of which were founded by women or have women leaders—have drawn much inspiration from ancient Shinto. "Today," says Yusa, "there is no doubt that the status of women in Japan is rising, making the primordial images of women remembered in Shinto myths and legends not so strange nor surprising to the modern Japanese once again."

Finally, with the new awakening of native American Indian religions and traditional African ones, there is often proud recovery of ancient feminine symbols. Hackett reports that there is a surge in the popularity of Mami Wata, an African female water spirit worshiped from Senegal to Tanzania; women in many new religious movements, moreover, are playing important new ceremonial and healing roles, and some women have even founded religions. The authors of this book have helped to tell the dynamic story of women and religion.

Kathleen M. Dugan

AT THE BEGINNING WAS WOMAN: WOMEN IN NATIVE AMERICAN RELIGIOUS TRADITIONS

Corn Grinding Song
(Hopi)
Oh, for a heart as pure as pollen on corn blossoms,
And for a life as sweet as honey gathered from the
flowers,
May I do good, as Corn has done good for my people.
Through all the days that were.
Until my task is done and evening falls,
Oh, mighty Spirit, hear my grinding song.

(Qoyawayma:5)

Recovery of the feminine dimensions of Native American religious traditions shares the difficulty of study in this field in general. In our era, we have a significantly better opportunity to reach an accurate understanding, for several reasons. The first encounters with the native peoples of this continent were marred by prejudice, considerable ignorance of their cultures, and substantial linguistic barriers. When the burgeoning sciences of ethnology and anthropology began to survey the scene, many ancient cultures had already been altered by the shock of Euro-American encounters. Understandable reticence on the side of Native Americans muted the images even more.

It is remarkable that there are as many excellent accounts as there are under these circumstances. That they exist is a testament to those in both cultures who believed that mutual tolerance and cooperation could only be gained through true knowledge of the other. Today there are new voices added to tell the story. Significantly, many of these are native women, who, as writers and poets, reflect on their traditional roots and search for ways to integrate the riches of their past with the challenges, opportunities, and defeats of the present. These voices remind us that we know only a portion of the story, and urge us to see more broadly the native cultures and persons in our midst. In their strong outcry for justice and a fair hearing, they represent a feminism of a special kind. For woman's power and influence in the various spheres of Indian life is not something revolutionary or novel; rather, it has been an intrinsic part of Native American life.

American Indian religious traditions took shape in cultures deeply rooted in the earth and linked in a web of interdependence with all of nature. The very elements of tribal cultures, whether dependent on hunting or farming, or a mixture of both, opened them to intimate association with forces that have traditionally been perceived as feminine by all cultures. In prehistoric and early historic times, Indian economy was reliant on hunting, and on a precisely calculated expenditure of natural resources. This was not natural to them, surely, but a knowledge gained over centuries and generations of struggling for survival. To succeed in such an economy demanded atunement to nature and the seasons, to the life cycles of animals and of plants to supplement their diet. Their astounding capacity to find and acquire game was noted early by the first explorers. No less impressive was the skill employed by women in maximizing the uses of the game they killed. Unlike their white contemporaries, Indian hunters displayed unusual reverence for the animals, and showed by this that they did not consider themselves superior to their prey. Quite the opposite; the sense conveyed is one of gratitude to animals.

With the advent of agriculture, the southern tribes and the woodland peoples undertook the task of planting and harvesting. It is especially in this context that the deeply feminine aspects of Native American religion emerged and took a sharper definition. Perhaps it is inevitable that any people who work with the earth comes to regard it as a mother-principle, and to speak of her identity and appearance in feminine terms. In the beautiful Cheyenne creation story, Maheo labors with the assistance of his early creatures to create the earth. Once fashioned, he adorns her with vestments—the plentitude of vegetation that covers the earth. Then, says the myth, he looked at her and saw that she was very beautiful. This vibrant image of a living and dynamic presence is native to North American religions, whether a culture be thoroughly agricultural or not. The

earth is a nurturing principle in this religious vision, and it is in her
ambiance that all beings have their lives. This has many exponents.

For example, one major view of Native American religions sees
human life as intimately nurtured and lovingly embraced by this
mother. Thus, it strongly forbids harming of the earth through dis-
respectful actions, or careless wastage:

> Every part of this earth is sacred to my people. Every shining
> pine needle, woods, every clearing, and every humming insect
> is holy in the memory and experience of my people. . . .
> Whatever befalls the earth befalls the sons of the earth.
> Man did not weave the web of life; he is merely a strand in it.
> Whatever he does to the web, he does to himself.
>   (letter of Chief Seathl [Seattle] of the
>   Suwamish tribe to the president of the
>   United States of America, Franklin
>   Pierce, 1854)

This principle of economy is based on an insight that has only
recently come into view in the modern West, as scientists experiment with the Gaia principle. Yet it has had profound repercussions
on the whole of Indian life, from determining the ways that are permissible to till the earth (the Hopi do not dig furrows for their corn,
but instead drill small round holes into which the seeds are placed),
to the rationale behind the strong arguments made in every treaty
council by the Indians that the earth cannot be owned.

In many other ways more germane to our discussion, the feminine principle has shaped the self-image of women in an enduring
way and provides for the spiritual realm an abundance of powerful
feminine symbols. It has also structured the polity of Indian life in
interesting ways; for it is clear that women have occupied positions
of influence and power in most Indian societies. They range from
the significant political influence of women among the Iroquois and
the Cherokee, to the matrilineal lines of inheritance of the land
among the Hopi and many other cultures. It is crucial to note that
these structures existed for profoundly spiritual reasons, rather than
simply human ones. They are born of a conviction that women occupy a place in the order of things that is very close to the center of
reality—to its very heart. In their role as mothers who give birth to
new members of the tribe, and whose nurturing influence touches
every member of the family and the entire people, their very being
was (and is) regarded as a dimension of holiness.

That nurturing influence also supported and gave vitality to the deep interconnectedness of life that is so much a mark of these peoples. Attuned in their very being to nature's cycles, women were the teachers in a society of how intricately woven is the web of life. It was the women who kept the clan together and strove to increase unity and peace, as among the Iroquois, where women had the power to name the chiefs. It was they who taught the children how true it is that we are related to every living thing. This social function is tightly linked with another: the transmission of the oral tradition. It has been said of these peoples that over their long history they have achieved a level of genius that is verbal and oral. Indeed, into modern times, the entire weight of historical memory and religious understanding was transmitted by oral techniques alone. Contemporary Scandinavian research has demonstrated how accurate such traditions can be, and Native American culture represents a high peak of its achievement.

Both men and women engaged in telling the stories, though there is somewhat of a division into what concerned each. To the men belonged the public oration of sacred history and military history; to the women, folk wisdom and stories meant to educate in behavior. But it is difficult to determine where the line is drawn between those stories proper to women and the sacred stories, for it is the latter that establish all the rules of order in Indian society. More tellingly, as in most traditional cultures, the telling of stories is deeply linked with the wellsprings of memory, and women are the keepers of the flame—literally and figuratively. It was upon the memories of women, especially those who achieved old age, that the people relied, and their trust was not misplaced. Memory of this kind—that deals with the web of life—is especially a feminine trait. Women of all cultures have learned to keep the most important stories of life in their hearts, ready to share them when the opportunity arises.

The use of memory is related to yet another feminine quality of Indian life; it is that which emphasizes the development of psychic powers. Shamanic Indian cultures have not separated intelligence from deeply psychic abilities and have traditionally sought to enhance both ways of human knowing. This is abundantly clear in any overview of Native American religious practices. Depth exploration of the psyche is a natural drive of profound intensity, a quality that was cultivated in many ways by Native Americans. The solitude engendered by their location in a vast land living in small bands, for the most part, awakened the spirit to its great inner resources and reserves of power.

It was long ago noted by Charles Alexander Eastman that one of the most treasured qualities of life for his people, the Sioux, was silence. This silence permitted the spirit to hear and respond to the mystery surrounding it, and so prayer became the most essential act of the Indian. Fecund silence is also the condition for the seeking of visions and the recognition of the significance of dreams, both of which played a large role in Indian spirituality—it could almost be said to be the core.

Closely aligned with it is the marked stress on individuality that makes Indian communal living such an interesting sociological model. It is well known that tribal and, especially, clan-based peoples lived tightly together, so much so that modern notions of privacy are absent. Yet from childhood the Indian boy or girl was trained to find and develop an authentic and unique identity. This attitude made possible high goals of achievement for men and women, and these goals were frequently met. Thus the cultivation of strong personalities and qualities was exemplified by women and men who vied to excel in realms such as sports. Ruth Landes noted that the Ojibwa athletic games offered women the same recognition as men, though this represented the sole sphere in which such striving was allowed. But girls were noted to have visions empowering them to be runners (just like boys). In more egalitarian societies, women could excel in the arts of war and leadership, as the story of the heroic Cheyenne woman, Buffalo Calf Road Woman, illustrates (Powell 445–46). It was not unusual for women among the Plains tribes to shoulder the burden of defending the people when their men had fallen. Indeed, sometimes the women behaved more fiercely than the men.

In a very special field women were in many tribes allowed to seek the power (and respond to it when it was given) that fashioned shamanic personalities. Here, where sacred power was focused to become most helpful in healing the wounds and sicknesses of the community, women served as channels of sacred knowledge and power. In some peoples the shamanic role fell mostly to women, as among the California Indians. But in all tribes it was expected that a woman be called to serve her people in this way once her childbearing years were over.

There is a profound significance in this development of the feminine role. It has already been noted that women were viewed as daughters of Mother Earth, and like her were granted the power of bearing life and nurturing it to maturity. During these years of potency, a woman was regarded as filled with holiness and terrifying power—the power of life itself. This is frequently obscured by the taboos surrounding menstruation, which have become well known. Rather than indicate disgust or uncleanliness, the mandated isolation of the woman in her lodge was believed to be for the safety of the men whose power as hunters and warriors could be countermanded by this primal force. So powerful was she considered to be that she could not practice medicine or shamanize until menopause, since it was believed that there would be a conflict of competing powers if she attempted it (Allen 47). This was the general rule, though exceptions could occur.

The transformation from mother to healer is a natural progression, for the powers inherent in the feminine are simply refocused and freed (or enlarged) to allow a broader field of action. As Eliade noted, the shamanic transformation is from the personal to the cosmic level, for both men and women. For women, qualities long in preparation are elicited to reach a peak of action that is the summit of creative energy, the arrival at wholeness that integrates all the powers of the person and releases healing energy to the world around that person.

It is no coincidence that the way into such a transformation is through visions and dreams, for the feminine predilection for such states is well known. Indeed, it is possible to say that American Indian religion is not only permeated by symbols of the feminine, and revelatory of that dimension in nature and in life, but that it has, as every authentic religious way, opened up the possibility for its followers to discover and develop the feminine in themselves, whether they are male or female. Not all religions are successful at liberating the feminine. Native American religious traditions have always demonstrated a high degree of awareness of the necessity of this task and a good rate of success in achieving it. Today, more than ever, this is one of the most important lessons that the traditional way brings to a people so often alienated from their best selves and disoriented because of the long history of abuse and dislocation that has been their lot.

Thus the center of this chapter shall deal directly with the feminine symbols and energies of the Native American spiritual world, using specific examples to illustrate the vital role that women and the feminine have traditionally played, and are beginning to assume again. First and most fundamental is the omnipresent image of the earth as divine mother, and the encompassing power that flows from her and embraces all her children. In the dynamic web that is the Native American experience of life, all is living and related, resonating to the rhythm of the whole. As the Hopi view it, this challenging view of life announces the plan of the creator, who is the ground and witness of all the living. As Spider Woman told it to her children, human beings are called to live in harmony and sing in gratefulness from the tops of the mountains. Only when this is done does the plan of the creation reach fruition.

The ancient image of the Earth as Mother is present everywhere in North America. With the rest of reality she is perceived as having identity and personality, will and emotions. Her place in the order of creation is that of original primacy, though different stories of the people place her variously in relation to the creator. Where there is no distinct concept of a creator, the role of Mother Earth is quite sharply defined. Yet even where there is a strong creator figure, as in the Cheyenne story of Maheo's act of creation, the earth remains a sacred principle and is the dimension of reality to which the individual can feel most intimately related.

It is interesting to note the differences of cultures from those of the northern plains. The southern agriculturists demonstrate a marked reference to the earth and vegetation, especially corn (in itself, a mother-principle for many cultures). The northern tribes derived their subsistence mainly from hunting of migratory animals (the buffalo, in particular, in the early modern period) and intermingled strong images of the feminine earth with very masculine images of teeming faunal life and sky-references. Yet no clear line can be drawn, nor should it be. The earth emerges as one of the universal aspects of Indian awareness of the sacred, and a host of related images follow from that recognition.

The Plains tribes' concept of a medicine wheel or sacred hoop signifies the insight Joseph Brown received from Black Elk when he spoke at length on the meaning of the circle and its repeated use in Native American art and ritual. In essence, all life occurs in a circle, and individuals can find self-definition and harmony only by consciously placing themselves within this sacred circle. This hoop is the hoop of the universe, manifested in more proximate form in nature: the earth in particular, but also stones, which have a sacrality uniquely their own, and in the variegated forms of nature. Black Elk told Joseph Brown that nature loves roundness and delights in the circle. Much analysis of mandalas and Jungian archetypes in modern times has enabled those outside primal traditions to discover the profound power of such symbols as they occur in nature and are replicated in culture.

To take the illustration further, it should be noted that among Black Elk's people, the Oglala Sioux, and all the plains tribes, a concerted use of symbols linked all the acts of the individual and the community in a profound response to the need to acknowledge and respond to the presence of the holy. Walker was told by Sword that in the forms taken by the mystery, the sun holds a very high place (among the superior gods, he is the chief) (Walker 79–81).

The manifold use of sun symbols is striking, and nowhere more telling than in ritual and in the honored discipline and craft of the warriors. The sun dance, the great thanksgiving ritual among the Plains Indians, is a ceremony steeped in the earth and her plentitude, and all its elements bespeak this fact. From the offering of the Pipe to the seven directions, to the realistic representation of the sacred circle in the ritual arena itself, as well as in the entire camp surrounding it, the circle is everywhere present. The dancers, whose desire and commitment are to sacrifice self in thanksgiving and renewed prayer for continued abundance, are painted with sacred figures, among which the circle predominates. They perform their sacred actions, circling around the magnetic center of sacred reality, the Sun Pole, which simultaneously refers to the sun, Wakan Tanka, the earth, and the buffalo.

Here, as in every ritual, the act of dancing in the circle is an effective sacrament of reestablishing contact with one's past, with the sacred center of all reality, and with all one's relatives who are the children of "one Mother and one Father." That these rituals are viewed as earth renewal ceremonies is indicative of the effort to concentrate human knowing and willing upon a fact that has saving significance. To know that the earth is sacred is *the* abiding principle of Native American religions, and it acts as a moral catalyst as well.

The symbolism of the circle appears in the warriors arts as well. No warrior was considered prepared or adequately fitted without a shield. This was a circle obtained from the buffalo's hide and directly related to the sun by its shape and function (here, the preservation of life). Foremost among the medicine bundles a person could possess, the shield could be fashioned only by someone who had had a medicine dream or vision, and this person alone had the power to make a truly powerful shield. The spirit helpers seen in the vision were thus believed present within the shield design, and the shield radiated a sense of the protective power that the warrior believed he had been given. These were power-objects of great value, and they present clear evidence of the embracing presence of the mysterious world order, which the Indian peoples image through the primary archetype of the circle.

The relation of women to this infrastructure of reality is everywhere manifest. Their biological function as bearers of life, and thus the extension of the people in time and history, was a respected role. So too were the arts by which they nurtured life and wisdom among the people, while they provided for their physical needs. It is not surprising that an extraordinary number of feminine images people the myths, or that women consistently play such crucial roles in rituals. Examination of both these avenues permits a fuller appreciation of the role of women in Native American religious life.

The profound unity between nature and human beings is complemented, balanced, by the superior and exemplary unity that exists on the plane of spiritual beings. Indeed, the Indians were taught to regard the spirit beings as relating to humans in familial bonding terms, so that it is proper to think of them "as they think of their fathers and their mothers" (Walker 1980:69). Their natural experience taught them that this relationship extends throughout the universe, uniting human beings to the rest of creation in strong kinship. This situation was not original, according to the Sioux and other peoples. Long ago, the plains buffalo were said to have been wild and ferocious, deeply antipathetic to humans (De Maillie 31). Yet at chosen moments the reconciliation between the species was brought about by a spirit being who, very tellingly, comes in the form of a sacred woman. The frequent presence of such an intercessor can be found throughout North America, and a study of several examples illumines the role and value of the feminine in native myth.

The sacred White Buffalo Calf Woman, so central to Black Elk's recording of the seven rites of his people, the Sioux, mysteriously appears in a time when the people are beset by hunger and without clear direction. As the story reveals, she comes among them as thoroughly sacred, one of the Wakan Tanka, who has clothed herself in the form of an arrestingly beautiful woman. Of the two young warriors who encounter her, only one perceives that she is more than human, and wins the right to announce her coming by his reverence. During her visit she imparts to the Sioux the priceless gift of the sacred Pipe, which becomes the means of lifting their prayer to Wakan Tanka, and the first of seven rites that will become the ceremonial center of their life. It is in departing from them that she reveals the complexity of her being, for she takes the form of a white buffalo calf, bows toward the four quarters, and then disappears (Brown 3–9). With them she has left her sacred bundle, and through her guidance she has established a new bond between the people and the creator, and between them and all beings.

Specifically, her gifts are outfitted toward filling the physical and spiritual hungers of the people. She is, thus, quintessentially a feminine principle of salvation. The manner of her coming emphasizes this in that she is received both as a buffalo, the symbol of sacred providence in regard to the source of food, and as a woman, representing the power inherent in all women to generate new sources of life.

Other peoples cherish stories that preserve deep reverence for a sacred woman who is instrumental either in original creation or in enhancing the condition of creation along its history. The Abanaki speak of First Woman who came to live with a spirit being called Kloskurbeh and a disciple. She offers them her power and love, and she and the disciple have many children. However, a famine interrupts their peace. In the suffering that is created, First Woman begs her husband to slay her. Then she instructs him to have her body dragged through a field until all her flesh is gone. He was to bring her bones to the center of the field and let them alone for seven months. When that time was over, they were to return and gather the food produced by this act. All that is accomplished is done by the power of this sacred woman and by her sacrifice. The food is the tangible sign of her love and concern, and they are reminded that they are to eat it with thankfulness and in peaceful harmony, for thus will the love of the first mother be fulfilled (Allen 23,24).

Similar stories abound in Native America. In each the gift of food (corn, preeminently, and also squash and beans) comes from a sacred woman who is foundational in the history of her people. There is a logic so persistent here that it cannot be dismissed: the feminine in creation is the power for life, and for its continuance. As she is in the natural order, the myths seem to say, so is she in the cosmic web of the spiritual world. All life is linked to her, of necessity.

Spider Woman is one of the most familiar embodiments of this spiritual power. In the Hopi story of emergence, it is she who is responsible for breathing life into first man and first woman, the parents of the Hopi. Her role is crucial to the long migration of the people as they struggle onward to find their home in the worlds of the creator. The myth portrays her as announcing the creator's plan for creation (significantly, he asks the people to live in harmony among themselves and with all creation, and to praise and thank the creator). She accompanies them as they stumble and fail, and it is she who provides paths of emergence from one world, as it is being destroyed, to the next. Though she is of the earth (Huruing

Wuhti), she lives in the worlds above where she empowers the moon and stars (Allen 14). She also shares with White Buffalo Woman a strength and solidity that "grounds" the life of the people.

The Keres of Laguna Pueblo tell of Tse che nako, Thought Woman, who is at the center of all things. This image refers to a spirit who is the power of intelligence, without whose blessing nothing is sacred. Multifaceted in appearance, she emerges on the plains, in the forests, on the mesas, in the canyons, and deep in the seas. She is a true creatrix, for she is that (thought itself) from which all else is born. She alone makes material creation possible and is female—the spirit of creative power, from whom comes right balance, and right harmony. It is she who orders all things in relationship to the cosmic law (Gunn 14). Here, in Thought Woman, we find a clearly defined creator-spirit, described as feminine. It is of telling interest to relate this image to the shape of Pueblo life, which sees women as sharing power with men, creative in agriculture as in art, and holds the feminine aspect of existence in high regard.

A similar example of a myth informing and molding the social structure of a people comes from the Seneca. Among these peoples we have a clear record of a society that has, from very early times, given enormous respect to women and allowed women to play significant roles in the political life of the tribe. In their story of becoming a people upon this earth, a spirit being from the world above, Sky Woman, falls to earth, pregnant and alone save for the help of the creatures of the skies and the sea who respond to her cries for help and form a net to break her fall. Through their help, she at last stands on an earth, and becomes fruitful in two ways: she gives birth to a daughter who will become the mother of the sacred twins who eventually create the beings of this world, including the human; and she plants the seeds that she had grasped in desperation as she tried to break her fall. It is compelling to note that the ancestry of the people is traced in this story through *women* who are the link between the Seneca and the Sky People (or the Spirit World). It is not surprising that the feminine becomes highly developed and cherished among these people. In fact, they present a most consistent example of how fully the feminine can emerge when there is openness to its power.

Very early in the European encounter with Native America, it was noted by the Jesuit missionaries in New France that dreams held a unique and revered place in Iroquois life. From the pages of the *Jesuit Relations* comes rich testimony about the centrality of the inner life of dreams and the important significance that it received. Fr. Ragueneau notes of the Seneca that so critical is the role of dreaming that it exercises an irrefutable power upon the people. Thus, he testifies that everything in their lives is governed by their dreams. Resisting the strong impulse to regard this as superstition, Ragueneau listened more carefully and has left us a remarkably clear explanation of what this people believed about dreams. Long before Freud, they had learned that dreams conceal (and reveal) the deep wishes of the soul, and that they express inborn desires that must find expression, if one is to find health and wholeness. So they created a ritual that would enable private dreams to be publicly expressed (in symbolic gestures) and to find appropriate fulfillment. This ritual, the dream-guessing rite, was held at New Year's. It marked the occasion for spiritual cleansing and regeneration in the spirit of the new birth always represented by this feast in the human cycle. The Iroquois recognized another type of dream, that which was a point of revelation from the sacred and was intended for all the people. Here is the source for myths and rituals.

This assiduous attention to the inner psychic and spiritual life, so focused and articulate among the Seneca, is a testimony to the feminine dimension of human experience and clearly manifests the honor given to it. Thus the origin myth and subsequent tribal history and practice acknowledge the power for good that resides in the feminine, and which is especially visible in the woman. This power is viewed as spiritual in origin, and creative and transforming in its dynamic presence. In an entirely healthy way, this people not only gave tribute to women but tried to nurture the feminine qualities of the dream-life in all. This provided a valuable balance for the strict discipline expected of the warrior, as A. F. C. Wallace notes (Wallace 59–75).

CHANGING WOMAN

Perhaps the most perfect symbol of the sacred woman in Native American mythology is Changing Woman of the Navajo emergence story. The myth speaks eloquently of the connections between her and the earth, and tells of her role in generating specific forms of life, among them the human beings who will become the historical Navajo. So rich a figure has attracted much commentary and analysis, from Berard Haile to Gladys Reichard and the psychologist Sheila Moon. Changing Woman has always spoken deeply to the Navajo, and these scholars sought to express her multidimensional significance. She is the archetype of womanhood for the Navajo, and is born, like them, into an extended clan structure of sisters and other relatives. The limits of this chapter forbid a thorough exegesis, but we can indicate some of the genealogy and role of this powerful spirit-woman who plays so great a role in Navajo life. In a universe where the gods are always ambivalent and quixotic toward human beings, she alone is thoroughly benevolent, and is the most revered.

First, it is important to note that Changing Woman is not present at the beginning of the story. She is preceded by First Woman, who, with First Man, is among the nine holy ones present in the first world of darkness. It is inferred that she and First Man come from primordial ears of corn. She is a creator and closely linked with earth; for instance, she receives the seed basket of Mother Earth for the first crops. But she does not act alone; a primary Navajo principle states that male and female must be co-present and work harmoniously for life to flourish. The Windway chant describes her as the one who gives birth to earth. Reichard concludes that earth is either Changing Woman, or is the mother of Changing Woman: to her is given the privilege of caring for the greatest Holy Woman, Changing Woman (Moon 30–31). Thus the Navajo myth opens with a tribute to the primordial feminine at the heart of creation.

The story of Changing Woman, as Haile translated it, occurs in a later period of history when a child is heard crying for four days. After the people failed to find the child, First Man discovered a mysterious baby girl. He recognized that Darkness was her mother and Dawn her father. This was Changing Woman. At first the child thinks that First Man and First Woman are her parents, but the winds tell her otherwise. She is extraordinary from her first entrance, arriving at her full growth and womanhood in twelve days. She eats only the sacred pollen. Eventually she quarrels with First Man, First Woman, and the other inhabitants of the lowest world, and separates from them to make her dwelling in the west. Her twins (who will play such a great role in ridding the earth of monsters) are born here (Moon 155–56).

Of all the gods, she is the most beloved. In her role of making human beings from pieces of her own skin, she becomes a symbol of the mystery of reproduction of life renewing itself perpetually and, very likely, of the life-giving earth itself. From the evidence given by the myths, Reichard concludes that the close association described between Changing Woman and earth and its renewal leans toward identification of the two. For example, she speaks of avoiding being trampled upon, and is depicted as decorated "with all kinds of herb-age and flowers wherever they grew" (Reichard 407).

Though she miraculously gives birth to twin sons who become warriors against the evils of existence, she herself is a symbol of peace and restoration and healing. In the intricate patterns of Navajo ceremonials, the theme of bringing persons and the earth back to wholeness is the central intention. In her very being, Changing Woman represents that power for harmony; she exempli-fies it. And the mysterious image of her that we see through the eyes of her sons shows us a being who goes through all the changes of the life-cycle and returns always to youth and beauty. It is this splendid and inspiring image that each Navajo girl is called to "become" in the ritual of initiation, which is Kinaalda. Birth and rebirth are her realms, and she teaches the Navajo how to traverse the dangerous path that is this life, and supports them by her protective power and benevolence:

> It's lovely indeed, it is lovely indeed . . .
> I, I am the spirit within the earth; . . .
> All that belongs to the earth belongs to me,
> It is lovely indeed, it is lovely indeed.
> (Moon 172–73)

CEREMONIAL PATTERNS

The second most obvious source about the role of women in In-dian society and religion can be found in the rich ceremonial pat-terns of tribal life. Eliade made clear the essential relationship between myth and ritual, and this is vividly apparent in Native American traditions. The major rituals dramatize the foundational religious events and remain the sources of power as the people con-tinue their history. It is significant to examine some representative rituals to demonstrate how sacred a role women have traditionally played in the religious life of their people. We have already seen that rituals derive in some instances from encounters with the feminine embodiment of the holy (The Sioux Sacred Buffalo Calf Woman). Perhaps more tellingly, women are often found in the mystic telling of a ritual's origin, and are instrumental and necessary receivers of the initial experience.

Two examples will demonstrate this. Among the Cheyenne the great story underlying the rituals of the Sun Dance relates that it was given to the culture hero, Erect Horns, and to his companion, the Sacred Woman, who went with him in a spirit-inspired journey to the sacred mountain where the Maiyun awaited them. They remained four years, during which time the powers instructed Erect Horns in the Sun Dance ritual. Then the woman received instructions in her role. The moment of completion came when Erect Horns received the Sacred Buffalo Hat. From the beginning, the Cheyenne version of the sun dance (incidentally considered to be probably the prototypical form on the plains by some scholars) featured the presence of the Sacred Woman who is essential to the success of the ritual. She represents clearly the vital and fecund source of life on the earth, and she is adorned with symbols that illustrate her high place in creation and her sacred nature as giver of life—and in this ritual, giver of the power that makes it possible. It is not an exaggeration to say that she is, with the sun pole, one of its centers.

Is'siwun, the Sacred Buffalo Hat, is the symbol of Maheo, the all-father's love for his children, and the living source of female power (Powell 444). Given to the Suhtaio, one of the original bands that formed the historical Cheyenne people, the Sacred Hat was one of the sacred mysteries that convinced the people that Maheo and the Powers willed creation's renewal through the ceremonies commemorating his gifts, in which woman plays an essential, complementary role to man. In a quintessential Native American insight that humans participate most intensely in supernatural power through sacrifice, the woman's role in ordinary life is lived to its fullest in her role in the Sun Dance. The wholeness of Cheyenne life depends on generous participation in this offering of life and a person's very being, and in the typical Cheyenne way, women offering their special sacrifice, complementing that of the men. Fire Wolf stated to Powell in 1961 that "the law is this: the woman is above everything because Maheo has given the woman power to spread people to cover the face of the earth" (Powell 444).

Thus, in an age-old tradition that shows a relation to the insights gained in primal societies' rites of regeneration, a woman vows the sun dance along with the Pledger. Her seat in the medicine lodge is one of honor, situated behind the buffalo skull altar. Her sacrifice is offered in the buffalo and massaum ceremonies. Moreover, Is'siwun's keeper shares his duties with a counterpart, the Sacred Hat Woman. Woman and the sacred buffalo are thus intrinsically linked in the Suhtai ceremonies, and this influence penetrated eventually all the ceremonial life of the Cheyenne tribe (Powell 445). That act of sacrifice expresses the human capacity for receiving, and communicating, the love and favor of the creator. It should be seen in the full context of the high respect accorded chastity in Cheyenne women—a clear indicator of the holiness of woman's ritual role. In the sun dance, the Pledger's wife is called the Sacred Woman or Offering Woman. Fire Wolf illustrated this for Powell: "Through her, the earth and the people are replenished" (Powell 448). Thus, when the great center-pole or the medicine lodge was set in its place, it was time for the woman to perform her most sacred role among the Cheyenne.

When the medicine lodge was completed, the chief priest and all the priests filed from the lodge, led by the sacred woman. Their procession halted east of the lodge and just inside the camp circle, where a solemn invocation was made. Blessing was implored for the welfare of all creation. The priests returned to the lodge, leaving the chief priest and the woman alone. These two then purified themselves with incense and prayer with the sacred pipe. Then they had intercourse within a buffalo robe with the prayer that, as a consequence of their act, all lives may be born (Gunnell 2:57).

This act was considered sacred and had the power to regenerate the earth and all the people. This was clearly expressed in the words of the woman returning to her husband: "My husband, my prayers and wishes have been approved by Maheo. I have brought you back power" (Powell 119). She also shared this power with the sun dancers, who joined the pledger in thanking his wife for gaining new life for all. This extraordinary act among the highly chaste Cheyenne was originally performed publicly, but is now done in private. It affirms the full measure of sacredness attributed to women among the Cheyenne, and this ritual dignity flows out into the rest of life. Cheyenne women have always had great influence, freely debated with their husbands, and generally have been successful in getting their way. Moreover, traditions of women chiefs and women who were politically creative exist, and there are memories of women gifted with great supernatural powers. Feminine influence has always been so great that Grinnell opined that they were the final authority in the camp, despite the fact that men usually spoke in councils (Powell 445).

The sun dance is truly an exemplary ritual of earth renewal, and the woman's role in it is appropriate, a surviving link with a much older time. What is especially striking about the Cheyenne is the perfect consistency reflected between the overall place and value accorded women in society and their intricate role in the sacred ceremonies. The Cheyenne were a renowned and rigorously disciplined warrior people, yet the place of women is extremely high. There is a careful balance established in the spiritual life of the Cheyenne by this dynamic, revealing a basic harmony between male and female. It gives a fascinating insight into the fecund and mysterious power of the sacred. The woman thus becomes a sacrament of the life-giving power of Maheo and is enveloped in the profound mystery that lies at the heart of the ritual of cosmic regeneration that is the sun dance. Like Is'siwun, she brings life!

Another example of women's ancestral role in ritual comes from the Siksika (Blackfoot). Beverly Hungry Wolf shares her recollections of the holy women among her grandmothers by describing the overall attention given to praying and living their religion. But the object of special reverence were those women who sponsored the Sun Dance. This rite, called Okan, was the highest religious event among her people, and it was *always* sponsored by a noble woman, true to her husband. This has contributed to the special standing given women in the tribe. The sacred story tells how long ago, the ancestors of the Siksika were taken up to Sun to bring back blessings from the creator. Every holy woman who sponsors a sun dance has represented one of these messengers from Sun. In the rite holy lodges are built into which everyone could go before the holy woman to receive the blessing for which she is the channel (Hungry Wolf 31). The women who vow the sun dance do so in the intention of offering a sacrifice (usually of four days in length) and wear a special headdress, the Natoas, given long ago by a sacred elk to a great holy man and worn by his wife (Hungry Wolf 42–45). The conjunction of male and female power is represented here, and in the Siksika ritual the woman is linked with Sun, on the plains the perfect symbol of nature's life-giving power. Here, too, the natural ground for regeneration is consciously linked with the highest power in nature to reveal woman as a bearer of divine life.

In another example, a most ancient ceremony took place among the Omaha—the Ho⁻ Hewachi initiation. In it chiefs and members of the society were formally called to consider the merits of a man aspiring to enter the Ho⁻ Hewachi. The candidate was expected to publicly present the record (or "count") of his acts. During this telling, a young girl who had been chosen to receive the mark of honor entered and danced before the society. (This was the fourth and last step of the initiation.) This act dramatized the awakening of the feminine element, believed by the Omaha to be necessary for a fulfillment in tangible form of the power of life. Generally the girl was the candidate's daughter, and if there were none, he could ask the daughter of a close friend or relative. It was necessary that she be a pubescent virgin. In the sequence of the ritual, she was laid on a luxurious bed and placed facing the west (lying, that is, sunwise). She was then ceremonially tattooed. A round spot (representing the sun) was first put on her head. In the narrative song, the sun is described as speaking to her, and descending on her with life-giving power. Next, a four-pointed star is placed on her chest (signifying the night, the dark mother force). The four directions represent the life-giving winds. This time the song speaks of the serpent, emblem of the teeming life that "moves" over the earth. Sometimes a crescent moon was tattooed on the back of her neck, and a turtle on the back of her hands.

This process was perceived (and experienced, no doubt) as an ordeal, a test of the girl's virtue. Only women danced at these meetings, for the central recognition was that of night, and of the feminine principle. The deeds recounted by the men were meant to assure the woman of protection so that she might be able to fulfill her responsibilities as wife and mother. Thus the rite of the Ho-Hewachi clearly manifested the fundamental ideas on which tribal organization and well-being was based. It simultaneously affirmed the essential role of women in promoting the general welfare (Fletcher II: 502–8).

The woman given the privilege of this sacred role carried the "mark of honor" in the recognition of all for her entire life. By it her family had achieved tribal status, and of her it was believed that she would become the mother of many (surviving) children. She alone could dress the skin of a white buffalo chosen to renew the sacred white buffalo hide of the sacred tent, which was the home of the Sacred Pole, the greatest object of reverence among the people. It was regarded as a sacred person, given honor, and stood in its holiness as guardian of the people (Fletcher 509). Here again the feminine component of ritual life is seen as the necessary partner with the masculine, and the essential action by which life is renewed and made harmonious and whole.

Native American women also had access to means of exercising power in the critical role of practitioners of medicine. Maintaining health and restoring it when lost was, and is, a vital part of Native American religion. There were two possible causes of illness, each requiring a specific treatment. The first kind resulted from natural causes, and were receptive to healing through herbs and other natural means. The other were physical and mental illnesses that were diagnosed as due to supernatural causes; these could be healed only by spiritual means. Knowing the difference was critical, and the office of diagnostician was highly regarded. It is interesting that among the Navajo, women are esteemed as having superior faculties in this area and thus serve to direct the patient to the proper ritual in a highly specialized ceremonial order. This tribute is more than an admission of female experience in "listening" to the subtle voices of the body and spirit. It is deeply related to the spiritual role of women in the life of people, as they continue to embody Changing Woman's creative presence.

Once the diagnosis was made, then the proper treatment could be determined. If herbal medicine was indicated, women were frequently the keepers of their powers. This was not exclusively the function of women, but generally women seemed to be more adept at making herbal potions and infusions. Usually the practice of medicine belonged to older women, who were considered freer from restrictions since they were past childbearing and raising years. Ancient insight held that the power of a menstruating woman could vitiate the healing strength of any medicine she prepared (Niethammer 146). A vast knowledge of medicinal herbs formed the pharmacy of native women, and highly effective curatives were known. This in itself is a testimony to the close relationship between women and the earth, for such extensive knowledge could be gained only by penetrating attention to the wealth of nature. Indeed, many accounts indicate that the relationship was typically a spiritual one, in which the herb or plant revealed itself to the healer. In taking it, the appropriate procedure mandated a prayer of beseeching and of gratitude for the life the plant was surrendering.

The process of becoming a healer was usually twofold. In some societies a woman could only practice medicine by assisting her husband. Among the Comanche, wives of medicine men often helped their husbands and were the approved persons to approach to ask for healing. Such a woman acquired power to heal from her husband and was not permitted to practice by herself until after his death, and then only after menopause (Niethammer 147). In other societies, women were allowed to practice medicine by themselves, but could learn it only from men (for example, the Nisenan of northern California) (Niethammer 148). In other tribes, women were instructed by their mothers or grandmothers. For others, the call would come in a vision or dream in which a spirit would invite the woman to enter into the difficult vocation of medicine woman.

However, as was true for all who were called to practice medicine in North America, even an inherited entry into the profession had to be validated in a spiritual experience in which a spirit spoke in distinctly personal terms and verified the supernatural call, which lay at the heart of medicine power. In some tribes, the vision or dream would come unsought; but in general the path was to go upon a vision quest in which the elements of ordeal functioned to initiate a person into another plane of existence from which she could draw the powers to heal. Thus, in the exemplary fashion of shamanic formation, women throughout America were transformed for the service of their people.

The visions that were the matrix of this vocation are remarkable for their color, individuality, and interest. R. L. Olson heard from the Quinault a story of a young woman who wanted to become a medicine woman. Characteristically, she sought solitude in the mountains, where she fasted for ten days. Each day she gathered wood until she had a large pile. On the tenth night she ignited it and waited. As the fire engulfed the wood, she heard a mournful howl from a nearby mountain. She looked and saw the peak begin to sway. The cry came closer as the fire intensified. When she drew back from the heat, a huge animal "something like a wildcat" appeared. It had a sharp nose, and a face so long it dragged on the ground. When it approached the fire, it howled. Fearful, the young woman rejected that spirit saying she did not want that kind of power. So it retreated, but then the water of a nearby lake began to hiss and boil, and many kinds of animals came swimming toward her. She was so terrified that she fainted and had a vision in which the animals brought her five kinds of spirits from which to choose. At length she chose the spirit who could recover lost souls (Niethammer 150). It is notable that this woman was given a choice. It was not unusual for Indian women who had supernatural dreams to reject certain powers offered in favor of others. Individual freedom is preserved even in the grasp of a spiritual encounter, and there was latitude in choosing one's power. But a call to be a medicine woman was highly prized and won the person great reverence. Traditional wisdom held that it must be followed, in one way or another.

THE SHAMAN

The role of shaman, or healer, is the preeminent spiritual calling among Native Americans. As Eliade has noted in the broader scheme of early religions, the shaman is the religious expert who becomes so by a unique and transforming experience in which he or she is remade on a higher plane, reconstituted as a cosmic person able to bridge the gap between the physical world and the spiritual realm. The shaman alone can move freely between these realms and is thus an invaluable source of wisdom and knowledge, and a functionary able to mediate diseases, suffering, and even death. Among the extraordinary powers given to such persons were control of the weather, and of animals.

A wonderful story from the Salish tells of a grandmother who helped lure salmon into her grandson's weir. Since he was having no luck, she decided to help him. So she took a walk by the weir and lay down on the opposite riverbank. Not long after dark a kingfisher flew by, and then she slept. During the night the weir began to catch salmon, and by dawn it was overflowing. The old woman called to the people and the fisherman to gather the more than two hundred fish that had been captured. Then the weir broke. The woman, Sikuntaluqs, claimed responsibility for the catch (Niethammer 157).

The conditions of Native American societies have changed greatly from the pristine times in which traditional ways were followed by all the people. Depending on the geographical location of each tribe, anywhere from four hundred to one hundred fifty years of cultural disruption and change have produced people struggling to retain the uniqueness of their culture while surviving on the economic level. The early parts of that history are dark and shameful chapters of colonial history. But for the past three decades there has been a notable renaissance occurring all over America. In it art, politics, literature, and religion have reemerged as means for an ancient people to express themselves in new ways that draw the attention of the mainstream population. It is not surprising that women have played, and are continuing to play, critical roles in this process. Nor is it remarkable that the heart of this renaissance has been the rediscovery of traditional religious values.

That tradition has a strong heritage of wisdom and practical skill to offer, and these are no less effective today than they were in their original setting. For example, contemporary Native American women have recognized that maintaining one's ties to the traditional past, to ritual, and to the symbolic structures of one's culture confers a significant sense of power, for it contributes to a firm sense of identity, kinship, and self-confidence (Tsosie 17). The tradition recalls that women have always had considerable power, and this empowers many contemporary women to assert their leadership (Winona LaDuke, founder of Women of All Nations, comes to mind) (Tsosie 23). Others retrieve the ancient role of women as faithkeepers and speak the oral tradition in poetry and literature (Paula Gunn Allen, Louis Erdrich, Joy Harjo). In these eloquent voices the themes of the feminine spirit of Native American religions clearly emerges.

Among them is a recognizable "first principle": the Indian woman's unique relationship to the land. There is as well the sense of the individual's relationship to the universe felt as an ancient and vital bond, and the sense of continuity with the ancestors as a vivid part of life (Tsosie 13, 25). Paula Allen has beautifully reaffirmed the symbol of the Sacred Hoop, signifying the awareness of the need to protect and enhance the harmonious bond that unites humans with all living things. As she recalls the forms of that awareness in Laguna Pueblo life, her own homeland, she allows the reader to see how pervasive this sense was to Native America, and how innate it was and is to women's spirituality. Thus native women today are retrieving the older values and discovering anew their power to heal and nurture the children of the one who is the mother of all.

Rosalind I. J. Hackett

WOMEN IN AFRICAN RELIGIONS

> The Great Mother has power in many things. . . . [She] is
> the owner of everything in the world. She owns you.
> We must not say how the whole thing works.
>
> (Drewal and Drewal 1983, 7)

The belief in women's creative and mystical powers is widespread
in many parts of Africa. Such powers may be channeled in a variety
of ways through ritual authority, spirit mediumship and possession,
divination, healing, and mythical knowledge. As attested to above
by the elderly Yoruba participant in the Gẹlẹdẹ festival in western
Nigeria, which pays tribute to and seeks to derive benefit from
female mystical power, these powers are frequently perceived as
shrouded in secrecy and mystery, and both venerated and feared. It
is this very complexity, secrecy, and ambiguity that render our task
of studying women's religious lives in Africa a very challenging one.

There is an urgent need to be aware of the religious factor in African women's lives, not just because of the intrinsic interest for
scholars of religion, but because of the capacity of religion to construct meaning, shape community, and influence behavior and self-
perception. Religious beliefs and values also provide an excellent
insight into a society's gender ideology and attitudes to women
(Strobel 1984, 88). Such concerns are regrettably absent for the most
part from the consideration of women's issues and development in
Africa in general.[1] More generally, as Zuesse rightly emphasizes, we
may note that the boundaries and interrelations between humans
and spirits, village and forest, children and adults, and male and fe-

male are matters of the deepest spiritual significance to Africans (Zuesse 1979, 11).[2]

This essay examines what is known of women's religious roles and experience in traditional African societies, attempting to do justice to both the unity and diversity therein. The survey type of approach, while much needed given the dearth of such comprehensive studies (Kilson 1976; Ezeanya 1976; Strobel 1984; Mbon 1987), has significant limitations. It runs the risk of being static and synchronic, ignoring the dynamism, subtleties, and complexities of the forms of women's religious expression and experience. It may lead to oversimplified generalizations about women's religious status (or lack of it) or unnecessary sentimentality about their fertility and virtue. It may lead to an overemphasis on the exceptional rather than the ordinary, focusing on overt, elite religious authority rather than the more covert, everyday forms of power and experience.

In order to avoid such possible shortcomings, I have sought, wherever possible, to draw on firsthand and indigenous sources. Examples are also drawn from my own fieldwork among the Yoruba, Efik, and Ibibio peoples of Nigeria. While not proceeding as systematically as Marion Kilson does in her article "Women in African Traditional Religions" when she selects religions from societies on seven different levels of social differentiation (Kilson 1976, 134), a range of examples has been selected from the various regions of Africa. The main focus is on the "traditional" religions of sub-Saharan Africa,[3] but some mention will be made of the transformations of African religions in the New World, and in the newer religious movements in Africa,[4] as well as the changes engendered by Islam and Christianity.

To ensure a well-rounded approach to women's religious lives in Africa, rather than being limited to theological concepts or ritual participation as a way of organizing the diverse and abundant data on the subject, Ninian Smart's six-dimensional model of religion is used (Smart 1983).[5] This divides the phenomenon of religion into its doctrinal, mythical, ritual, ethical, experiential, and institutional aspects. While any such divisions may be artificial, Smart is keen to emphasize the organic nature of religion—the interdependency between beliefs and practices, for example. Alternatively, themes or types of religion (such as hunting or agricultural religions, as used by Zuesse in his book on African religions, *Ritual Cosmos* [1979]) or regions, as suggested above, could have formed the basis of this study. However, for comparative purposes and given the orientation of the present book, the six-dimensional model provides a more illuminating and productive approach.

Most importantly, however, the present essay is informed by a more flexible approach to gender and sex roles, and the way these are reflected in or shaped by religion.[6] Gender should be viewed as a cultural construct and sex is the term for biological differences (Strobel 1984, 88). Ritual is an important forum for the articulation of the discourse, or even the dialectics, of gender (Glaze 1986). Representations of "maleness" and "femaleness," together with the crossing of boundaries and reversal of roles may be an integral part of the performance. We need to recognize the multiplicity of signs of female religious power and authority—iconography, verbal and musical expression, dress, dance, architecture, rather than just public office.

Women's religious roles and activities in Africa may be sexually exclusive, parallel, or complementary. They deserve a more thorough and adequate treatment than they have enjoyed in the past, and to some extent the present. For, as D. Amaury Talbot astutely observed in the introduction to her book, *Woman's Mysteries of a Primitive People*, in 1915, "primitive woman is still unknown save through the medium of masculine influence." This requires, as outlined above, the descriptive analysis of women's religious participation and symbolic differentiation, but also an awareness of the interplay and complementarity of men and women and the expression of their power conflicts through the medium of religion.

First, some discussion of the characteristics of African "traditional" societies and their religious systems is required, for this has methodological implications. Despite the enormous geographical and cultural diversity of the African continent, including diversity in the status of women, an underlying asymmetry (of various kinds) between men and women is a recurring feature.[7] Prior to the imposition of European rule, most African economies were based on agriculture, trade, or iron technology. Some were made up of pastoralists or hunting and gathering peoples. Women were (and still are) responsible for much of the agricultural and domestic labor. The majority of slaves in precolonial Africa were women. Women played an important commercial role, particularly in terms of the retail food trade, which they dominated in West Africa. They were able to achieve some degree of economic autonomy often because they were able to retain control of their property in marriage. Women's position was also affected by varying family structures. Most African peoples are broadly patrilineal, tracing descent through the paternal line, but there was a greater incidence of matrilinearity in Africa than elsewhere. Even in patrilineal groups, descent through women still often constitutes a "submerged" line of descent through which spiritual qualities can be carried. Marriage was, as now, predominantly a social, political, and economic affair.[8] Nuclear families were rare, as polygyny served to generate wealth and children for men.

In many African societies women's and men's spheres have traditionally been distinct.[9] The delimitation of these spheres is fluid and varies according to ethnic, social, geographic, and historical factors. Women frequently act collectively within their own sphere, either through voluntary associations or through institutions that parallel those of men. In many parts of the continent it has been demonstrated that women had considerable economic independence and a political voice, but they were not dominant, nor were they equal. Some observers attribute this to a general bias toward male superiority, others to unequal access to resources, while some would point to the various cultural restrictions that may keep women subordinate, such as long puberty and mourning rites involving seclusion, menstrual and childbirth taboos, and male secret societies, which are culturally legitimated ways of suppressing women.

It is generally agreed that colonialism weakened the position of African women, both politically and economically, with the importation of Western culture, bureaucratic structures, and military technology. It served to heighten gender stratification, adding European sexism to the patriarchal elements in indigenous cultures (Robertson and Berger 1986, 6).

Since women's religious roles and experience are embedded in their socio-historical context, it is impossible to isolate their religious lives from their lives in general. Religion is such an integral part of traditional societies that many African languages (if not all) have no word for "religion."[10] Zuesse, in his book on African religions, *Ritual Cosmos,* describes the main focus of African religions as being "the transcendental significance of everyday life" or the "sanctification of life" (Zuesse, 3,7). He further observes that "All energies are directed to the ritual sustenance of the normal order— "normal" in two senses, as imbedded in norms going back to the beginning of time, and as usual and commonplace reality (Zuesse, 3). Therefore it is important to include (wherever feasible given the comprehensiveness of the present essay) the possible interpretations and explanations (both internal and external) that point to the embeddedness of women's religious roles, such as the therapeutic benefits of spirit possession or the function of ritual in validating bonds between women beyond the domestic sphere. We now turn to ideas concerning female mystical power.

IDEAS REGARDING WOMEN'S
RELIGIOUS POWER AND FEMALE DIVINITIES

Ambivalency seems to characterize the ideas about women and their mystical powers in Africa. They are respected for their procreative powers and nurturing role, and their links with the earth and the ancestors. However, in some societies, women may be regarded as the purveyors of evil and misfortune, often in the guise of witches, and polluters of the sacred. This is attributed by some to the uncertainty about women's allegiances to their husbands' lineages. Their generative powers are often associated with the uncontrollable forces of nature. On account of their perceived greater affectivity, they are often believed by certain peoples to be more subject to spirit possession. Their powers of intuition are associated with clairvoyance and equip them in some societies to be diviners.

It is clear that there are strong links between the religious status and participation of women and their (perceived) physiology and psychology. Cultural perceptions of women's power vary from society to society, but some degree of mystery and fear is usually present. It is important to sound a note of caution here, since these are predominantly male perceptions of women recorded and reproduced by male anthropologists. According to Zahan, these dominant perceptions among the Bambara of Mali relate woman to the "night" and "darkness" because she is more enigmatic and unfathomable than any other creature. They relate this to her physical constitution, which is seen as mysterious and very different from that of the male.

In her entirety, the woman "is" the earth—that is, the inert matter that encloses "life within it, and supports all that is necessary for man's existence. She 'is' also water, the element of proliferation and abundance. Each of the woman's sexual organs, as well as its adjacent parts, reveals by the analogies it evokes the different parts of the creation, each as mysterious as the next." (Zahan, 94)

Thus, like the earth, woman is inert and passive. Like water, she is multiform and changeable (Zahan, 95) and does not let herself be mastered. Like the night and the shadows, woman is difficult to fathom, and like a cavity or hollow, she does not allow herself to be grasped. Alongside this is the view, as among many other African peoples, that women do not know how to impose limits on their words and speak too directly (Zahan, 114). Similarly the dominant ideology among the Dogon asserts that women's

chattering is a fault attributed to them by their nature, directly relating them to sickness and death, since a surfeit of words engenders
illness (Zahan, 113). This both reflects reverence for the power of
the spoken word in Africa, and men's fear of women's powers in
this regard.

It will be seen that the various ideas concerning female nature
and sexuality are translated into the ritual roles that are ascribed to
women, such as night sorcerers, shrine caretakers, "wives" of deities, healers, life cycle ritual specialists. These ideas also influence
their metaphysical status as witches or ancestors (all of which will
be dealt with in later sections). In some cases, women may only perform key ritual functions when they have reached the postmeno-
pausal stage or are childless, and have become "like men."[11] They
also account for why women are often restricted to neutral or domestic space, particularly for important ritual occasions, because
they are considered both vulnerable and dangerous (Douglas, 7).
Clearly, such an ideology serves male interests socially.

Sacred images also express ideas concerning female spirituality.
Yoruba religious art frequently depicts, in wooden sculptural form,
a kneeling woman with a child on her back or at her breasts or
sometimes uplifting her breasts, all symbolizing not just fertility
but devotion to the deity. The woman's dignity and devotion are regarded as exemplary for both men and women. Among the Igbo and
Ibibio, also of Nigeria, their "cool," female masks and masquerades,
which are usually colored white and emerge in the afternoon, dance
and move gracefully like women, in contrast to "hot" male aggression. Certain priests of the Yoruba thunder god, Ṣango—whether
male or female—are known as the wives (iya) of Ṣango and are endowed with the power to soothe and placate the god, just as females
are believed to have a soothing effect on their husbands (Drewal and
Drewal, 166). Their hair is plaited in a bridal coiffure to communicate that their heads (the site of one's personal essence, potential,
and destiny) have been prepared for a special relationship with the
deity. The Yoruba perceive patience to be inherent in femaleness
(Drewal and Drewal, 15). The Great Mother epitomizes patience—
in other words, her inner head is composed. She is believed to
exact covert revenge and does not display visible anger. These ideas
about women are expressed in the channeled and controlled steps of
the female Gẹlẹdẹ festival dances, which are powerful yet re-
strained. The mothers—that is to say, all spiritually powerful
women whether elders, ancestors, or deities—"who are united with
all women by the 'flow of blood,' embody the concept of balance, a

female quality that men must understand—indeed emulate—in order to survive" (Drewal and Drewal, 15).

Another important idea that needs to be mentioned here, although it will receive fuller treatment below and in the section on mythology, is that in former times women had much greater mystical and creative power, and were superior to men. They were held to have founded the great secret societies or even been the prime movers of creation. Whether because of their perceived inability to keep secrets or their loquaciousness, or their unwillingness to wage war (Tonkin 1982), men appropriated the mystical secrets and wrested the power from women.

Turning to conceptions of the divine as female will enable us to examine how some of the above beliefs and ambiguities are reflected and manifested in the form of spirits and divinities. Even in the absence of convincing statistics (Dime, 39), scholars have little doubt that male conceptions of the divine predominate in Africa. As we shall see, this may not always have been the case and the issue is, in fact, more complex than might be assumed. Let us begin by considering some of the classic examples of female deities that are still extant.

Contrary to the pantheons constructed by most studies of African traditional religions, it is exciting to discover that there exist a number of female creator gods. The Uzo (or Ijo), a matrilineal people of the Niger Delta region of Nigeria, for instance, speak of God in strictly female terms.[12] They have four principal names for the supreme being—namely, Temearu (Tamuno is a variant of Temearu), "she who is the molder of all," Ayeba (or Ayebaarau), "the foundress" of the universe," Woyingi or Oyin, "our mother," and Oginarau, "she who dwells in the heavens." There are also references in a ritual context to Ayo, which also means "mother," and to Pere Bau, meaning "the sovereign queen." Temerau is therefore believed to be the primordial mother, uncreated and the ground of all being, as illustrated in the following drum poem:

> Oloma N'Ogina, Oloma N'Ogina
> Oloma N'Ogina who creates before she kills;
> Creatrix of cities, Creatrix of humanity
> Creatrix, Creatrix, Creatrix, Creatrix Being.[13]
> The eternal Fountain,
> The sovereign Queen,
> who, with only one breast,
> gave birth to all mankind.

Among some peoples, the godhead is considered to be female as well as male. The Ewe people of the Republic of Benin (formerly Dahomey) believe in a bisexual supreme deity, known as Mawu-Lisa.[14] Mawu is female and identified with the moon; Lisa is male and identified with the sun. Mawu is generally held to be the creator god; she is the elder, the mother, although occasionally the consort or twin of Lisa. While she has no regular worship or temples, there are many myths that connect her with creation. It is told that she created earth and then withdrew, because of trouble with men. Lisa, as her only son, was sent to clear the forests and make tools. Mawu is considered to be gentle and forgiving, as illustrated in the oft-cited proverb, "When Lisa punishes, Mawu forgives." Parrinder reports that the image of Mawu in the ancient royal collection at Abomey (capital of the ancient kingdom of Abomey) was the only image of a supreme god that he had seen. It was a wooden statue, colored the red of dawn, with large breasts and a crescent in one hand, symbolizing Mawu's creator role and association with the moon.

In some parts of the central republic of Benin and neighboring Togo, Nana Buku is the chief creating deity.[15] She is female and sometimes paired with Osha who may be the same as Lisa. Parrinder records similar beliefs among the Yoruba in Nigeria, where Oriṣanla (or Ọbatala), and his wife Odudua,[16] appear to be supreme creating beings, independent of, or prior to, the normal Yoruba god, Ọlọrun or Olodumare. The female identity of the creative figure of Odudua or Oduduwa, while contested by some scholars, is emphasized by Idowu (1979) and Lawuyi (1988). Nyame, although often regarded as male by the Akan of Ghana, is also referred to as a lunar goddess (sometimes as the female aspect of a bisexual deity), who gives birth to the universe without the help of a male partner.[17] The waxing moon symbolizes her as a giver of life and increase, while the waning moon symbolizes her as killer-mother. She is often represented in the form of the *akuaba*, a statuette given to barren women by a priest so that they may bear children. A similar statue, with upraised arms, is placed on the graves of headwomen of clans. It symbolizes the lunar *kra* (or life-giving power) of the deceased. The *akuaba* consists of a rectangular or triangular body (symbolizing Nyame as ruler of the sky, earth, and underworld), surmounted by a straight bar, and the head in the form of a disc. The disc represents the moon and the circle within the larger circle is the *kra* or life-giving power of the goddess. Meyerowitz (23) argues that the position of the Akan queen-mother in the state and the rites and customs that reflect the identification of the divine life-giving queen mother with the moon, point to the belief that in the beginning, a mother-goddess, visible as the moon, was held to have given birth to the universe.

Similar ideas about a female primordial deity exist elsewhere. In the early part of this century, D. Amaury Talbot (who was the wife of a British colonial administrator in southern Nigeria), conducted a field study of Ibibio women, which resulted in her book *Woman's Mysteries of a Primitive People* (1968). One of her most exciting discoveries, she claimed, was that (contrary to prevailing beliefs) a female creator deity, known as Eka Abassi (Mother of God), was at the fount of Ibibio religion (Talbot 1968,9). This was fearfully revealed to her by elderly women, who themselves had heard it from their grandmothers. They described Eka Abassi or the Great Mother as the mother of all created things including Obumo, the thunder god. She was also his consort, but believed to be above all the other gods in the pantheon and so could not be spoken of (Talbot 1968,10). She was commonly believed to manifest herself in the "unhewn stones set amid sacred waters" or the great trees "the givers of babes." Her supreme attribute was "bestower of fertility," hence many barren women prayed to her and parents of deceased children would bring a lock of their children's hair to place in a hole in the rock dedicated to the goddess, known as Abassi Isu Ma (the face of the Mother) (Talbot 1968, 12). As source of life, she was also the source of death; people would say "Eka Abassi has taken our brother." Even then it was regarded as a jealously guarded secret that, in earlier times, it was woman, not man, who was the dominant sex (Talbot 1968, 13) and source of creation. Today, among the Ibibio, Annang, and Efik peoples, Eka Abasi is viewed less as the primordial mother of all children and more as a spirit agent, mandated by the supreme being, Abasi Ibom, to deliver unborn babies from the spirit world into the wombs of would-be mothers (Mbon 1987, 16). Each *Eka-Abasi* must be properly placated, otherwise sickness in the newborn child may result. The role of earth goddess has been taken over by Isong (Talbot 1969,II,62).

After Chukwu, the supreme being in the Igbo pantheon, in southeastern Nigeria, the earth goddess, Ala (or Ani or Ajala), is the most eminent.[18] Ala is provider and protector, and owner and mother of her people; her special province is the land. She not only controls its fertility and productivity, but is also queen of the underworld. She is responsible for public morality in conjunction with the ancestors and will punish violently any defilements of the land such as incest, adultery, stealing of yams, fighting, birth of abnormal children, or murder. Shrines to Ala are communal and the cult is an important focus for social unity. Among the Owerri Igbo, when the equilibrium of the entire community is threatened by sickness, war, famine, or drought, a *mbari* is built, usually for Ala. These are shrines filled with painted mud sculptures. Ala is always seated in the *mbari* house with her feet on an iron rod, reflecting both her status and people's desire to control her by rendering her immobile (Cole, 201ff.). She is greatly feared for the wicked side of her character; she often bears a knife in her right hand, which denotes malice, beneficence, and strength. This type of ambiguity of power is also found in Matu, the night-hag Mistress or Mother of the Dead among the Mbuti Pygmies, whose name signifies genital, especially menstrual, blood (Zuesse, 22). She is also associated with the moon and releases animals into the forest (Zuesse, 21–22, 35). Ala is depicted by her people in a dignified, seated position. The breasts of her life-sized body droop because she is a great woman, "past childbearing, older, a man among women" (Cole, 204). The unnamed children beside her are those whom she controls, for whom she peels yam.

These symbolic and mythical ambiguities are an important indication that male/female spirituality and power are a contested issue. These differing voices are addressed by Robert Armstrong, who, while attending a sacrificial ceremony among the Idoma of Nigeria in 1952, recorded the following ritual statement: "They gave (the sacrifice) to the East. The East said they should give it to the West. The West said they should give it to God. God said they should give it to Earth, for Earth is senior."

As a result of his ensuing years of research, he concluded that the seniority of Earth is a strongly held ancient view among the Idoma of Nigeria (Armstrong, 9). The Earth ceremony with its attendant taboos is the only one that affects the entire population simultaneously. Yet people dispute Earth's seniority over God (generally conceived as male) even though she is the source of Earth-dwelling spirits (Morton-Williams, 245).

The dialectics of gender approach that we have espoused is well illustrated in the intercommunication and interaction between Ọlọrun and Onilẹ.[19] This ongoing rivalry (Ọlọrun is generally considered to be in the dominant position, which Onilẹ continually seeks to reverse) is reflected in the tensions between the Ọba or king and the Ọba's chiefs respectively. In other parts of Yorubaland, divination verses attest to female suzerainty at the beginning of the world. Woman was given control over the gods and all good things of the earth at the time of creation (Drewal and Drewal, 9). McKenzie has argued that a more flexible, localized view of Yoruba ideas and rituals is required ("subjective theisms"), since in reality he found that there is no fixed pantheon (McKenzie 1976). Varying *orişa* achieve supreme importance for particular localities, families, or individuals, and this may be subject to change over time. In other words, a woman may have been born into a family that worshiped Ogun, the god of iron and war, but developing infertility, she may turn to the cult of Oşun, the river goddess, who has a reputation for helping barren women.

Thus far, some common characteristics of female mystical power and conceptions of the divine as female have emerged. These are generally associated with procreation and fertility, but also with death and morality. I have emphasized, however, that a rigid and ahistorical approach to these issues, which, as we have seen, are often shrouded in secrecy and ambiguity, fails to appreciate the dynamics of the gender factor in religious ideas. Likewise the ideas about female religious power are influenced, but not determined, by such socio-economic considerations as matrilinearity, demography, and livelihood. For example, the primary religious orientation of the Efik of southeastern Nigeria, prior to trading contact with Europeans, was numerous river god cults (which were predominantly female). By the end of the eighteenth century, it was the male-oriented secret society, known as *Ekpe*, which proved more suitable for the changing political and economic conditions (Hackett 1989, 36). Amadiume has argued that the original supremacy of the cult of the goddess Idemili among the Nnobi Igbo declined in favor of the patriarchal ancestral cult, when Idemilili was domesticated and transformed into the wife of a less powerful god, Aho (Amadiume, 99).

MYTHOLOGY

The previous section already addressed some of the myths concerning an original mother of humankind. To this might be added the myth in eastern Africa of a virgin woman known as Ekao, who fell on earth from the sky and bore a son; the son married another woman and founded human society.[20] Even if woman did not act alone, but rather as an agent of God, there are many myths that describe her sharing in the mysteries of life and creation. Several origin myths, such as those of the Akamba, Turkana, Luo, and Luhyia and others in Kenya, recount how the first human pair were lowered down by god from the sky to the earth.[21] Other myths describe how woman was created after man. However, the focus here is rather on myths that address women and their specific powers, needs, and transgressions.

One myth tells about the Great Mother, Eka Abassi, of the Ibibio people of Nigeria, how she is the teacher of and guarantor of fertility for earth women (Talbot 1968, 13):

> When, therefore, she saw that all the first earth-women were barren, long she pondered; then sent to them a great white bird, which on reaching earth, laid a gleaming egg. . . . Old women tell that, after showing the people how, by honouring eggs and oval stones, and making sacrifice to the Great Mother, the gift of fruitfulness might be won, the magic bird flew back to its home in the sky; whence with folded wings, soft brooding, she still watches over the children of men. . . . The Moon-bird floats down from her place in the sky and pecks up grains or other food . . . she looks round to see that all is well with the earth-folk, and that the *tabu* on fowl and eggs is still being observed. (Talbot 1968, 13–14)

The myth serves to account for various taboos as well as going on to remind people of the consequences of breaking these taboos (barrenness). In some myths, women are credited with the discovery of or invention of fire or foodstuffs and their preparation, emphasizing their nurturing aspect. For the Mbuti Pygmies, fire was the possession of Matu, the old woman herself, mistress of the night forest (Zuesse, 34). According to one legend, it was a woman who stole fire from either the chimpanzees or the great forest spirit (Turnbull, 156).

Many African myths of origin tell how humans initially lived in conjunction with the gods, usually in the sky. The ensuing division or separation of earth and sky, and humans and gods, explains the conditions of human life as people now find it. Some have described this as a form of "paradise lost," while there is evidence that a number of peoples (Mbuti Pygmies, San peoples of the Kalahari Desert, Zulu, Fang) celebrate the removal of God from their midst, because of the danger of "divinity's unrestrained proximity" (Zuesse, 55). Mbiti claims that there are several myths that place the blame on women for the separation of earth and heaven. An Asante myth from Ghana describes how a woman, while pounding *fufu* (a regional speciality), kept on knocking against God, who lived in the sky.[22] So God moved higher up. The woman instructed her children to construct a tower by piling up mortars. The tower almost reached God, except for a gap that could be filled only by one mortar. The mother advised the children to take the mortar at the bottom of the pile to fill the gap. The whole tower tumbled down, killing many people. One version of the Yoruba creation myth states that God withdrew because a woman wiped her dirty hands on the sky. The Dogon attribute the coming of "real" death into the world to a woman's discovery of the fibers that had previously clothed earth (African-American Institute, 11). Satimbe masks representing the woman, Yasigne, are worn at funeral rites by Dogon men.

A myth of the Dinka of the southern Sudan, which tells of division in the world, states that Divinity (and the sky) and men (and the earth) were originally contiguous; the sky lay just above the earth.[23] They were connected by a rope, by means of which people could clamber at will to Divinity. There was no death at this time. One day a woman "because she was greedy" decided to plant or pound more than the amount of one grain of millet a day that had been permitted by Divinity to the first man and woman. In raising her pestle or hoe to pound or cultivate, she struck Divinity who withdrew, offended, to his present great distance from the earth. He then sent a small, blue bird to sever the rope that had previously given access to the sky. The Dinka believe that they now suffer death and sickness as a result of their separation from Divinity. Lienhardt remarks that it is significant that a woman should be the cause of the separation, since women are considered by the Dinka to be responsible for setting up factions leading to the separation of peoples, and in dividing the lineage. This is not necessarily a bad thing, it is somewhat inevitable, since people are cramped by Divinity's presence. Women are therefore the agents who allow people to "grow up" and develop continuously. As Lienhardt emphasizes, an awareness of the total *mythos* is required, for in myths of the first master of the fishing spear a woman suggests the means whereby his lethal power may be counteracted. Women therefore appear in complementary roles.

Some interesting myths surround the relationship between women and the origins of secret societies and certain festivals in Africa. The Mbuti Pygmies believe that it was a woman who once "owned" the *molimo* (their most important festival), but the men stole it from them and since then women have been forbidden to see it (Turnbull, 156). In the case of the Ibibio of southeastern Nigeria, the Ekpo Society, now exclusively a men's secret society, was originally discovered by women in Cameroon who went fishing early one morning.[24] The secrets and "image" (probably the masquerade costume and mask) of Ekpo were taught to them by a "divine woman" who came down to earth to share this knowledge with her human sisters. The women later bore the image in triumph to the town and established the rites of the cult there. After a time the men noticed the importance of the new institution and persuaded the women to admit them to their mysteries. Once initiated, the men slew the women and passed a law that only men could become members or witness the rites. Until today, women and non-initiates are still subject to harassment should they look upon the rites or sacred symbols of the cult, in spite of government measures in this regard. The myth described above (similar accounts may be found among the Dogon and Gola, for example [Tonkin, 169]) together with its ritual implications, is an important metaphor for, and cause of, male-female hostility (Isichei, 62).

Similar patterns are described for the development of Ekpo Njo, the most feared of all Ibibio secret societies, which represents the ghosts of the dead. Men strove to find a way to overthrow women's power and knowledge of the "old, old days." Following internecine warfare, they were able to appropriate some of the masks and ritual paraphernalia, eventually wresting the mysteries of the cult from the younger women. The older women continued to practice the cult in secret, but were eventually discovered and beheaded. When the Talbots were conducting their research in Nigeria in the early 1900s, they were able to witness the female heritage of this cult in the form of a terrifying Kali-like figure—Eka Ekpo, the Mother of Ghosts, Bringer of Death. Her colossal, ill-proportioned, and coal black mask emerged principally at the time of the New Yam Festival. She was seen as the dread counterpart of Eka Abassi (Mother of God). As D. A. Talbot (1968) comments, here was the symbol of motherhood as the source of both good and evil, life and death. She links this queen of the underworld figure with the belief found elsewhere that women introduced death into the world and that what creates may also destroy.

It would be unwise to draw any conclusions from the above myths, since they are very fragmentary and our selection is limited and focused on those that contain some reference to women. We also need to be aware that the majority of myths were created by men; those produced by women are often muted. However, it is possible to see the patterns of mythical explanation for women's ritual power or exclusion and place in the social order. We have also seen some examples of the more widely held belief that women once held power and were overthrown by men (Hafkin and Bay, 9). While there would seem to be no evidence of earlier matriarchies, hunting and gathering peoples with matrilineal descent tend to be more egalitarian than agricultural peoples with patrilineal descent.

RITUAL

In this section on ritual, I shall first treat women as ritual specialists, then as ritual participants, examining the rites associated with womanhood. Examples of women playing primary ritual roles, with their attendant political power in the traditional African context, are relatively few. One of the classic examples is the Lovedu Rain Queen of the Transvaal.[25] The queen was believed to be of divine origin; her mystical powers were linked to the welfare of society. Her powers were not absolute; combining her own divinity with the use of medicine and charms, she worked in conjunction with the ancestors to control rain and ensure the cyclic regularity of the seasons. She was believed to be so bound up with nature that her very emotions affected the rain. Various royal institutions preserved her sanctity, such as celibacy, seclusion, and suicide. Her death was considered to dislocate the rhythm of nature, causing drought and famine, and necessitating rites of purification, to ensure the harmonious succession of the new queen. The prestige of the queen as ruler helped maintain the high status of women in a patrilineal society. Heads or "mothers" of districts (who might also be men) also served as mediators to the queen. The queen's feminine attributes—appeasement, reciprocity, reconciliation—were viewed as positive, diplomatic qualities.

Among the Yoruba, women are admitted into the priesthood of the main cults such as Ṣango (thunder god), Ọbatala (god of creation), and Ọṣun (goddess of fertility). Women are more likely to predominate as officials in cults devoted to female or bisexual deities, or where there is a powerful consort, such as in the case of Ọya (wife of Ṣango).[26]Opinions are divided about whether these women who held high religious office, such as head of the king's market, the worship of departed kings, or the cults of Oduduwa or Ọṣọṣi and the royal women, were exceptions to the rule and whether they wielded any real political authority. Afonja argues that the religious roles offered these women as advisers to the king are in addition to the general respect accorded their office as intermediaries between people and the divinities (Afonja, 151).

The existence of a strong female deity is no guarantee of female ritual authority. The majority of Igbo cult groups are exclusively male preserves, even that of Ala, the earth goddess (Arinze, 73). Possible exceptions could occur at the family cult level, when elderly women could sacrifice directly to their personal *chi* (guardian spirit) in their compounds, but never at the public level. Igbo women may become diviners, *ndi dibia*, but usually as elderly widows.

In order to gain ritual authority, women sometimes need to have exceptional status or they must lose the characteristics of womanhood. For example, the figure of Mother Ndundu, the female overseer of the Kimpasi, is sometimes an albino (*ndundu*), but is generally an old woman past childbearing age, and who had not given birth to children or they had died. In ordinary life, therefore, she is an unfortunate figure, yet within the context of the cult she is given an elevated status. Her infertility provides her with a central ritual role as mother of the cult members (Janzen, 91; Lewis, 95). Among the Azande, certain women diviners gain authority to mediate between the human and spirit world following a symbolic death, where they claim to witness and experience their death and resurrection (Zahan, 83). No training is required in this type of initiation.[27]

Let us turn now to the role of women as spirit mediums and diviners, both of which are widespread phenomena in Africa, but sometimes difficult to distinguish.[28] Frequently the call to mediumship begins with psychological or physical disturbances, which may worsen if the call is ignored (Horton, 34). Sometimes mediumship is expressed in marital terms—the woman becomes a "wife" of a spirit or deity. The main deities in the Bunyoro and Buganda kingdoms in East Africa had women dedicated to them as wives (Berger, 174). These women were to remain unmarried while in the deity's service. Two of the most important were Mukakiranga, wife of Kiranga in Burundi, who played a major part in the great national ceremony and annual spiritual renewal of the Rundi kingdom, and the medium of Mukasa, the god of Lake Victoria, who was popularly held to have the power to cure the king and work miracles (Berger, 175–76). Gã mediums of southeastern Ghana have been studied by both Field (1937) and Kilson (1972, 1975). Traditional Gã religion (or *kpele*) consists of a number of cults, addressed to particular divinities, which are served by two categories of specialists: priests and mediums. The priesthood is a kinship-ascribed male status chiefly concerned with representing humans to the gods; mediumship is an achieved female status concerned with communicating the messages of gods and humans to one another. Priests and mediums cooperate to perform certain calendrical rites (priestly authority tends to be greater), but the medium (woyei or wongtse) may operate independently, as a diviner, to serve clients. Field argues that these women have no authority except when possessed. Kilson states that most of the mediums are illiterate, and often childless, women; yet their ritual possession and success as insightful mediums may serve to redress much of the inferiority they would normally experience in Gã society.

Berger lists a number of varied ways in which East African women achieved higher status as mediums, symbolized through their use of male stools, male ceremonial dress, and spears, for example, and expressed through the authority they were able to exert over women's (and sometimes men's) affairs in the community (Berger 1976). For two years (1971–1973) during the war for independence in Zimbabwe, an aged female medium, known as Kunzaruwa, serving the great spirit Nehanda, gave advice to the guerillas on how to win the war. She imposed ritual prohibitions, told them what food to eat and which paths to take—"she hated all European things" (Lan, 3–7). There was a tradition of resistance and liberation associated with Nehanda mediums, which dated back to Shona resistance against colonial oppression in the 1890s and was expressed in many important works of Shona literature from the 1950s onward.

Let us now turn to those women who practice divination. Among the BaLuba specialists who serve as intermediaries between the souls of the dead and the living, there are numerous women who serve in the highest class (Zahan, 83). All Gusii diviners in Nyansongo in Kenya are female. Following an apprenticeship and elaborate initiation ceremony, the diviners of a given area are said to meet secretly from time to time. As Levine states: "The parallel between the female diviners meeting together, training and inducting novices, and the female witches who also meet, recruit and train, is a striking one" (Levine, 232–33).

Sandobele (female diviners) among the Senufo of Côte d'Ivoire believed to mediate between land spirits and clients, are generally revered for their ability to "cool" or heal people from the illnesses and troubles resulting from their unintentional offences against the spirits (Glaze 1986, 37). Yoruba women are not excluded from the divination system known as Ifa. In fact, in Yoruba mythology it is told how the goddess Ọṣun was initiated into Ifa. Some would claim that several verses (odu) of the Ifa corpus, particularly those associated with female or androgynous deities (Ọya, Olokun, Oduduwa), were composed by women.[29] However, few women attain the status of babalawo (father of mysteries; sometimes the term, iyalawo is used) because of the lengthy and rigorous apprenticeship involved. Many families consider divination to be an undesirable and impractical career for women.[30] Barber (288–90) maintains that women are not debarred from becoming babalawo, only that they choose not to—preferring to avoid likely accusations of witchcraft. Among the Temne of Sierra Leone, distinctions between male and female are reflected in the contrasts between private/public and individual/social divination (Shaw, 289). In private divinations, the majority of clients are women and, apart from a few female private diviners, divination is predominantly a male preserve. Public divination, the domain of men, is more positively evaluated, since it is performed in the open and is associated with the upholding of community interests.

Numerous rituals and accompanying taboos concern women alone.[31] Women's religious devotions among the Igbo of Nnobi in southeastern Nigeria begin with private worship known as ilo chi (remembering the deity) at their personal shrines before proceeding to group worship, ilo chi Idemili (remembering the goddess Idemili) (Amadiume 1987, 103–4). Ekwe titled women have their own exclusive day of worship. In a number of parts of Africa, it is commonly believed that pregnant women need special protection from witches and evil spirits. Gã women (Ghana) would bathe in a bath of herbs and morsels of food (believed to deceive the preying witch) (Field 1937, 164). To ensure a safe delivery, libations might be made to the gods, the priest might draw symbolic markings on the body, and rites to ascertain the wishes of the unborn child might also be performed. The Ila of Zambia forbid pregnant women from entering the hut where a woman has just given birth, from entering a calabash garden, and from getting too close to a nest of eggs. Zuesse explains this in terms of a basic antipathy between the not-yet formed (primordial) and the formed (cosmically structured) (1979, 83). Death in childbirth is greatly feared; the Asante of Ghana remove the undelivered child, for they believe it will prevent the dead woman's soul from entering the place of the dead, transforming it into a vengeful ghost (Field, 122).

Barrenness, the fear of women throughout Africa, is generally attributed to witchcraft or the failure to propitiate regularly family gods and spirits. Many women turn to fertility gods or goddesses. Ibibio women might still supplicate Eka Abassi as they did in the past, going with their husbands to lay a sacrifice at her rock shrine:

> O Abassi Ma! Keeper of Souls! What have I done to anger
> thee! Look upon me, for from the time I left the fatting-
> room in my mother's house I have never conceived,
> and am a reproach before all women. Behold! I bring gifts,
> and beg Thee to have pity on me and give me a child.
> Grant but this prayer, and all my life I will be thy servant!
> (Talbot 1968, 19)

In some societies such as the Efik and Ibibio, women were os-tracized if they gave birth to twins—the sign of a woman's associ-ation with evil spirits. Twin killing was a major target for reform by Christian missionaries. Among other peoples such as the Yoruba, Bambara, Dogon, and Senufo, multiple births are viewed as sacred and special rites may be performed in the event of the death of a twin (Houlberg 1973).

Menstruation is often the source of ritual seclusion and numer-ous taboos, reflecting the ambivalent attitudes toward women's re-productive powers. Ndembu women have to go and live in special huts and are advised to throw the water used for washing the cloth used at such times in the river, not in the bush, where it might im-pair hunters' medicines or be used by sorcerers (Turner, 248). Among the !Kung Bushmen of the Kalahari Desert, menstruating women are supposed to keep away from their husbands and not touch their husband's weapons, for fear of destroying their power. The Ila of cen-tral Zambia do not allow menstruating women to tend the fire, for fear of polluting the ancestral essence (Zuesse, 82).

Yet the first menstruation is often a sign of rejoicing and marks the beginning of the ritual preparation of the young girl for wom-anhood and marriage. Throughout the matrilineal central Bantu cultures, these initiation rites for women are basically similar, in-dicating their importance (Zuesse, 83). Everywhere the novice is separated from her mother, taken from the hut, and in the bush and later in an instructress's hut is reshaped into the archetypal fertile woman.[32] The culmination is often the wedding of the young woman. Ritual serves to delineate this transition, dramatizing and resolving the social conflicts. Ndembu women in Zaire believe that the shades, mukishi, will be angry and cause infertility if a girl does not pass through the rites before her marriage (Turner 1968, 200).

The focal point of the Ndembu girls' puberty ritual, *Nkang'a*, is the sacred *mudyi* tree, whose milky white latex symbolizes both the mother's milk and the matrilineal and social customs of the Ndembu. The tree also serves to delineate womanhood from manhood, and mother from daughter (Turner, 17).

The importance of these rites in symbolically expressing female identity and defining women's domestic roles is attested to by their persistence in the urban context. In Lusaka, Zambia, for example, these initiation rituals are on the increase, often being jointly performed by several ethnic groups (Bemba, Ngoni, and Crewa). Modified forms have been incorporated into the life cycle rituals of the indigenous or independent churches (Jules-Rosette 1980).

Fertility rites are often celebrated exclusively by women at strategic times of the agricultural year. Ibibio women and girls would go naked, unseen by men, at the time of the New Yam Festival to the shrine of the (male) deity, Isemin, protector of women and bestower of fertility (Talbot 1968, 109–10). They would present sacrifices of corn and fish, symbolizing fertility of earth and the waters. Because of their association with life, women often have major responsibilities at the time of death. Among the Gã of Ghana, an old woman assists the surviving partner to perform the *kwa* or separation ceremony, to convince the dead of the grief of the survivor. The woman is not a priestess (although the appointment is hereditary), just an old woman belonging to a family that the dead know and respect (Field 1937). The difficult and important task of identifying a particular reincarnated ancestor among the Anlo of Ghana, known as *megbekpokpo*, the rite of reincarnation, is a female diviner's prerogative (Gaba, 181). Women are also the principal or key functionaries in a number of other Anlo rituals associated with birth and death. In the past, Ibibio women had responsibility for the burial of their dead warriors in a ritual reminiscent of the Isis and Osiris myth of regeneration. Secret rites were performed, which involved the drawing of sacred boughs over the body of the deceased in an attempt to extract his virility for the community (Talbot 1968, 206–8). Efik women, also from southeastern Nigeria, are responsible for announcing the death of the king or *obong* to the community.

In many parts of Africa, women may be subjected to numerous rites of purification at the death of their husbands. These were often condemned by Christian missionaries, for they involved months of seclusion for the woman, where she was not allowed to wash, plait her hair, or wear clothes; she was expected to wail publicly and sometimes undergo physical ordeals by way of purification. Among

the Efik and Ibibio these mourning rites (*mbukpisi*) have been much
reduced and modified in recent times.

As many have observed, it would seem that women are generally relegated to subordinate ritual roles in the central, communal,
and public cults. They rather dominate in the personal rituals of
status transformation or life cycle rituals (Kilson 1976, 138–39; Richards 1956). Even when women's involvement appears to be peripheral, in the rituals that men dominate and control, it may be
subtle and strategic, pointing not only to men's recognition of female mystical and procreative powers, but also their former higher
status. For example, the new ruler, or Ntoe, of the Qua people of
southeastern Nigeria is crowned by the Queen Mother, who represents the populace. A senior, royal woman may be called upon to
retrieve the *ekpe* (leopard) or mysterious and invisible being from
the forest, upon which the Ekpe society is founded (Hackett 1989,
35; Talbot 1968, 193). As part of one of the main festivals of the
Ekong or warriors' society among the Ibibio, on the periphery of the
proceedings, sat singing a man dressed in women's clothes. He represented "The Mother of Ekong" ensuring blessings for the coming
year and reminding people of the female origins of the society (Talbot 1968, 203–4).

The use of ritual space may be significant in understanding perceptions of gender. The Lele of Zambia regard the forest as almost
exclusively a male sphere; women are generally prohibited from
entering it on all important religious occasions until the proper
rites have been performed by men. Women are allocated to the neu-
trally perceived grasslands. Douglas explains this ritual exclusion in
terms of religious conceptions of women's fertility powers—they
are both highly vulnerable and highly polluting (Douglas, 7). The
Yoruba Gẹlẹdẹ festival to appease the "mothers" or witches of the
society is appropriately conducted in the marketplace, at once the
domain of women and the worldly domain of spirits, where homage
can be paid to the special powers of women (Drewal and Drewal, 10;
see also Lawuyi and Olupona 1988).

RELIGIOUS EXPERIENCE

The area of women's religious experience yields little information. This is attributable to the fact that most accounts of women's
religious activities are androcentric, generally viewing women as
insignificant or subordinate. In addition, there is a general lack of

interest in (or avoidance of) the experiential dimension by researchers. The intangibility and psychological nature of experience, especially when related to the divine or the spiritual, represents a
methodological challenge. There is a need for more biographical and
autobiographical accounts, such as the one of Julia, an East African
diviner, whose extraordinary calling brings about a reversal of an oppressive family structure (Binford, 3–14) and that of Nisa, a !Kung
woman, who describes the trance states of women during the drum
dance and their intimate connection with n/um or the power of
healing (Shostak, 297–300). In the absence of such accounts, artistic
images offer visual statements—kneeling, nurturing, offering, paying homage, uplifting breasts—of female emotions—namely, seren-
ity, devotion, submission, calmness—in the presence of the divine.
The product of male sculptors, these images nonetheless condense
and articulate through female symbolism the ideas and norms of di-
vine/human relationships.

The marginalized and privatized world of women may be decep-
tive and misleading to observers, whether inside or outside the culture. Women may not always be center stage, but their experiences
in ritual seclusion may not necessarily be characterized by power-
lessness and fear. Instead they may display tolerance of male coer-
cion, such as in masking traditions, and enjoy ideological freedom
(Tonkin, 171). Women are not supposed to know the secrets of male
cults and associations, but they frequently do.

Since it is the spirit-mediumship cults that have offered women
some of the greatest possibilities for active participation, it is here
that we are provided with accounts and interpretations of women's
religious experience. Berger rightly distinguishes between spirit mediumship (discussed earlier), where the person is conceived of as
serving as intermediary between the divine and human realms, and
spirit possession, a form of trance in which the behavior indicates
spirit control (Berger, 161). The latter has engendered the formation
of a number of cults, which Lewis has labeled marginal or "peripheral" since they provide therapeutic assistance to the powerless. He
describes the Sar cult among Muslim women in Somalia, where women's ailments are interpreted by them as possession by traditional
sar spirits. These spirits demand luxuries and finery from their husbands and expensive cathartic dances to effect the recovery of the
women. The men generally acquiesce to these demands, which usually occur at times of neglect and abuse in a conjugal relationship.
Through the cult Lewis argues that women are able to air their
grievances and gain some measure of redress in a world dominated

by men. Similar patterns of possession are observable in Ethiopia (where it is known as the Zar cult), Egypt, other parts of northern Africa and Arabia, as well as in the Bori cult in northern Nigeria and Niger (Lewis, 75–79).

Wilson disagrees with Lewis's interpretation of these cults in terms of sexual antagonism; he proposes instead that spirit possession is linked to tensions between women, often caused by marriage (Wilson 1967). Spring is critical of the above social/functional perspectives, because they depict women negatively as "pawns" or "agents of conflict." Based on her research among the Luvale of Zambia, she argues that spirit possession is a way of treating physiological disorders among women and binding them together into a wider symbolic community (Spring 1978). Mernissi shows how Moroccan women seek material power through saint cults, the type of power denied to them through trade unions and political parties. She maintains that this form of religiosity, while offering some therapeutic benefits, only serves to entrench their marginality in an "ever-strengthened" patriarchal system (Mernissi 1977). In his examination of spirit possession among the Kalabari in southeastern Nigeria, Horton (1969, 35ff.) provides important information on women's possession (oru kuro), particularly the circumstances of its onset, the ensuing consequences for behavior and life-style, and acceptance or rejection of the possessing spirit (oru). He regards such possession as a response to childlessness, terming it more generally as a "loophole for the socially miscast." However he does see this type of spirit possession as a means of recasting social roles, and also as a platform for the introduction of innovation into a highly conservative culture.

TABOOS AND VALUES

As already seen, the discourse of gender relations is worked out through the domains of religious ideas, myth, ritual, and experience. Notions of morality are frequently related to conceptions of relationships between dominant and nondominant groups. The focus of this are the ambiguities surrounding perceptions of women's moral nature and their moral actions, and how religious beliefs and rituals shape and express this morality. These ambiguities are linked to women's biological and social roles in providing continuity of the lineage and yet being external to it. Women are seen as the link between nature and culture (Zuesse, 230). Because of their generative powers they are linked to the forest, to wilderness, and as a potential threat to culture. Yet as nurturers they are instrumental in transmitting culture. The woman is nonetheless integral to the highest ethical value—the community. Many African proverbs glorify the role of the woman as wife and mother.

Yet the power to create also entails the power to destroy, and women are frequently blamed for infertility, adultery and witchcraft. The same innate powers that create can also destroy, particularly when frustrated by jealousy or infertility. Zahan attributes the association of women with the night, witchcraft, and sorcery to their mysterious and unfathomable character and physical constitution (Zahan, 94). Blood is a powerful and pervasive symbol of the ambivalent attitudes toward women's powers (Gaba, 185). Among the Dogon, the prohibitions on women at the time of menstruation—that is, confinement to a menstrual house or *ya punune ginu* at the edge of the village—are linked to a primordial offense. It is believed that the Earth Mother gave birth to animals and humans. She cohabited with her firstborn, the mythical ancestor, Dyougou Serou. This incestuous act resulted in the appearance of menstrual blood, the first form of death in the world and universal disorder (Calame-Griaule, 288).

As Kiernan has shown, African ancestral spirits can be focal points in the articulation of a moral system. Among the Swazi of southern Africa, a mother joins her husband's ancestors in death (in many African societies a woman's status in the next life is dependent upon that of her husband's). However, the mother as ancestor is anomalous—while absolved of moral evil, she can be the direct source of natural evil. This ambiguity is reflected in the location of her burial place, which is just outside the entrance to the cattle kraal. This signifies her dissociation from her own natal ancestors, yet stops short of identifying her with her husband's ancestors (Kiernan, 194–95). Among the Bamana, women are venerated as ancestral spirits (African-American Institute, 10). Carved wooden female figures, suggesting fecundity, represent primordial ancestor figures.

Women are commonly viewed as agents of conflict. Their transgressions are considered to be more polluting (Zuesse, 64; Gaba, 181; Shaw, 292). Men justify their control of women on this basis. A good example of this comes from the Hune, an acephalous, egalitarian people of northwestern Nigeria (Salamone, 522). Adultery is considered a serious offense for both sexes, yet women are the ones subjected to religious sanctions. A woman accused of adultery has to swear an oath, in front of her husband and the chief priest, on a stick used for killing goats in religious sacrifices and take a poison-ous medicine. Men are fearful of women destroying the family as source of cultural identity. Women have great cultural power as the repository or embodiment of Hune values and the Hune believe that "purity" and "fidelity" in women hold their society together and justify male control and religious legitimation. Among the Nyole of eastern Uganda, who explain suffering in terms of dislocations in social or ritual relations, unrelated or "foreign" or "little" spirits are particularly associated with women (Whyte, 175). These spirits are generally perceived as dangerous and undesirable, and are treated by being sent away. They represent women's movement from one place or husband to another, and justify men's manipulation of such un-controlled movement in the interests of marital stability.

Witchcraft is an important area in connection with ethical be-liefs and practices. It is widely held that women are more frequently associated with witchcraft than men. Among the Temne, for in-stance, a barren woman is the primary suspect if her co-wives' chil-dren fall ill and die (Shaw, 294). She is believed to have contributed her womb to a communal witch feast and to be continuing to sac-rifice her co-wives' children as victims. Among the Tswana of Botswana, for example, night witches are believed to be elderly women who conduct their nefarious activities in small groups at night, wearing virtually nothing and smeared with ashes and the blood of the dead (Schapera, 111). It is interesting that women are more frequently stereotyped as witches even when, in terms of actual accusations, there may be an equal sex distribution (Mar-wick, 284).

In Nupe society in northern Nigeria, witches, who are always held to be women, are dependent on men's power to function. Yet men can block the evil witchcraft of women, particularly through the male secret society. In Nadel's view, this reflects a sharp sex an-tagonism, "which assigns the evil intention to the female, and to the male a benevolent and ideally decisive—if somewhat utopian—role" (Nadel, 265–66). He emphasizes the social context of these be-liefs, since Nupe wives occupy a strong economic position as itinerant traders. Men are often indebted to women and fear their withholding their procreative power for professional reasons. This threat to male interests because of their dependency on women also finds expression in men's fears about types of hidden supernatural power inherent in women and their fear of women's secret powers and knowledge (Shaw, 291). It is interesting and significant, as Shaw notes in her work on Temne diviners and clients, that women themselves view their secrecy as both positive and necessary to marital and social harmony (Shaw, 293). Shaw also demonstrates how female clients may to some extent, through private divination, negotiate and validate their life experience (1985, 300).

Some consider the stereotyping of women as witches with fearful mystical powers as deriving less from restricted social worlds and economic independency and more from their generative powers and their mediatory role. The association of women with transitions, links, and opposed realms promotes fears of divided loyalties, expressed in demonic images and justifying the enforcement of taboos and male control (Zuesse, 231). Whether these taboos prevent menstruating women from entering the forest or associating with hunters or not eating certain foods or animals, it is important to see them not solely as repressive mechanisms, but rather as tacit symbolic affirmations of the implicit divinity and power of women. In other words, taboos are a means of ordering and patterning, not so much that which is different (sacred and profane), but that which is similar (women and forest, for example, among the Lele of the Congo forest), resulting in a differentiation of the sacred and recognition of transcendental otherness (Zuesse, 68).

Despite the tendency to project disorder and inexplicability onto women, there are examples of women serving as agents of social order. For example, Yoruba festivals honoring particular deities provide a ritual context for women to serve as social critics. Using songs, dances, and ritual role-reversal, groups of women (though not exclusively women) parade the streets lampooning social miscreants of the past year as part of the annual Oke'badan festival in Ibadan, Nigeria. This festival honors the founding goddess of the city and solicits her continuing protection for the forthcoming year. Among the Wè of Canton Boo in the Ivory Coast, *woodhoe*, female counterparts to male masqueraders, *gela*, perform antisorcery functions (Adams, 54–55). However, painted faces in lieu of face masks limit their powers.

INSTITUTIONAL ROLES AND AUTHORITY

The institutionalized aspect of women's religious roles will necessarily be the smallest section because many of women's religious activities are private and domestic. Also women's institutionalized and legitimated religious authority has to some extent been dealt with in the section on ritual. So the focus of this discussion will be women's socio-religious associations. Among the Senufo in Côte d'Ivoire the Tyekpa or "women's secret society" or "women's poro," which strikingly parallels the men's Pondo or Poro secret society, engages in prestigious visual display for large audiences in funeral and initiation rituals (Glaze 1975, 65). During the funeral ceremonies, a large, painted figure sculpture of a seated woman, representing the Ancient Mother, Maleeoo, is carried aloft by a woman.

The female adult initiation society, known as Bondo or Sande, found among many peoples in Liberia and Sierra Leone, is a powerful female association with political, social, religious, philosophical, and educational aims (Boone, 13). It is one of the few known instances in Africa in which women wear masks. The society's classic mask or *sowo* plays a key role in Sande ceremonial and ritual activities, and embodies the society's precepts and ideals. In her study of the Sande aesthetic, Boone recounts how:

> According to tradition, the root source of all fertility, productivity and wealth is female, so Sande exerts its strong spiritual influence over both men and women. Sowei, the high-level leaders of Sande, are adepts with access to spirit ancestors and forces of nature; they have a monopoly over certain sacred knowledge crucial to the development, happiness and success of the individual and the well-being and prosperity of the community. (Boone, 16)

The sanctioning power of Sande in the community is dramatically represented and reenacted by the appearance of the masked female ancestral figures in the village at the close of the initiation season (MacCormack, 35). In addition to the figures clothed in black, helmet-type wooden masks and black raffia capes, symbolizing healthy, virtuous, and serene womanhood, there is also a second type of mask. Blotched and diseased, with snail shells containing Sande "medicine," this masked figure publicly remonstrates against wrongdoers of either sex and all ages. This reminds all who watch the public ceremony of Sande's power to apprehend and punish transgressors even if they sin in secret.

In addition to the deep feeling of social solidarity that Sande provides for women as both producers and reproducers in settled agricultural societies such as Sierra Leone, Sande laws articulate the respect that should be shown to all women (MacCormack, 34). These laws are generally respected by all men and women, being legitimated by religious sanctions and pragmatic political action on the part of women organized locally into a hierarchy of offices (MacCormack, 34).

Among the Igbo of the northeastern region, in a particular village group—Nkaliki—women's public roles altered dramatically in the mid-1970s.[33] The oracle of Uke, in a dream to the priestess, asked women to organize and dance *Ogbodo Enyi* (a male age-grade mask, which comes out at funerals and dry season festivals) in return for intercession. Now well established throughout Nkaliki, women's masquerade is a collective, nonhierarchical representation with a single mask (elephant mask and bell-shaped raffia costume). It differs from the male version in that it is not competitive, but is similar in that the masker is chosen by the *ogbodo* through divination and dreams. The masquerade is controlled by women and generally approved of by men.[34] It is a public symbol and celebration of the social identity and contributions of women, but it serves to complement the male *Ogbodo Enyi*, by paying the debt of gratitude to the oracle for the whole community, a function which the male spirits cannot satisfy.

CONCLUSION

It may be argued that the distinction between men and women is the primary social distinction for many societies (e.g., Whyte, 182; Shaw 1985). Sometimes myths and rituals serve to emphasize and explain these contrasting categorizations of reality, sometimes they are more implicit. It has been demonstrated that social models and their representation through religious ideology and related ritual practice are elaborated from the dominant male position (E. Ardener 1975). This view represents men as central and identifies them with the essence of society itself. Such ideological discourse defines women as "other" than men, either by placing them peripherally in nature, or as possessed by spirits that are marginal, foreign, or little (Whyte, 180–81; Lewis 1971). Several authors have argued that despite social differences, men and women still share the general social model and are part of the same social structure (Whyte, 189). The counterpart models and alternative views generated by women, which seemingly repudiate the male subject, are not completely independent or autonomous. They are interactively shaped by the general ideological and structural model. We have seen throughout this chapter how this complementarity, rather than equality, is expressed in a number of ways both symbolically and ritually, transcending everyday hierarchical social relationships. Religion serves both to legitimate male dominance as well as to provide a (sometimes subtle or covert) channel of communication for the muted or subdominant groups such as women to express their interests, to challenge male control and revalidate their identities. African ritual has been aptly described as "dialogic in form, and always a process of competition, negotiation and argumentation" (H. J. Drewal 1988, 25). West African secret societies and their attendant masquerades represent particularly rich contexts for such processes and perceptions (Glaze 1986).

When studying African traditional religious systems and women's roles in these religions, it is important to guard against the too ready imposition of Western values and over objectified interpretations (Holden, 3–4). It is too simplistic to dismiss women's ritual roles as subordinate because they are linked to their sexual status and biological functions (Hoch-Smith and Spring, 2–4) or to say that women achieve authority only by becoming and behaving like men. Complexities and ambiguities abound. We are challenged to be attentive to the female symbols atop male masquerades, the sexual metaphors of architecture, the cross-dressing of ritual participants, the androgynous character of many religious leaders, the transformative capacity of spirit possession. Both perceptions and behavior are marked by fluidity—men, as well as women, may become "wives" and "cooks" of the deity, just as women may be "husbands" and "kings." Exclusion from the religious life, such as initiation rites, may not necessarily entail exclusion from the spiritual life, since it may be held that women naturally carry (spiritual) knowledge within them (Zahan, 54–55).

It is this very ambiguity and fluidity that generates debate, such as over whether ritual segregation gives women a greater or a different power or serves to alienate them, or whether female ritual authority shapes, questions, or even undermines male authority in any way. More research is required in this field. It must treat women as subjects and not just as objects. It must seek to hear the multiplicity of voices involved in order to see more clearly, even reconstruct, women's religious worlds not just in contradistinction to, but also in interaction with, men's religious lives. Likewise, the historical perspective is integral to an appreciation of the dynamic of gender discourse.

It seems appropriate to end this chapter on women and religion in Africa, not so much by looking back, but rather by looking forward, by highlighting areas of persistence and transformation. Evidence abounds for the demise of traditional religious institutions, yet there are some interesting examples of women playing strategic roles in preserving and revitalizing religious traditions both in Africa and the New World.

For example, the annual festival of the river goddess, Ọṣun, in Ọṣogbo, western Nigeria, has become a very popular event, drawing thousands of people from all over Nigeria. They come to seek her blessings since "she is the wisdom of the forest where the doctor cures the child and does not charge the father. She feeds the barren woman with honey and her dry belly swells up like a juicy palm fruit."[35]

Susanne Wenger, an Austrian artist who settled in Yorubaland in the 1960s, and became a priestess in Ọṣogbo, has done much to revitalize the traditional festival of Ọṣun (Wenger and Chesi, 1983). Yoruba goddesses have an appeal beyond national boundaries. In her book *Oya: In Praise of the Goddess*, Judith Gleason traces the various manifestation of Ọya in nature—the great river Niger, strong winds and tornadoes, lightning and fire, and the mighty African buffalo, and her associations with funerals and masquerades constructed of secret, billowing cloth, from Africa to the New World, where she has devotees in Brazil, the Caribbean, and New York City (Gleason 1987). Ọya is also linked to market women, to transformations, to the dynamic interplay of edges, to concealment, and to female leadership. African goddesses have tremendous appeal for African-American women (Sojourner 1982).

In both Zimbabwe and Nigeria, white women have been active in revitalizing traditional cults. In addition to Susanne Wenger, referred to above, a white spirit medium, Elsie Thompson, in eastern Zimbabwe, claims to have been possessed by and ordained to bring back the spirits of Mzilikazi and Chamunika (*New African*, May 1989). A white American woman, Norma Rosen, whose initiation into the Olokun cult in Benin has been well-documented (Nevadomsky 1988), has established a shrine in Long Beach, California.

Mami Wata, an African female water spirit worshiped from Senegal to Tanzania, is currently experiencing a dynamic growth (H. H. Drewal 1988). Mami Wata is a Pidgin English term for "Mother of Water." In her more contemporary transformations, she represents Africans' attempt at understanding or constructing meaning from their encounters with overseas strangers. Mami Wata is an independent, foreign spirit, free of any social system. She is believed to dominate the realm of water and those who come under her sway. She relates to her devotees more as a lover than a mother, and offers rich financial rewards. Africans incorporated the concept of the mermaid, characteristically depicted as emerging from the water, combing her long, luxurious hair as she contemplates her reflection in a mirror (H. J. Drewal, 162).

The many new religious movements (mostly Christian-related), which abound in places like South Africa, Kenya, Nigeria, Ghana, and Côte d'Ivoire, exhibit both continuity and innovation. In the independent churches, women have found important new ceremonial functions. This leadership and responsibility is both an extension of and reinterpretation of traditional priestly roles and spirit mediumship (Jules-Rosette 1987; Callaway 1980). It contrasts with the submission and dependency advocated by the mission-related churches. Several women have founded their own movements, such as Alice Lenshina and the Lumpa Church in Zambia, Christianah Abiodun and the Cherubim and Seraphim movement in Nigeria, Marie Lalou and the Eglise Déimatiste in Côte d'Ivoire, Mai Chaza in Zimbabwe. Indeed, the very first recorded African religious movement was founded by a woman, Dona Béatrice (Kimpa Vita) in the late seventeenth century in the former kingdom of the Kongo (now Zaïre). Because of her challenge to the Portuguese Roman Catholic Church and its doctrinal and liturgical hegemony, and her advocacy of indigenous leadership, she was burned at the stake in 1706. It has been argued, however, that despite their increased ritual participation (in part linked to the fact that healing is a central focus of these movements), women's political authority and public leadership are restricted in the independent churches (often through taboos), short-lived (female successors are rare), and chiefly symbolic (Jules-Rosette 1987; Hackett 1987, 191–208).

Within the mainline churches or the mission-related churches, it is generally not as priests or pastors that women may exercise influence, but as leaders and participants in the various women's associations and prayer bands. These semi-autonomous groups are a feature of many of these churches; they allow women to organize their own religious and social affairs. In many cases, they constitute a powerful voice within the respective churches and a force for church development (women are renowned as effective fund raisers) (Hackett 1985, 259). As a corollary of this, a number of Methodist and Anglican women in Nigeria have built up compound healing ministries. As in the case of "Ma Jekova," a well-known Methodist healer in Calabar, southeastern Nigeria, they see their work as complementary to that of the larger, more official church.

The position of women in African Islam has been largely neglected by researchers or they have been portrayed as absent or marginal within Islam (Coulon, 113). Islam is presented as a male religion; women's involvement is rather in the (pre-Islamic) spirit-possession cults such as *bori* and *zar* (described above). However, several women with special powers or *baraka* have become revered or even worshiped as saints, *marabouts* or *khalifa*. Such an example is Sokhna Magat Diop in Senegal, who took over her father's Mouride community in 1943 (Coulon, 127–29). Information is coming to light about female *shaiks* who were renowned for their scholarship (Boyd 1989). Boyd and Last show how there is more open activity among Muslim women in northern Nigeria in the twentieth century (1985). Based on their research in Sokoto, they describe the activities of formal women's organizations, where women serve as *agents religieux*. Focusing on the actions and thought of learned women, they claim that women have helped transform the character of West African Islam through their encouragement of the use of vernacular languages and the use of popular songs and poetry for religious instruction and devotion.

The New World offers exciting possibilities for the study of continuities and transformations of African women's religious experiences. In Haitian Voodoo, women possessed by female spirits act out the social and psychological forces that define, and often confine, the lives of contemporary Haitian women (Brown, 1989; 1981, 237). These spirits or *lwa* are derived from African religious traditions (such as Mami Wata) and identified with Roman Catholic saints (such as the Virgin Mary).

This chapter has sought to identify and discuss some of the main areas of women's religious experience and expression in traditional Africa as well as in the newer African religions. Much research remains to be done, not just to enrich and challenge our understanding of the African context, with its rich and varied religious traditions, but also to complement the many valuable studies that have emerged and continue to emerge on women and religion in related contexts.

Michiko Yusa

WOMEN IN SHINTO: IMAGES REMEMBERED

The sun rising over the sea is one of the prototypical images of Shinto and traditionally has been worshiped as the goddess Amaterasu. So the soaring Mt. Fuji, the symbol par excellence of Japan, is worshiped as the goddess Konohanasakuya. The feminine presence in the deep recesses of the Japanese psyche, and hence in Shinto, is something undeniable. In the following, we shall look into the roles women played in the Shinto tradition.

My discussion will first focus on the political leadership and power held by the women of antiquity. Those women derived their political power from the realm of the supernatural, largely thanks to their shamanic abilities. We shall also examine Shinto myths and legends and see how the images of ancient powerful shamanesslike women were remembered. Then we will turn to the historical development of the institution of high priesthood, the unifying symbolic power of Amaterasu, the emergence of egalitarian movements during the latter half of the Tokugawa period, and finally the rediscovery of the place of women in Shinto by modern scholarship. But before going into these points, let us first ask what Shinto is.

WHAT IS SHINTO?

Can we call Shinto a native religious tradition of Japan? Some argue against it because of the multiracial ancestry of the Japanese people. The fact remains, however, that Shinto is a term given to designate the native cult of deities (*kami*), which stood in clear contrast with Buddhism when the latter was introduced to Japan from

Korea in the sixth century C.E. The word Shintō literally means "the way of gods/deities," which was coined in contradistinction to "Butsudō," "the way of the Buddha"—that is, Buddhism. The first mention of this word Shinto appears in the *Nihon shoki* (Chronicles of Japan, hereafter cited as *Nihongi*, Aston 1972, II, 106).

The Shinto religion centers in the worship of ancestors and *kami* deities, and emphasizes ritual purity (both physical and mental) of the worshipers. Shinto maintains the worldview that human beings are basically good, sharing the goodness of *kami* deities, and that the world in which we live is a good place, where we ought to pursue happiness and prosperity, and establish peace. Shinto does not have any set creed or credos. It focuses on *here and now*, affirming life on earth, and it asks of people to purify their heart and live with the everrenewed sense of gratitude for the benevolent protection of *kami* deities. The Japanese may not particularly think of Shinto as a religion, but rather a way of life. Annual Shinto-related events, such as the year-end general cleaning (from the Shinto ritual of *harai*, "dusting") and the ceremonies of the New Year, are deeply ingrained in Japanese culture and continue to punctuate the lives, however hectic it may be, of the contemporary Japanese people.

The *kami* spirits may manifest in human form (anthropomorphized) or in any other natural forms, including animals, stones, trees, rivers, winds, thunder, lightning, and so forth. *Kami* are the mysterious powers that pervade nature and affect the affairs of the human world. In ancient days, whatever defied the comprehension of the human mind was conceived to be *kami*. Heroes, gifted artists, poets, extraordinary scholars, as well as ominous characters, fear-invoking spirits, and all sorts of natural phenomena belong to this category of the mysterious things. Motoori Norinaga, the scholar of the eighteenth century, characterized *kami* as resembling Rudolf Otto's *mysterium tremendum* (see *The Idea of the Holy*). Motoori wrote:

> *Kami* signifies . . . the deities of heaven and earth that appear in the ancient records and also the spirits of the shrines where they are worshiped. It is hardly necessary to say that it includes human beings. It also includes such objects as birds, beasts, trees, plants, seas, mountains, and so forth. In ancient usage, anything whatsoever which was outside the ordinary, which possessed superior power, or which was awe-inspiring was called *kami*. Eminence here does not refer merely to the superiority of nobility, goodness, or meritorious deeds. Evil

and mysterious things, if they are extraordinary and dreadful, are called *kami*. It is needless to say that among human beings who are called *kami* the successive generations of sacred emperors are all included. (Tsunoda 1958, 23–24)

Kami deities are set off from the ordinary human world by their *sacred* quality. Traditionally, they are considered to be endowed with four different powers or efficacy: gentle spirit (which protects the worshiper), rough spirit (which brings about war victories, for instance), miraculous spirit (which performs miracles), and blessing-conferring spirit (which brings about happy life on earth). Motoori Norinaga interpreted that these powers could be exercised by one and the same deity as necessary and as called upon (Chamberlain 1981, 290, n. 9).

The number of *kami* deities is enormous. It is said that there are eight million deities (*yao yorozu no kamigami*); of course, the figure eight million means "innumerable." So great is the number of Shinto deities. Certain *kami* are local deities, while others are known for their ability to manifest themselves (sort of theophany or, better, hierophany—*yōgō* in Japanese) at various places without being confined to one specific place. An example of the latter *kami* is the deity Hachiman, the god of war. *Kami* are often worshiped at shrines (*jinja*). In every small ward of a Japanese town, there is a local *jinja*, and every village has its *jinja*. We cannot begin to list the names of the shrines in Japan, the number of which being as great as the number of deities. The Grand Shrine of Ise, enshrining the Sun Goddess Amaterasu, assumes a special position among all the Shinto shrines in Japan, together with the Izumo Shrine, which enshrines the great earth deity, Ōkuninushi.

Shinto and Women, A Brief Overview

That the chief deity, Amaterasu, is a she seems to say something about the power women had in antiquity. Pioneer ethnologists such as Yanagita Kunio and Origuchi Shinobu did much to advance the study of the role of women in Japanese folk tradition, and currently many scholars are following their footsteps.

It appears that women's position declined with the separation of the political and religious domains. The offices of politics and religion were gradually separated with the institutionalization of *ritsuryō* system (an administrative and governmental system, including a land-distribution plan, the idea imported from Tang

China) in the mid-seventh century and under the modified *ritsuryō* system of Heian aristocracy. Women, formerly having derived their political power from their spiritual and religious ability, were gradually shut out from the political sphere. In this process, controlling power shifted to the hands of their fathers. Along with this change, shamanesslike spiritual power went underground from the point of view of official history. Women's status in general declined even more under the rule of the warrior class (*samurai*) and was devastated under the Neoconfucian ideology (especially the stream of Zhu Xi's thought) adopted by the Tokugawa Shogunate (1603–1867). Some scholars of the Tokugawa period firmly believed in the inferiority of women, so much so that they flatly rejected that Amaterasu was a goddess. How could a member of the inferior female sex be the supreme deity of the Shinto pantheon?, they asked. Indeed, some documents, going back as early as to the Muromachi (1336–1573) as well as of the Tokugawa periods, reveal that Amaterasu was regarded neither male nor female but as a "parent." Amaterasu, when called the "great deity of Ise" (*Ise Daijin*), sounded more masculine, and people held a vague notion that the great deity of Ise was male. Such was the dominant current of male superiority of the recent past. But with the development of the critical study of the ancient texts, especially of the *Kojiki* (Records of Ancient Matters, hereafter cited as *Kojiki*), the views of the remote past came to be rediscovered.

THE SHAMANIC QUEEN, HIMIKO

We know from such documents as the *History of the Kingdom of Wei* (*Weizhi*, c. 297 C.E.) and the *History of the Latter Han Dynasty* (*Houhanshu*, c. 445 C.E.) that a queen by the name of Himiko (or Pimiko) ruled the country of Yamatai, otherwise called Wa, which was one of some thirty countries on the Japanese islands in the third century C.E. The *History of the Latter Han Dynasty* records that the country of Wa was in great turmoil from 147 to 189 C.E. and there was no ruler; thereupon they agreed on a female ruler, Himiko, and the confusion subsided. Himiko secluded herself from the public. She received divine oracles and communicated these oracles to her younger brother who was the only male allowed to see her. The *History of the Kingdom of Wei* describes Himiko:

> She occupied herself with magic and sorcery [i.e., shamanic practices], bewitching the people. Though mature in age, she

remained unmarried. She had a younger brother who assisted her in ruling the country. After she became the ruler, there were a few who saw her. She had one thousand women as attendants, but only one man. He served her food and drink and acted as a medium of communication. She resided in a palace surrounded by towers and stockades, with armed guards in a state of constant vigilance. . . .

When Himiko passed away, a great mound was raised, more than a hundred paces in diameter. Over a hundred male and female attendants followed her to the grave. Then a king was placed on the throne, but the people would not obey him. Assassination and murder followed; more than one thousand were thus slain.

A relative of Himiko named Iyo, a girl of thirteen, was then made queen and order was restored. (Tsunoda 1958, 8–9)

The description of Himiko found in the *History of the Latter Han Dynasty* is quite similar. "Remaining unmarried, she occupied herself with magic and sorcery and bewitched the populace. Thereupon they placed her on the throne. She kept one thousand female attendants, but few people saw her." It adds that her younger brother "was in charge of her wardrobe and meals and acted as the medium of communications" and that "the laws and customs were strict and stern" (Tsunoda 1958, 9). In 238 C.E., during the reign of Emperor Ming, it is recorded that Himiko sent an envoy to Taifang, the capital of Wei. Again, in 240, missions were exchanged between the courts of Wei and Himiko. In 265 the successor of Himiko, Iyo, sent a tribute of twenty people to West Jin (265–316). From these records, we have a glimpse of the country of Yamatai, which was headed by powerful shamanesslike queens, which had the technology and the wealth to send envoys to the distant land of China, and which was recognized by the Chinese court. The leadership exercised by women must have appeared strange to the Chinese officials, so the court recorders especially made a note of the fact.

As we turn to the Japanese sources of early history, we are struck by the curious lack of any reference to Himiko in any of the documents, including such main sources of ancient Japan—the *Kojiki*, the *Nihongi*, the *Kogoshūi* (*Gleanings from Ancient Stories*), local records called *Fudoki*, and the *Man'yōshū*, the anthology of ancient poems. These sources contain Shinto myths and legends, and are considered sacred books by Shintoists. The conspicuous absence of reference to Himiko in these classics raises speculations as to how Himiko or her likeness might have been treated in these early sources. Various opinions have been advanced as to the possible identity of Himiko with such figures as the sun goddess Amaterasu, the shamanic Princess Yamato, the charismatic Empress Jingū, and so on (Hori 1968, 191; Ellwood 1986 argues the identity of Himiko with Empress Jingū). The uncertain identity of the Queen Himiko adds an aura of mystique to this shamaness queen.

SUN GODDESS, AMATERASU

The main Shinto myth concerning the sun goddess Amaterasu may be relatively late in making. The reason for this speculation is that Amaterasu was the clan deity (ujigami) of what later became the imperial family. It was with the rise to power of the imperial family that Amaterasu was accorded the highest position in the Shinto pantheon. It is also likely that her story presupposes the actual existence of shamanesslike Queen Himiko.

Amaterasu was the daughter of Izanagi and Izanami, the primal couple. The name Izanagi means "he who invites," and Izanami "she who invites." They are the Adam and the Eve of the Shinto tradition in the sense that they are the primal male and female. (It should be noted that the comparison stops here, since there is no Shinto myth that corresponds to "the fall.") The names of six divine couples who existed before Izanagi and Izanami are mentioned in the Kojiki and Nihongi, but Izanagi and Izanami are the first divine couple around whom mythic tales unfold. They descended to the earth to create the islands of Japan. To begin this task, they stood on a heavenly floating bridge and stirred the ocean below to coagulate the sea salt to make a little isle. They went down onto it, performed a marriage ceremony, and gave birth to islands through the act of procreation. Izanagi and Izanami created eight islands of Japan and all sorts of natural features on them. When Izanami gave birth to a fire god, she got burned and consequently died. Enraged, Izanagi killed this fire god and proceeded to the land of the dead to seek for her.

To make a long story short, Izanagi was unable to bring his wife back to earth and had to return empty-handed. Upon his return from the underworld, he went to a river to perform purification because he came in contact with the world of the dead. Amaterasu was born when he washed his left eye. Susano-o, the wind god, was born as he washed his nostril, and Tsukiyomi, the moon god, was born as he washed his right eye. These three deities are called the "three noble children." Amaterasu was endowed with brightness, limpidity, and purity. Izanagi entrusted his daughter the domain of "high heavens," Susano-o the domain of the ocean, and Tsukiyomi the domain of night. Tsukiyomi never appears in any significant way in the subsequent myth.

Amaterasu was put in charge of the affairs of heaven and presided over myriads of deities. She eventually descended onto Ise to be worshiped there first as the imperial patron deity, and later as the patron deity of the country of Japan. Susano-o, on the other hand, represented something of a chthonic (i.e., earthly) character, and eventually descended to the land of Izumo to rule the world below heaven. There may well have been political overtones associated with these divisions of the domains to rule, as Susano-o may represent a patron deity of a powerful rivaling clan that vied power with the imperial family. At any rate, in the myth, Amaterasu and Susano-o interact as a kind older sister and a good-hearted but unruly younger brother. Amaterasu has understanding like the benevolent sun, while Susano-o possesses a violent temper like a storm.

The Incident of the Heavenly Rock Cave

The incident of the heavenly rock cave amounted to the expulsion of Susano-o from heaven and the elevation of Amaterasu to the throne of absolute sovereignty. The story begins as Susano-o is doing nothing but wailing and crying, saying he wants to see his mother, Izanami, whom he has never seen. Finally, Izanagi concedes. Before he descends to the underworld, Susano-o first goes to heaven to visit his sister Amaterasu to bid farewell. Amaterasu was alarmed at his coming; she armed herself, clad in man's clothes, and met him at the entrance to heaven. Susano-o claimed that his intention of visiting her was pure. In order to prove his innocence, he asked Amaterasu to agree on producing children by saying oaths to each other. Five male children were born of Amaterasu's breath, and three female children of Susano-o's. Because he produced "delicate female children," Amaterasu judged that Susano-o was innocent. Having proved his innocence, Susano-o was elated with joy and began to act rambunctiously in heaven. He broke down the divisions of the rice field and filled up the ditches (thus rendering ineffectual the irrigation system, which was essential for the good harvest of rice), strewed excrement all over the sacred palace where Amaterasu was to observe the ritual of the first harvest of the year (thus defiling the sacred rite performed by the queen, or king, whose proper obser-

vance of rites was considered necessary for the good harvest of rice),
and finally, he threw a colt, which he flayed alive, into the sacred
weaving chamber (thus blocking the sacred rites of the queen, or
king, and defiling the palace with death and blood, also interfering
with the process of weaving new clothes needed for the observance
of rites). The last incident greatly upset Amaterasu. She locked herself up in the heavenly rock cave and would not come out. The
world plunged into utter darkness and eternal night ensued.

Deities gathered together in front of the heavenly rock cave and
discussed how to bring Amaterasu out. They bade the wise deity
Omoi-kane to think up a plan, which he did. Various deities were
put in charge of making a mirror, curbed jewels, and a sacred rope.
Some gathered the branches of sacred *sakaki* tree, a sort of evergreen
tree, and tied the sacred jewels onto them. A sacred cock was made
to crow to signal the arrival of the dawn. When the preparation was
completed, they lit a bon fire and gathered around a goddess, Ame-
no-uzume. She stood on a sounding board, stamped her feet on it,
and began to dance. All the deities, who sat around her, sang and
cheered her by clapping their hands. Ame-no-uzume went into a divine trance. Her breasts were unclad, and she tucked up her skirt,
exposing her private parts (all symbolizing agricultural fertility). At
that moment, heaven shook, and the myriads of deities roared with
laughter. Ame-no-uzume's dance was a shamanic dance of prayer to
entice the life-issuing force to return to the earth.

Having heard the happy merriment outside the heavenly rock
cave, Amaterasu grew curious. "Why is Ame-no-uzume dancing,
and why are the deities laughing while I am here?" She slid the rock
a little to see the scene outside the cave. At that moment, two deities, Ame-no-koyane and Futotama, put out a mirror in front of her
face. Amaterasu saw a radiant beauty in front of her. Not knowing
that it was her own reflection on a mirror, she was lost in her be-
wilderment. At that moment, Ame-no-tajikara-o, a god with strong
arms, took her hand and walked her away from the cave, while Futotama tied the sacred rope at the entrance to the cave so that she
could not return to it any more. The light came back to the world.

This episode of heavenly rock cave, some observe, depicts the
scenes of the imperial enthronement ceremony (Saigō 1967, 85–87).
The temporary disappearance of the sun goddess into a solitary confinement and her reappearance from it can be interpreted as an en-
actment of the birth of a divine child, and hence a new divine ruler.
When the sun goddess reemerged into the world, she was no longer
the benevolent sister of Susano-o but the sovereign who was to pre-

side over the political affairs of heaven. The daughter of Izanagi went through the rite of passage and reemerged as the reigning queen. She now had Takami-musubi, a male deity, at her side whenever she made political decisions. The partnership of Amaterasu and Takami-musubi reminds one of the relationship between Himiko and her brother, in which Himiko dealt with religious matters, while her brother saw to political matters (Yanagita 1962, 7–22).

As for Susano-o, he was vanished from heaven and descended into Izumo. There he became a local hero, killing an eight-headed serpent. He found a sword in the tail of the serpent and sent it as a gift to his sister Amaterasu. Susano-o married Princess Kushinada, who had been offered to the serpent as a sacrificial maiden. They bore a child, Princess Suseri, who fell in love at the first sight with a handsome earth deity Ōnamuji or Ōkuninushi, and married him at once. Ōkuninushi had a magical power and a medicinemanlike quality, and was a powerful local deity of Izumo, to whom the Izumo Grand Shrine is dedicated. To the chagrin of Princess Suseri, Ōkuninushi married many other maidens, who bore him numerous deities all associated with certain place names, and Ōkuninushi expanded his territory—a mythological description of the conquest of local tribes by a powerful clan. It was with his two sons that the heavenly court of Amaterasu negotiated for the sovereignty of Japan. Finally, Ōkuninushi's sons yielded their lands to the sun goddess. This episode implies the growth of the imperial power and its attainment of the position of supremacy over other vying powerful clans.

The Descent of the Imperial Grandchild

In the *Kojiki*, the land of Japan is called the "luxuriant reed plain land of fresh rice-ears" (*Toyo ashihara no mizuho no kuni*), suggesting that Japan was already in the stage of wet rice cultivation by the time these stories were told. Amaterasu thought that the land of luxuriant reed plain should be ruled by her offspring. Therefore, she first planned to send Ame-no-oshihomimi, the son who was born of the swearing that she and Susano-o conducted. Amaterasu and Takami-musubi sent messengers to the earth and negotiated with the sons of Ōkuninushi the possibility of their relinquishing the holding of the lands to the heavenly deities. The former eventually conceded to their request. Meanwhile, a son was born to Ame-no-oshihomimi and Takuhatachichi, the daughter of Takami-musubi. Thus, the duty of ruling the land below befell on this grand-child of the sun goddess, Ame-nigishi-kuni-nigishi-amatsu-hi-daka-hiko-hono-ninigi, the long name signifying that he was the prince bounty, who shines high in heaven and is prosperous in heaven and on earth (hereafter he is called Ninigi). Ninigi was accompanied to earth by five deities, Ame-no-koyane and Futotama (who put out the sacred mirror in front of Amaterasu's face), Ishikoridome (who made the sacred mirror), Tamanoya (who made sacred jewels), and Ame-no-uzume—the deities who had been meritorious in bringing Amaterasu out of the heavenly rock cave.

Prior to Ninigi's departure, Amaterasu and Takami-musubi gave him the sacred jewel, the sacred sword (which Susano-o discovered in the serpent's body and sent to Amaterasu), and the sacred mirror, which was used to bring Amaterasu out of the cave. (These three items are called the "three divine regalia" and have been the sacred objects handed down from emperor to emperor, as the symbol of imperial power.) Amaterasu and Takami-musubi commanded Ninigi, saying: "Regard this mirror exactly as if it were our august spirit, and reverence it as if reverencing us" (Chamberlain 1981, 130). In a different version found in the *Nihongi*, Amaterasu's famous utterance is recorded: "This Reed-plain-1500-autumn-fair-rice-ear Land is the region which my descendants shall be lords of. Do thou, my August Grandchild, proceed thither and govern it. Go! and may prosperity attend thy dynasty, and may it, like Heaven and Earth, endure forever" (Aston 1972, I, 77). According to tradition, Ninigi's grandchild became the first emperor of Japan, Jinmu, who suppos-edly reigned from 660 to 585 B.C.E. This is the mythohistoric ac-count of the direct descent of the imperial family from the sun goddess Amaterasu. This is why Amaterasu is the ancestor goddess and the clan deity (*ujigami*) of the imperial family.

The imperial line of succession from the sun goddess is sum-marized in Figure 1.

EMPRESS JINGŪ

According to the ancient records, Empress Jingū was the wife of the Emperor Chūai (*14), and the mother of the Emperor Ōjin (*15). She is credited with the conquest of Korea. She probably was not a historical figure but a mythohistoric presentation of an imagery of powerful female leaders of antiquity. Her imagery curiously over-laps that of Himiko mentioned in the Chinese documents, which

Figure 1. Imperial Succession

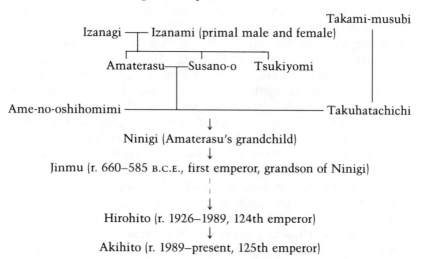

we have seen above. Many scholars speculate that the compilers of the *Kojiki* and the *Nihongi* were conscious of the existence of a Himiko and superimposed her image onto Empress Jingū or created Jingū in her image.

The *Nihongi* records Empress Jingū to have lived from 169 to 269 C.E., but the entries under her reign would better match the historical events by moving her dates to the fourth century. It is pointed out that since the Chinese calendar is organized in a sixty-year cycle, we should adjust the dates of Empress Jingū by two cycles (i.e., 120 years) to get the proper historical correspondence. For instance, Japan invaded Korea and conquered it in 391 C.E. and was active on the Korean peninsula for about two hundred fifty years thereafter, holding its administrative seat called Mimana on the southern tip of the peninsula until 562.

Empress Jingū was capable of receiving divine oracles. The time was the age of theocracy, when kingship was regarded sacred and supported by the divine presence, and the leader had the obligation to know the divine will and act according to it. The *Kojiki* notes that one night, the Emperor Chūai, the Empress Jingū, and the Prime Minister Takeuchi Sukune set up a purified court in the garden of the imperial residence in order to receive the divine command. The emperor played the lute to invoke the divine spirit, the prime minister requested the divine orders, and the empress was possessed by the deity and uttered the oracle, which the prime minister in turn interpreted. The deity invoked said that "there is a rich country in the west. The country abounds in gold, silver, and other riches. I shall give you that country." The emperor, incredulous of the oracle, charged the deity by saying, "there is no country in the West that I can see. You must be lying." Having thus gone against the divine oracle, the emperor mysteriously expired shortly thereafter. Concealing the death of the emperor lest the country fall into confusion at the untimely news of his death, the empress surreptitiously assumed the throne, and with the assistance of the prime minister, they carried out a thorough exorcism of the country. Having done so, they again consulted the divine oracle. The answer of the deity was the same. This time, the deity revealed her identity as Amaterasu the sun goddess, and said: "This western land will be reigned by the imperial august child who is in the empress's womb." The sun goddess gave the empress and the prime minister detailed instructions as to how to prepare their way to the West, and enjoined them to pay due respect to the deities of heaven and earth, mountains, rivers, and ocean. The empress followed her instruction, gathered the troops, arranged ships, and commanded the fleet herself, dressed in man's clothes and assuming a man's role (just as the sun goddess Amaterasu did when she met her brother Susano-o) to cross the ocean. The ships were aided by the favorable winds sent by the great goddess, and they arrived at the country of Silla in no time. The king of Silla, having heard of the divine land that existed in the East, surrendered his country without any resistance. At that time, the imperial child was due to be born, but the empress picked up a stone and tied it over her skirt to prevent the baby from being born. She gave birth to a child upon her return to Japan, when she arrived at the coast of northern Kyūshū. The conquest of Korea is attributed to the charismatic empress, whose image resembles the shamanlike female rulers of the past.

Empress Jingū was not only a war heroine but the mother of the heir to the imperial throne. Upon her return to Japan, because she feared the dispositions of the halfbrothers of her son, she cleverly deceived them and drove them to their eventual demise. The older brothers did raise their armies against the youngest halfbrother but were killed by the empress's army. The empress was a determined mother who would protect the interests of her son, resorting, if necessary, to any means. The empress's son was enthroned as the fifteenth emperor, Ōjin.

A miraculous episode in the *Kojiki* further confirms the shamanic quality ascribed to the empress. In early April of a certain year, the empress went to a riverside to have a picnic. At that time she pulled a thread from her skirt, prepared a bait out of rice, and fished trout with it. The *Kojiki* adds that women of that region still fish trout in every April using rice as the bait (Chamberlain 1981, 291).

Six Empresses

It was not uncommon until the eighth century for an empress to succeed the imperial throne. Empresses Suiko (*33, r. 592–628, during whose reign the *Kojiki* was compiled), Kōgyoku (*35, r. 642–644, whose prayer for rain was granted by the deity; she rereigned as Empress Saimei, *37, 655–661), Jitō (*41, r. 686–697, the wife of the Emperor Tenmu [*40]), Genmei (*43, r. 707–715, Empress Jitō's sister), Genshō (*44, r. 715–724, during whose reign the *Nihongi* was compiled), and Kōken (*46, r. 749–758, the daughter of the pious Buddhist Emperor Shōmu [*45]; she reassumed the throne as Empress Shōtoku [*48, r. 764–770]; she was well-known for her admiration of a Buddhist monk, Dōkyō) succeeded the throne.

Origuchi asserts that many of these empresses were regarded as intermediaries and endowed with a shamanic ability so that they were able to communicate with the divine being (Origuchi 1956, 12), just as we saw in the characterization of the protoempress Jingū.

Besides these six women, two more empresses assumed the throne during the Tokugawa period: Empresses Meishō (*109, r. 1629–1643) and Gosakuramachi (*117, r. 1762–1770). But they were enthroned because of their connection with the ruling Tokugawa family, and not because they had charismatic power or anything of that sort (Ueda 1973, 22).

THE GRAND SHRINE OF ISE

The Grand Shrine of Ise, dedicated to the sun goddess Amaterasu, is the holiest of all Shinto shrines. Actually, it has two shrine complexes, the inner and the outer. The inner shrine (*naikū*) is the shrine of sun goddess Amaterasu, and the outer shrine (*gekū*) is that of the food goddess Toyouke. The tradition of rebuilding the sanctuaries of the Grand Shrine every twenty years, called *sengū*, began in 690 during the reign of Empress Jitō (*41), and it has continued to this day, the next *sengū* taking place in the year 1993 (Watanabe 1964, 43). The custom of *sengū* was actually interrupted during the Sengoku (warring) period, the time of civil wars, but was revived in the sixteenth century thanks to the effort of Buddhist nuns who actively engaged in fund raising (Fujitani and Naoki 1960, 114–15). The sentiment behind this periodic rebuilding of sanctuaries is that the divine presence should be continually renewed.

The account of how the sun goddess eventually decided to descend onto Ise is found in the *Nihongi* (but not in the *Kojiki*). During the reign of Emperor Sūjin (*10), a great pestilence broke out and more than half of the population died. The plague was followed by rebellion, and the country was thrown into chaos. The emperor feared that these calamities were caused by the wrath of gods. He had hitherto worshiped two deities, Amaterasu and Yamato no Ōkunidama, within the imperial residence. The *Nihongi* reads:

> [The emperor] dreaded, however, the power of these Gods, and did not feel secure in their dwelling together. Therefore he entrusted Amaterasu to Princess Toyosuki-iri to be worshiped at the village of Kasanui in Yamato, where he established the sacred enclosure. (Aston 1972, I, 152)

The emperor entrusted the worship of Yamato no Ōkunidama to another imperial princess, Nunaki-iri, but according to the *Nihongi*, she was "bald and lean, and therefore unfit to perform the rites of worship." The emperor further inquired by divination into the will of myriads of deities. They told him to worship them reverently. As he did so, the pestilence ceased and order was restored to the land.

The account tells us that the physical separation of the emperor and the imperial ancestor deity took place sometime in the early history of Shinto, and that the rites of worship of deities were entrusted to the imperial princesses. Moreover, these princesses had to be healthy and femininely intact to be able to serve the sacred duty.

During the reign of the Emperor Suinin (*11), the duty of the worship of Amaterasu was taken from Princess Toyosuki-iri and entrusted to Princess Yamato. Princess Yamato is considered a sacred woman in the Shinto tradition and ascribed all sorts of legends. For instance, she is supposed to have lived several hundreds of years (Chamberlain 1981, 228, n. 7). The *Nihongi* accounts:

> The Great goddess Amaterasu was taken from Princess Toyosuki-iri, and entrusted to Princess Yamato. Now Princess Yamato sought for a place where she might enshrine the Great goddess. So she proceeded to Sasahata in Uda. Then turning

back from thence, she entered the land of Ohomi, and went round eastward to Mino, whence she arrived in the province of Ise.

Now the Great goddess Amaterasu instructed Princess Yamato, saying "The province of Ise, of the divine wind, is the land whither repair the waves from the eternal world, the successive waves. It is a secluded and pleasant land. In this land I wish to dwell." In compliance, therefore, with the instruction of the Great goddess, a shrine was erected to her in the Province of Ise. Accordingly, an Abstinence Palace was built at Kawakami in Isuzu. This was called the Palace of Iso (*Iso no miya*). It was there that Amaterasu first descended from Heaven. (Aston 1972, I, 176)

Princess Yamato was the aunt of Imperial Prince Yamato Takeru, a heroic figure who subdued powerful contending clans of East and West under his father Emperor Keikō's (*12) command. When Yamato Takeru was about to set off by the imperial decree to pacify eastern Japan, he visited his aunt at the Grand Shrine of Ise and revealed his lamentation regarding his father's heartless treatment of him. Princess Yamato "bestowed on him the sacred sword [*kusanagi no tsurugi*, which was sent to Amaterasu by Susano-o] and likewise bestowed on him an august bag, and said: 'If there should be an emergency, open the mouth of the bag' " (Chamberlain 1981, 260). In the bag was a flint, which saved Yamato Takeru's life when he was caught in a fire set off by his enemies. He cut enough grass around him with the sacred sword and, using the flint given by his aunt, ignited the counter-fire which spread and burned down the village of the enemies who tried to kill him. Princess Yamato thus saved the life of her nephew with her foresight. This episode is just a hint of how she was no mere princess but had a quality of "medicine woman" and shamaness. Indeed, the wandering she undertook in order to find a place to enshrine the sun goddess would seem impossible by an ordinary person. She must have been possessed by the spirit of the sun goddess and led by it.

High Priestess of Ise: Saigū

Imperial Princesses Toyosuki-iri and Yamato were the precursors of the *saigū*, the high priestess of the Ise Shrine. The office of *saigū* was filled by an unmarried imperial princess, who represented the emperor and served the great goddess Amaterasu at Ise. The high priestess, if she was the daughter of the emperor, was called *saigū* or *itsukinomiya*. If she was an imperial niece, she was called *saiō* or *itsukinomiko*. The original term for this office, *mitsueshiro* (lit., "august-cane-substitute"), signifies that the high priestess was the one on whom the great goddess relies as if on a cane—that is, she communicates her will through her. The office of *saigū* at Ise reveals the nature of ancient imperial authority—that is, the emperor was required to maintain an intimate divine connection if he were to be truly an emperor. Princesses were the ancillary of the deity, the intermediaries (*miko*), and the necessary extension of the sacred imperial authority (Yamakami 1980, 89–108).

The office of *saigū* was somewhat sporadically filled at first, no doubt reflecting the yet to be firmly established power of the imperial family. Nine princesses were sent to Ise during the reign of thirty-three sovereigns. After the reign of the Empress Suiko (*33), no princess was sent to Ise for about half a century, but the office was revived in 673 under the Emperor Tenmu (*40, r. 673–686), and the system continued until the time of the Emperor Godaigo (*96, r. 1318–1339). By the time the last *saigū* retired in 1336, Japan had entered the period of the divided court between the south and the north (Nanbokuchō period), and the imperial authority considerably weakened due to the schism regarding the successional matters of the imperial throne. The imperial court was unified in 1392, but the office of *saigū* was never again revived (although some unsuccessful attempts were made, once near the end of the Tokugawa period and another time immediately after World War II).

The specifics of the office of *saigū* were spelled out in the *Engishiki* (*The Code of the Engi Era*), proclaimed in 927. (Ellwood 1967 offers a detailed discussion of the *saigū* system.) Each time the new emperor succeeded the throne, the candidate for the *saigū* was chosen by divination from among his unmarried daughters; and if none was available, from among his unmarried nieces. The chosen candidate would first go into a ward called *shosaiin*, which was set up within the compound of the imperial palace, and lead the life of strict seclusion and abstinence for one year. Abstinence included total seclusion from the outside world, avoiding taboo words, observing a vegetarian diet, making offerings to the deities, and so forth. In the following year, typically in autumn, she would move into another palace called Nonomiya, "the palace in the fields," which was located in the lonely southwestern part of Kyoto.

A slight digression may be permitted here. In the famous novel, *The Tale of Genji*, written by Lady Murasaki Shikibu around 1000

C.E., the Imperial Lady Rokujō, an ex-lover of Imperial Prince Genji, was visited by the Shining Prince, Hikaru Genji at Nonomiya. Lady Rokujō resided there with her daughter, who was chosen as the next *saigū* and going through the second year of purification. Being unable to forget Genji's love, Lady Rokujō had decided to give up her life at court altogether and accompany her daughter to Ise, although such was a custom unheard of. Genji visited Lady Rokujō before her departure for Ise to exchange their past memories. This sad episode of *The Tale of Genji* was rendered into a noh play called "Nonomiya" in the fifteenth century, possibly by Zeami. With the technique unique to noh plays, the playwright brings out a girl, who actually is the spirit of Lady Rokujō, on stage and lets her recall:

> This is Nonomiya, the Shrine in the Fields, where in ancient days the virgin designated as the priestess of Ise was temporarily lodged. The custom has fallen into disuse, but today, the seventh day of the ninth month, is still a time for recalling the past. . . . This is the day when Genji the Shining One visited this place, the seventh day of the ninth month. He brought with him a twig of *sakaki* and pushed it through the sacred fence. (Keene 1970, 184–85)

After another year of observing strict abstinence at Nonomiya, the princess would go to the imperial palace to see her father to bid farewell. At that time the emperor would give her a comb, a symbolic token of farewell. That would be the last time father and daughter would see each other alive. After giving her the comb, custom forbade the emperor to even look back upon his departing daughter. The *saigū* would proceed to the abstinence palace in Ise in a grand ceremonial fashion, accompanied by about two hundred maids and officers. This procession, called *gunkō*, took five days, symbolically reenacting the sacred wandering that the Princess Yamato took (Ōbayashi 1984, 75). At each of the overnight stops, she dispatched Shinto officer-priests to perform a purification ritual (*misogi*) at a nearby river (Asai 1985, 118). She could go back to Kyoto only if her father abdicated the imperial throne or died, or her mother became seriously ill, or she herself fell seriously ill. She could also be dismissed from the office, if she should have any forbidden liaison with a man.

Because of the "air of the forbidden" surrounding these princesses, some romantic rumors as well as tragic stories have been told of them. In the *Nihongi* we read a story related to the fifth *saigū*, Princess Takuhata. A man named Kunimi made a slanderous accusation that a young man called Takehiko "had illicit intercourse with the Imperial Princess." Takehiko's father, being terrified of the cruel Emperor Yūryaku (*21, r. 456–479) and his revenge, killed his son. The emperor sent a messenger to Ise to inquire of the princess. She answered, "Thy handmaiden knows nothing." After that, Princess Takuhata took a divine mirror with her, went to the precincts of the shrine, buried the mirror, and hanged herself. The emperor sent people to search for her. When they came to Kawakami in the still of the night, a rainbow appeared. "When they dug the place from which the rainbow sprang, they found the divine mirror, and no great distance off, they discovered the imperial princess's body." Upon investigating the body of the princess, they found that she was innocent. The father of Kunimi feared the consequence of this incident, killed his son, and went into hiding at a shrine called Isonokami (Aston 1972, I, 341).

In another instance, Princess Iwane, the daughter of Emperor Kinmei (*29, r. 539–571), was dismissed from the office of *saigū* because she was convicted of an intrigue with the Imperial Prince Mubaragi, her halfbrother on her father's side and cousin on her mother's side (Aston 1972, II, 40). In *The Tales of Ise*, there is an episode of a courtier Ariwara no Narihira's escapade with a *saigū* princess (episode 69). The very impossibility of approaching a *saigū* princess added fuel to readers' imagination, and they wanted to believe the historicity of such fictions. Historians also tended to want to keep these stories alive.

There was no telling how long an imperial princess had to remain in Ise. The average length of their service was about eleven years, some shorter, some longer. Princesses could be only four or five years old when chosen by divination, and when they returned to Kyoto after serving the office for so many years, they still had good prospects of getting married and entering into normal aristocratic life. (In fact, some married the then reigning emperor.) Other princesses were already in their late teens or twenties when chosen, and by the time they returned to Kyoto after serving the office, they had very little to look forward to in their lives. (The thirty-fourth *saigū*, Princess Yasuko, the daughter of Emperor Uda [*59, r. 887–897], was at the office for thirty-four years.) Apparently, a princess could voluntarily serve more than one emperor: the Princess Nukade (or Sukade), the daughter of the Emperor Yōmei (*31, r. 583–587), served the office during the reigns of her father, the Emperor

Sujun (*32, r. 587–592) and the Empress Suiko (*33), for the total of thirty-seven years (Aston 1972, II, 107). (For a complete list of *saigū*, see Asai 1985, 104–6 and Yamakawa 1924, 308–9).

Once in Ise, the *saigū* resided at the abstinence palace, which was located about ten miles north of the inner and outer shrines. Her duty included the observance of three major annual festivals that took place in June, September, and December. At those times, she went to the grand shrine, taking two days to complete the rites at the inner and the outer shrines. Besides these major festivals, she had numerous Shinto rites to attend to at the abstinence palace. When finally the day of her departure from Ise came, she took a different route back to Kyoto, going through the present-day Osaka area, performing a purification ritual at the Bay of Naniwa.

The imperial high priestesses were required to observe pure Shinto rites and customs. For instance, they had to practice avoiding certain taboo words (*imikotoba*). Words associated with unwelcome events, such as death, illness, blood, and crying were respectively changed to recovery, rest, sweat, and brine-dripping. They had to also avoid the direct mention of any words related to Buddhism. The Buddha was referred to as the middle child (*nakago;* the reason for this word is uncertain), the Buddhist scriptures as dyed paper (*somegami*, because they often used artistically dyed paper to write scriptures on it), Buddhist monks and nuns as long-haired ones (*kaminaga*) and female long-haired ones (*mekaminaga*) respectively, because it was the Buddhist custom to cut their hair when ordained, and so forth (see *Engishiki,* book 5; also Aston 1907, 255). This observance of taboo words is just an indication of how the *saigū* system kept to the core of Shinto religiosity. It is especially remarkable in view of the fact that Buddhist-Shinto fusion was taking place even at the imperial court, and that many members of the imperial family embraced Buddhism.

Some argue that the institution of *saigū* was the "greatest defeat of feminism throughout the history of humankind" because it corresponded with the decline of women's social status (Saigō 1967, 37–38). Regardless of the virtue and shortcomings of this system, we must consider the possibility that the *saigū* system originally got started with the high spiritual esteem that women enjoyed in antiquity. Imperial princesses were believed to be able to communicate with the sun goddess, and this mediumlike ability was at the heart of the priestesshood to which the princesses were assigned. Imperial princesses by birth were related to the great ancestor Amaterasu and considered closest to her. These women served as the medium, while representing the imperial authority and rendering it the indispensable sacred power.

High Priestess of Kamo: Saiin

During the reign of Emperor Saga (*52, r. 809–823), a new office of *saiin* was instituted more or less after the fashion of the Ise *saigū*. The reason for this office seems more political than religious. The *saiin* priestesses were also chosen from among the unmarried imperial princesses by divination and sent to the Kamo shrines in Kyoto. The *saiin* took the same preparatory abstinence steps as the *saigū* princesses. The sixteenth *saiin*, Princess Nobuko (964–1035), the daughter of Emperor Murakami (*62, r. 946–967), served five emperors, En'yū (*64, r. 969–984), Kazan (*65, r. 984–986), Ichijō (*66, r. 986–1011), Sanjō (*67, r. 1011–1016), and Goichijō (*68, r. 1016–1036), staying in the office for fifty-seven years from 975 to 1031. She was rightly called the Great *Saiin* (*Daisaiin*), and her residential palace became a literary salon, gathering gifted aristocratic women around her. Murasaki Shikibu, the author of *The Tale of Genji*, describes the place of Great *Saiin* in her *Diary* as "famous for beautiful moonlit nights, marvelous dawn skies, cherries, and the song of the wood thrush" and "has an aura of seclusion and mystery about it, and they [i.e., ladies-in-waiting] have very little to distract them."

Murasaki happened to mention the *Saiin* of Kamo because she was secretly shown a letter written by one of the ladies attending the Great *Saiin*. In that letter, this person wrote: "We are the only ones of note. Everyone else is as good as blind and deaf when it comes to taste." Murasaki, not without an ironical twist, writes: the *Saiin*'s place "naturally lends itself to poetry. Amid such perfect elegance, how could one possibly fail to produce anything but excellent poems?" (Bowring 1982, 123–31). At any rate, the Great *Saiin* commanded much respect and enjoyed inviolable prestige. Less grand yet relatively well-known princess who became *saiin* was Princess Shikishi, the daughter of Emperor Goshirakawa (*77, r. 1155–1158). She served the office of Kamo from 1159 to 1169. In her case, with the decline of the political fortune of her family, her post-*saiin* days were spent in melancholy, although she too held quite a privileged position. In her latter days, she embraced Buddhism and became a nun. She is better remembered by most of the Japanese for her poems and her alleged relationship with the celebrated poet Fujiwara no Teika, rather than having served the office of *saiin* (Baba 1969; for a complete list of *saiin,* see Asai 1985, 130–32 and Yamakawa 1924, 320).

The office of *saiin* was abolished after 1212 as Minamoto Yoritomo seized political power in 1192 and the Heian period came to an end.

AMATERASU:
SYMBOL OF SOVEREIGNTY AND NATIONAL IDENTITY

Amaterasu was originally the ancestor deity of the imperial family, and as such her protection was bestowed exclusively on the immediate members of the imperial family. But with the unification of Japan by the imperial family, Amaterasu gradually came to be identified with the country of Japan itself, and eventually she became the goddess who bestows her blessings on the people of Japan. From a historical point of view, it is interesting to observe how still unknown Amaterasu was in the eleventh century to a girl of an aristocratic stock. The author of *Sarashina Nikki (Diary of Sarashina)* recounts her dream in which an unknown person appeared and said to her to revere the Great Deity Amaterasu. Not knowing who this deity was, she later asked people about it: "Is it a *kami* or is it a Buddha?" (Taguchi 1969, chapter 49). We learn from this that in the eleventh century Amaterasu was still regarded mostly as the patron deity of the imperial family, but it was already possible for nonimperial members to worship her.

Relatively soon after, everyone in Japan knew the name of Amaterasu, the great deity of Ise. She was no longer the exclusive ancestor deity of the imperial family but the protectress of Japan. The earliest account is found in a letter written in the twelfth century by Minamoto Yoritomo, the first shogun of the Kamakura government. "Our country is the divine country," the generalissimo wrote (Fujitani and Naoki 1960, 82). Worship of Amaterasu lent the newly risen warrior-ruler the connection with sacred power, which was formerly reserved for the emperors. The incipient connection that later loomed larger of Shinto and nationalistic militarism was also established thereby. As Japan miraculously came out victorious of the Mongolian invasions of 1274 and 1281, thanks to the timely *"kami*-sent" typhoon storms (*kamikaze*) which swept away the Mongolian fleets, the belief that Japan was a divine land protected by *kami* spread widely among the people. Kitabatake Chikafusa, the supporter of the imperial court and the author of *The Records of the Legitimate Succession of the Divine Sovereigns* (1339), wrote, no doubt echoing the account found in the *Nihongi* (see above):

> Japan is the divine country. The heavenly ancestor it was who first laid its foundations, and the sun goddess left her descendants to reign over it forever and ever. This is true only of our country, and nothing similar may be found in foreign lands. This is why it is called the divine country. (Tsunoda 1958, 274)

As the supreme position of Amaterasu penetrated the minds of many, Buddhists also attempted to identify her with the Sun Buddha, Mahāvairocana, and to regard her as the manifestation of the Buddha-essence or sometimes as the protectress of Buddhism (Fujitani and Naoki 1960, 77–79). The cult of Amaterasu attained enormous popularity during the Muromachi period, largely due to the missionary activity of Ise-based traveling priests called *oshi*, who converted the people of distant villages, by taking each village as a unit (Fujitani and Naoki 1960, 101ff.). In the Tokugawa period the Grand Shrine of Ise became the center of pilgrimage for all Japanese. Even today, some six to seven million people annually visit the Grand Shrine, attesting to the popularity of the Ise shrine and the cult of Amaterasu for contemporary Japanese.

During the medieval period, Amaterasu, as the most encompassing symbol of Japan, transcended the division of powerful clans and *daimyō* warloards. Her unifying symbolic power was effectively exploited by the officials of the Meiji government who tried to put Japan onto the international stage of modern nations (Nishigaki 1983, 118; Fujitani and Naoki 1960, 160–207). As militarism became the fashion of the day in the 1930s, the nationalistic ideology of one mythic big "family," of which the emperor was the father-figure and the people his children, was advocated by the government, and its culmination was the kamikaze pilot of World War II. The word kamikaze ("divine wind") had a close association with Amaterasu and Ise, as the great deity herself described Ise as the place "of the divine wind" and "the land whither repair the waves from the eternal world, the successive waves. It is a secluded and pleasant land" (see above). It was also associated with the wind that Amaterasu sent when the Empress Jingū went to Korea to conquer it, and again when Mongolian fleets came to Japan. The militaristic side of the cult of Amaterasu was radically dismantled and toned down in the post-World War II period.

WOMEN AS THE UNCLEAN SEX

Japanese women born and raised before World War II would still today recall those days when they were regarded "unclean" and considered inferior to men because of menstruation. When and how such a view came to be prevalent has been the subject of recent studies. Findings show that the strong sense of ritual uncleanness originally came from India with Buddhism, and assimilated into the Shinto sensibility of cleanliness.

Coming into contact with death, childbirth, and blood were, by some time in the late Heian period, considered three major defilements to be avoided. These taboos were taken up by Shinto institutions. The avoidance of defilement agreed with the Shinto sensibility toward ritual cleanliness and purification, as demonstrated by the performance of *misogi* (water purification) and *harai* (lustration). We recall the story of Izanagi and Izanami in which Izanagi cleansed himself in the river after returning from the underworld because he came in contact with the dead. We also read in the *History of the Kingdom of Wei* an account of an ancient Japanese custom that after the funereal mourning of ten days, "all members of the family go into the water to cleanse themselves in a bath of purification" (Tsunoda 1958, 6–7). The pollution caused by coming into contact with death was the object of purification since early days.

Regarding childbirth, we read in the *Kojiki* and *Nihongi* the custom of building a separate hut for delivering a baby. But childbirth itself was never mentioned as a pollution. The idea behind building a separate hut was, some argue, the animistic belief of the ancients in nature as the source of life. They felt that at critical moments of life, typically those moments concerning birth and death, they could tap into the source of the life-bearing force of nature by coming close to the earth, grass, and so forth, and by so doing they could get the help of the *kami* spirits (Takatori 1979, 28). Later, childbirth came to be considered pollution, and the length of "unclean days" was specified as seven in the *Code of the Engi Era* (927). It was prolonged to thirty days in the Muromachi period. During the Tokugawa period, it was fixed at thirty-five days. While women were on their "unclean" days, they were not permitted to visit shrines. Even today, the custom of taking a newborn baby to visit a Shinto shrine to celebrate its birth is observed on the thirty-second day, if it is a boy, and on the thirty-third day, if it is a girl. The number of days is the vestige of an old taboo.

Blood associated with menstruation was not considered pollution in the *Kojiki* and *Nihongi*. Rather, menstruation was regarded a positive sign for a woman to assume the role of a medium (*miko*) or to become the bride of a *kami* (Wakamori 1964, 55; Makita 1981, 133–34). Anthropologists point out the double meaning of the word taboo—prohibition and awe-inspiring holiness (Makita 1981, 157). Menstruation was earlier regarded something sacred because of its association with life force, but it was later turned into a thing to be avoided.

The *Code of the Engi Era* referred to menstruation but did not specify the length of "unclean days" (book 3), nor did women writers of the Heian period particularly feel the need to mention it. It is hard to believe that the high priestesses at Ise and Kamo stayed away from their official duties during their menstruation. An author known as the Mother of Michitsuna, in her *Kagerō Nikki* (*The Diary of the Ephemera*, which covers the time span of 954–974), however, mentions menstruation as something of a bother and a taboo. When she went and stayed at a certain Buddhist temple of a Shingon sect in the western mountain area of Kyoto, she relocated herself to a different temple building during her "monthly thing" (Ōnishi 1971, chapter 142). From this we gather that menstruation was considered a taboo in the Buddhist context, and that court ladies were gradually becoming more sensitive to it. The *Shintō-shū*, the fourteenth-century compilation of Shinto-related legends and documents, refers to menstruation as a seven-day pollution (Kondō 1959, 164). The attitude toward menstruation worsened in the Muromachi period, when a Chinese apocryphal sutra was introduced, which talked about the horrible consequence of menstruation or childbirth—polluting the earth with blood—for which women were destined to go to the hell of blood pond (Makita 1981, 163–66). In the Tokugawa period at various places it evolved into a custom of segregating women during their menstruation from the rest of their family members. Their food was prepared with a separate heat source in order to avoid the pollution. This strong abhorrence of blood, bordering on superstition, was widespread among the people by the end of the Tokugawa period. The Meiji government ordered the abolition of such taboos in 1872 (Fujitani and Naoki 1960, 174). It is only after

World War II (1945) that taboos related to menstruation vanished completely and became things of the past.

QUEST FOR THE LIBERATION OF WOMEN

The underlining Shinto ethos calls for equality of the sexes. The idea that male and female are equally necessary and complementary appears to be a philosophical outlook often found in the Shinto-based sectarian movements, which became quite significant in the nineteenth century. Such an egalitarian view of men and women went against the official creed of the Tokugawa government, which in facile terms operated under the assumption that "the male is to be respected, the female to be taken lightly."

By the medieval period, women were forbidden to climb sacred mountains throughout Japan. (As to when this custom became prevalent is unclear; the taboo was lifted in 1872). But a religious society organized during the Tokugawa period called Fujidō or Fujikō, which worshiped the sacred mountain Mt. Fuji, permitted women to climb it every sixtieth year. Apparently, in the years 1800 and 1860, the scale of the event caused quite a social sensation. The sixth leader and the one responsible for reviving the Fujidō sect, Miroku (1671–1733), already gave a special permission for women to climb it in 1731, although it was not one of the sixtieth year. The doctrine of the Fujidō sect denied the view that menstruation was a pollution and advocated the view that the complementarity and harmonious unity of both sexes is the foundation of the world (Miyata 1979, 169–82; Murakami and Yasumaru 1971, 634–45).

Nakayama Miki (1798–1887), the foundress of the Shinto-based Tenrikyō, advocated the equality of husband and wife as the basis of ideal family life. Her career of a charismatic religious leader began with her experience of a *kami* possession. When she came out of the three-day possession by deities, she was inspired to preach the universal equality of everybody. For her, ancestor worship, the social system based on class distinctions, and the patriarchal family system—all of which supported the feudalism of the Tokugawa government—were far from the essential reality of humanity. She emphasized the realization of happy life based on the spiritual enlightenment of the equality of, and the care for, all human beings. Women were freed from the taboos and superstitions related to childbirth and menstruation that had hitherto bound them. Her teaching attracted a considerable number of followers. After much persecution by the government, it was finally recognized in 1908 as a religious sect (Murakami and Yasumaru 1971, 605–15). The followers of the Tenri sect established their own community near Nara, which is today's city of Tenri.

CONCLUSION

The primordial Shinto ethos seems to have been essentially egalitarian. Women played a crucial and indispensable role in the formation of Shinto as a religious tradition. As the domains of religion and politics were separated and rituals and priesthood were institutionalized, however, the spiritual vitality that women possessed, and with which they supported the Shinto tradition, passed into oblivion, or at best were obscurely remembered. Women held some important positions such as the high priestesshood at Ise (saigū) until the fourteenth century, but with the rise of the warrior culture, which was inherently male-oriented, Shinto institutions also underwent changes. The original Shinto ethos of egalitarianism cropped up in popular religious movements here and there, but it is only recently that such phenomena have been reexamined and reevaluated by scholars. Through the course of history, however, the image of powerful, spiritually-gifted women lingered on in the deep recesses of the Japanese psyche. Today there is no doubt that the status of women in Japan is rising, making the primordial images of women remembered in Shinto myths and legends not so strange or surprising to the modern Japanese once again.

APPENDIX

Names of the Japanese Historical Periods

Jōmon (ca. 8000–300 B.C.E.)
Yayoi (ca. 300 B.C.E.–250 C.E.)
Kofun (ca. 250 C.E.–552)
Asuka (552–645)
Hakuhō (645–710)
Nara (710–784)
Heian (794–1192)
Kamakura (1192–1333)
(Nanbokuchō) (1336–1392)
Muromachi (1336–1573)
(Sengoku) (1467–1568)
Azuchi-Momoyama (1568–1603)
Edo/Tokugawa (1603–1867)
Meiji (1868–1912)
Taishō (1912–1926)
Shōwa (1926–1989)
Heisei (1989-present)

Nalini Balbir

WOMEN IN JAINISM

Jainism, a religious movement born in India around the sixth century B.C.E., has survived as an influential minority of about three
and a half million followers until the present day. It has never excluded women as such, since one of its key concepts is that of the
"fourfold *saṅgha*," comprising monks and nuns, laymen and laywomen. The discussion of the religious status of women, however,
slowly became a crucial point, since it is at the background of the
ancient sectarian division between the Śvetāmbaras and the Digambaras (79 C.E.). In this paper I will constantly refer to these two
sects which, in spite of a common doctrine and much common religious behavior, have different scriptures. The fact that the Jains
were never numerous did not prevent the rise of subsects especially
among the Śvetāmbaras: namely, the Mūrtipūjaks (idolatrous), the
Sthānakvāsins (nonidolatrous) and the Terāpanthins.

On the other hand, it must be kept in mind that except in recent
times, when a few prominent Jain nuns have spoken of their own
lives, Jain women have not been able to speak for themselves: almost all the texts we read are written by monks or male-oriented.

THE JAIN NUNS' ORDER

It is quite likely that the place to be assigned to women was a
point of disagreement between early Hinduism (which denied
women access to the religious scriptures) and the ascetic movements born in the sixth to fifth century B.C.E. which, on the whole,
defended egalitarian attitudes. Women were permitted to enter the
early Buddhist *Saṅgha* (Schuster Barnes 1987, 106). They were also

allowed to enter the order of the Jains and the Ājīvika-sect (Basham
1951, 106). Ṛṣabha, the mythic founder of Jainism, or Pārsva and
Mahāvīra, who are both historical figures, all had among their followers numerous female ascetics and laywomen, some of whom became paragons of virtue in the later narrative literature (Candanā,
Sulasā, Revatī). It is interesting that the number of nuns given in the
texts is always more than twice the number of monks. This is probably a distinctive feature of Jainism. According to the Śvetāmbara
Jain books of discipline (the corpus of the so-called Chedasūtras),
only two types of women are forbidden to receive initiation: those
who are recognized as pregnant and those who are still very young
(under eight years old) or have a small child.

Now the question is whether the probably massive initiations
of women had any effect on the nuns' rank within the religious order. Data provided by Digambara sources on the organization of the
church are so scanty that they can hardly be used. The Chedasūtras,
on the other hand, contain a whole set of rules stating what is allowed or what is prohibited for both monks and nuns in their daily
routine. In most cases they are similar, but special regulations and
stricter restrictions are imposed upon nuns. They concern, for example, the type of alms that nuns can accept, the places where they
are allowed to stay, or the implements they can use. Further:

> A nun is not allowed to be alone. A nun is not allowed to en-
> ter alone the house of a layman for food or drink, or to go out
> from there alone. A nun is not allowed to enter alone a place
> to ease nature or a place for stay, or to go out from there
> alone. A nun is not allowed to wander about alone from one
> village to the other. A nun is not allowed to be without cloth-
> ing. A nun is not allowed to be without superior. A nun is not
> allowed to stand in [the ascetic posture called] kāyotsarga.
> (Bṛhat-Kalpa-Sūtra 5.15–21: Schubring 1977, 31)

Generally speaking, the nuns are more dependent than their
male colleagues and are subordinated to the latters' authority: "The
male-ascetic is governed by two persons: the teacher and the preceptor. . . . The female ascetic is governed by *three* persons: the female-
superior (*pavattiṇī*), the preceptor and the teacher" (*Vyavahārasūtra*
3.11; 3.12).

In the Chedasūtras the rules are simply stated. But from the jus-
tifications expressed in the exegetical literature, it seems that most
prohibitions are motivated by the wish to avoid all objects and con-

ditions of life that could endanger the vow of chastity. Although it is not always clearly stated, the belief that women are more fragile creatures in this respect seems to be all-pervading.

The inferior status of nuns results in the fact that, even when they have had a longer religious life, they may be subordinate to monks who have been initiated only a few years. Moreover, nuns require more years than their male counterparts to attain high positions in the religious hierarchy. To judge from the literary tradition, nuns probably never reached the same positions as monks. I can find no record of such high titles as *ācārya* and *sūri* being used for nuns. They have their own titles such as *gaṇinī*, "head of a *gaṇa*," of a small unit of nuns, *pravartinī*, and *mahattarā*, which appears to be a special designation conferred on a restricted number of very learned nuns. In the chronicles that record the lives of Śvetāmbara orders in the middle ages (thirteenth to fifteenth century), it is evident that both the decision and the act of conferring titles upon nuns always fell to male dignitaries.

Theoretical literature does not really provide any argument against equality between monks and nuns as far as learning and teaching are concerned. The only passage often quoted in the secondary literature as proving that nuns (and women in general) were forbidden to study the texts included under the heading Dṛṣṭivāda, because they are "empty, given to haughtiness, sensual and inconstant," cannot be relied upon. It has been convincingly shown that these commonplaces about feminine nature and other statements:

> Merely testify to a firmly established if somewhat naïve belief that "the Dṛṣṭivāda contains *everything*—a belief obviously betraying complete ignorance of the real contents of the long-lost text and, on the other hand, conveniently permitting to derive from 'the Dṛṣṭivāda' or 'the Pūrvas' any text or subject which it was desired to invest with canonical dignity." (Alsdorf 1974, 256)

From the literary evidence it is not possible to draw any conclusion about the general educational level of nuns in the past. Compared with the large number of monks who are known to us as scholars or writers from the often very detailed colophons of Jaina manuscripts, the number of nuns who did not remain anonymous is quite small: the most famous one is probably Yākinī Mahattarā, whom Haribhadrasūri recognized as his "(spiritual) mother." Very few are those who have signed a work, or even who have collaborated with monks in the writing of a book, or who have inspired them (Shāntā 1985, 140–42). However, as testimony that intellectual life could be brilliant among nuns, we can refer to the so-called *Kuratti Aḍigaḷ*, a teaching institution managed by female ascetics in Tamil Nadu (ninth to eleventh century: Shāntā 1985, 171ff.).

In spite of the rise of a fairly large number of sects and subsects in the course of history, the picture offered by the *contemporary* Jain nuns' order is fundamentally the same as the one described above. Except among the Digambaras, nuns are more numerous than monks in the three major sects:

	Nuns	Monks
Śvetāmbaras	3,400	1,200
Sthānakvāsins	522	325
Terāpanthins (1981)	531	164
Digambaras	50	125
(Jaini 1979, 247; Balbir 1983,41)		

Although the question should be examined further, factors related to social environment and restraints imposed upon women (such as the impossibility for a widow to remarry or the prospect of a very hard life in less developed areas of Rajasthan) play an important part in their decision to become nuns. The fact that religious life is an opportunity to develop one's own personality through study is also often adduced as a strong motivation.

In most sects nuns live in small groups under the leadership of one of them and conform to well-defined seniority rules. They are not allowed to wander alone (Misra 1972, 37ff.). However, an interesting example of the way the nuns' order is structured is provided by the vigorously organized Terāpantha sect, which originated in the eighteenth century in Rajasthan, as a reaction to the "lax" discipline of the time. In the beginning the patriarchal structure was centered around a single *ācārya*. He was the head of monks and nuns who were almost equally proportionate. But the regular increase of nuns led to the institution of a so-called *pramukhā*, "a (female) head" who became the religious superior of the smaller units. She is, however, by no means the equal of the *Ācārya*, who makes all the important decisions, but is rather a kind of coordinator, also subordinate to him.

A crucial debate centers around the nuns' education. Today there appears to be sectarian differentiation with regard to the canonical texts accessible to them. While the Sthānakvāsins and the

Terāpanthins make no distinction between monks and nuns, and profess that everybody can learn everything if he or she has the capacity for it, the Tapāgaccha school of the Mūrtipūjaks spreads among its female followers the idea that their abilities are less than those of men. As a result they study a very small number of the canonical texts and are in any case forbidden to have access to the Chedasūtras where faults and their punishments are recorded, lest it would give them bad ideas (Shāntā 1985, 377).

Even if today there are some prominent nuns such as Āryikā Jñānamati (Digambara), who actively contributes to the propagation of Jain law by her translations and educational pamphlets (Shāntā 1985, 513ff.), or Mahattarā Mṛgāvatī (Śvetāmbara, 1926–1986) who acted as an incentive for the establishment of some institutions, they are exceptional cases. The late Mṛgāvatī for instance (1989, 51) clearly articulated the importance of nuns being learned, lest an important potential be wasted, and recommended that before young nuns are initiated, they pass through a five-year curriculum where they would study Jaina basic texts as well as grammar, literature, and the like, with some learned pandits.

In this respect the steps taken by the Terāpanthins are probably a distinctive feature of this movement. Before initiation the girls have to undergo a period of probation during which they attend a full course in a boarding school and become familiar with religious scriptures. The daily routine of the nuns probably includes more time effectively devoted to the study or the copying of texts. Finally, for about ten years, the Terāpanthins have initiated within the order a particular category exclusively consisting of women who are released from certain rules (such as that of going exclusively on foot) and whose main function is to read and write (samaṇa śreṇi: Balbir 1983, 42–43). This innovation is a part of the claimed objective of the sect to improve women's conditions.

THE JAIN LAYWOMEN

The importance given to the laity was always an essential element of Jainism and is often said to partly explain the survival of the movement in India into contemporary times. As a matter of fact the laity is the economic foundation of the religious mendicant order, which it supports by its gifts, receiving in exchange the teaching of the law. Laywomen contribute to the sustaining of the community no less than the laymen do.

Jainism developed an immense corpus of texts devoted to the code of conduct of the laity (*śrāvakācāra:* Williams 1963). In these treatises, however, "the male is invariably taken as the paradigm" (Leslie 1989, 43) as can be seen from the wording of the fourth minor vow, which prescribes "contentment with one's own wife" and "avoidance of the wives of others" (Williams 1963, 85). No discussion is found on the question of whether the term *śrāvaka* also implies the feminine. Such information must be sought in the rare places where particular rules connected with womanhood are discussed. Other evidence is provided by the rich narrative literature of the Jains, the aim of which is to illustrate religious virtues through exemplary lives or by modern observation (Stevenson 1915; Mahias 1985; Reynell 1987).

I shall not deal here with the general duties of Jain women, which are obviously largely dependent on the Indian environment and much similar to Hindu rules (Leslie 1989). To put the matter in a nutshell, their dharma is summed up by the word *śīla*, which designates a perfect wife, such as Sītā or Draupadī (whom the Jains also recognize) or others who remained faithful to their husbands (Shāntā 1985, 181) and are glorified as *satīs*. As has been shown by Reynell (1987, 340), "physical chastity is believed equivalent to spiritual purity," and to some extent removes the boundary between a woman in the world and a woman outside the world.

The present section will try to analyze a few areas of religiosity that seem to concern women more than men. The distribution and complementarity of religious roles between men and women is obviously due to "the social construction of gender" (Reynell 1987, 313). As a general rule, men work outside to earn money, while women remain at home. Men manifest their prestige by giving money to the temple. Women are best fit to master all that is connected with food and, provided rather serious limitations, with the field of worship. On the other hand, they insure "the reproduction of the Jain community" through marriage and religious teaching imparted to their children (Reynell 1991, 59ff.).

Food

In a doctrine such as Jainism, which lays so much stress on dietary rules (Williams 1963, 50ff., 110ff.; Mahias 1985, 100ff.), the part played by women is obviously of primary importance (Reynell, 1991, 54). Since they are the ones who cook, they are in a good position to obey the rules or transgress them, as well as to make others do the same.

The first and foremost responsibility of a laywoman is to prepare food that is acceptable to monks and nuns though not specially meant for them. This is no easy task considering the number of prescriptions to be observed. When the canonical texts describe the donor, they use the feminine gender, because, as a commentator remarks, "she is the one who mostly offers alms" and is the donor par excellence:

> If a woman of the house wastes the food when distributing it, (the monk) should refuse [it, saying to] the [alms-]giver: "I may not accept such [alms]." [When he notices that] she crushes living beings, seeds [and] plants with her foot, he should avoid such [a house], knowing that she performs that which is not suitable to [his] self-control. . . . She brings food and drink having put her hand into the vessel and poured out [that which was inside]. [In all these cases] he should refuse. . . . If she brings food and drink having put down her crying boy or girl to whom she is giving the breast, that food and drink is not allowed. (*Daśavaikālikasūtra* 5.1.28–29, 31, 42–43: trans. Schubring 1977, 208–9)

One of the most popular stories in Jain literature relates how a woman caused the death of a *sādhu* because she had offered him some rotten vegetable, which he was obliged to eat in order to avoid the death of numerous ants attracted by its foul smell (*Nāyādhammakahāo* 16 etc.). On the other hand, among the most famous positive heroines is Candanabālā, a young girl who alone knew what type of food the twenty-fourth Jina Mahāvīra needed to break his fast. Instances of male donors are, however, also easy to find.

Even if normative literature prescribes the avoidance of eating or drinking at night for all, whether men or women, a perusal of narrative literature seems to show that it is actually observed mostly (if not only) by women, for they are the sole protagonists of stories devoted to this topic. Moreover, a common story-pattern stages a couple where the woman strictly keeps to this vow while her husband or her in-laws (sometimes non-Jain) first laugh at her and refuse to act similarly, then are later convinced of the need to follow her behavior under the pressure of events. It is remarkable that, while no specification is generally given about women in the case of other religious themes, some texts include a separate account listing the miseries or happiness awaiting any girl who would break this vow or keep it. Modern evidence shows the same trend (Misra 1972, 44, 54) and, as has been argued by Mahias (1985, 108–11), it may result in inverting the normal sequence of the meals, since the wife would then take food *before* her husband.

As constituting the penance (*tapas*) par excellence because it also implies sexual purity, abstaining from food in the form of fasts is indeed "one of the most important expressions of female religiosity" and "one of the key ways through which women demonstrate family honour" (Reynell 1987, 322; 1991, 56ff.). There is a large variety of fasts (Mahias 1985, 111ff.; Reynell 1987, 320–21), either implying total restriction (water but no food) or partial restriction regarding the type of food or the frequency of meals. Some types of fasts, such as the *ravivār vrat* ("Sundays' fast") among Digambaras, are specific to women (Mahias 1985, 116). The more fasts they perform during their life, the higher their reputation of religiosity is. Fasting women always arouse great respect among their relatives and are surrounded by great care (Misra 1972, 49). To quote Reynell (1987, 347), "through her fasting a woman makes a public statement about herself. Fasting becomes a statement of a woman's inner purity and by extension becomes a statement about the honour of her family." As a matter of fact, the breaking of a fast always involves a group celebration or a feast of some kind, which contributes to social cohesion (Misra 1972, 50; Reynell 1987, 348–51).

Worship

The question of worship is rather intricate with regard to the position of women. Except for the followers of the nonidolatrous sect of the Sthānakvāsins who pray or meditate privately in their houses, all Jains must go to the temples daily and worship the Jinas as "human beings who have achieved omniscience and final liberation and who teach the path of liberation to others" (Babb 1988, 67). The doctrine prescribes it for all and actual observation shows that women do it more regularly and more at leisure, adding to it the performance of other rituals at home (Reynell 1987, 319).

Nevertheless sporadic statements also imply that their rights possibly differ from those of men as far as the performance of rituals is concerned, or that women are submitted to more restrictions. Whatever its divisions, daily worship generally implies two categories of rituals: the first takes place in the cella of the temple and requires a perfect physical and mental purity from the worshiper since it implies direct contact with the image, which has to be washed or anointed with paste of sandalwood and flowers. The second ritual requires less purity since it takes place in the main hall, in front of the image but at a distance from it (e.g., Babb 1988, 70ff.). Woman being the paradigmatic "impure" creature, it happens that among Śvetāmbaras she may be excluded altogether from the first category of rituals (Stevenson 1915, 251). The followers of the Kharataragac-cha Śvetāmbara school do not allow women to worship images of the Jinas (Deo 1950, 25).

In front of a recently built temple dedicated to the god Ghaṇṭākarṇa Mahāvīra, a board says that no woman should enter the cella, and that no menstruating woman should enter the main hall (Lodurva, Rajasthan; see also Babb 1988, 69). Among Digam-baras she may not be allowed to wash the image (Mahias 1985, 254). To quote one of their treatises: "If a woman performs worship to the Jinas, she should follow the same injunctions (as men), but she is not entitled to touch the image. Thus do the knowledgeable people say" (Kiśansimha, Kriyākośa [18th century] vs. 1457).

Such details are important insofar as they represent an under-current tendency rather than a general line. They embody the con-flict between the fundamentally egalitarian religious doctrine of Jainism and the pan-Indian beliefs about womanhood.

On the other hand, it is well known that in Śvetāmbara temples the right to perform different sorts of pūjās first is determined by a system of auction. Though nothing theoretically prevents women from raising bids, there seems to be a kind of consensus that they can do it only along with their husbands (Reynell 1987, 327–28).

THE JAIN IMAGE OF WOMAN AND
ITS THEOLOGICAL CONSEQUENCES

The pan-Indian prejudices against women, who are said to be weak-minded, fickle, treacherous, and impure, are shared by the Jains (see extract p. 134). Except harsh criticisms against the wom-an's body, said to host innumerable subtle beings in constant danger of being crushed, which are obviously due to the specific impor-tance ascribed to ahimsa by the Jains, they are not of much interest as such.

What is relevant, however, is the way these prejudices are ex-ploited by a religion that advocates renunciation as the highest value, the way they are inserted in religious debates and used as ar-guments therein, and their consequences, which for the sake of con-venience I would term "mythology." Hence an overall impression prevails that the Jains have followed their own ideas through to their logical conclusions.

Woman as a Symbol of Attachment

In a religion like Jainism where asceticism is the central value and the quickest path to salvation, the woman is bound to be represented negatively: as connected with sexuality she is a living and insidious threat to the monk's fourth "major vow," the vow of chastity, which among the five "great vows" taken by mendicants is said to be very difficult to comply with. Therefore it is even prohibited to talk to her, as is expressed in the Prakrit term *itthīkahā*, "talks with/about women," one of the four forms of "bad talks" (*vikahā*). On the other hand, because it is emphasized that there exists a fundamental interconnection between the different vows, not observing chastity would mean going against the resolution to renounce possessions and against the vow of ahimsa, sexual intercourse implying injury to many living beings.

Hence the vehement outbursts against women as temptresses one comes across from the oldest texts onward:

(A monk) who leaves mother and father (and his) former (family) connection, (resolving:) "I will live alone, without companion, as one for whom sexual pleasure has ceased, seeking solitary places"—him approach, with crafty, stealthy step, sweet-spoken women; they know how to contrive that some monks will suffer a (moral) breakdown. They sit down closely at his side, they frequently put on holiday dress, they show him even the lower part of their body and the armpit when lifting their arm. . . . He should not fix his eye on those (women), nor should he consent to (women's) inconsiderate acts, nor should he walk together with them: thus his soul is well-guarded. (*Sūyagaḍanga* 1.4.1,1–3; 1.4.1,5: trans. Alsdorf 1974, 202–3; see also *Mahānisīhasutta* 2.10–16)

Schuster Barnes has observed that in Buddhism "most of the time the texts correctly direct their denunciation against a man's . . . attitude" (1987, 113) more than against external causes. This does not seem to hold true for Jainism where such statements are quite exceptional and where the account of the fourth vow generally forms a starting point for lengthy reflections on women's innate wickedness (Williams 1963, 176). At the same time, however, some writers probably felt that these were overstatements that should not be understood literally, since they indicate that their purpose is only to warn monks against danger and help them (see extract p. 134; Śubhacandra's *Jñānārṇava* 12:56–59).

Religious Debates about Woman

Woman and Emancipation. It has been argued that the period between 300 B.C.E. and 200 C.E. witnessed the eruption of "a doctrinal crisis wherein the spiritual capacities of women were challenged and a real effort was made to prove theologically that women are inferior to men" (Schuster Barnes 1987, 114). This had an impact on Jainism (as it had on Mahayana Buddhism) at a similar time. As a matter of fact the first evidence in support of men's and women's spiritual inequality is found in one of the religious poems ascribed to Kundakunda, one of the most revered Digambara teachers said to have worked toward the beginning of the Christian era. By establishing a direct connection between the fact that a woman cannot go naked and the affirmation of nudity as sine qua non condition for the attainment of emancipation, Kundakunda (*Sutta pāhuḍa* vs. 22ff.; Jaini 1991, 34ff.) put forward the central argument of a debate that subsequently became a *locus communis* of the Digambara/ Śvetāmbara doctrinal rivalry, which has continued to the present day. While the Digambaras advocate that a woman cannot attain emancipation, implying that rebirth as a man is a prerequisite, the Śvetāmbaras say that this transitory stage is not necessary.

Copious primary literature on the topic comes from both schools and, interestingly enough, is often inserted in treatises devoted to the discussion of philosophical or logical matters (Jambūvijaya 1974; Bhattacharya 1967; Jaini 1986, 204; 1991, 41– 108) as if the need was felt to lead the debate beyond mere postulates with the help of closely argued reasoning. The first complete book is apparently the *Strīnirvāṇaprakaraṇa*, composed in the ninth century by Śākaṭāyana, a member of the now extinct Yāpanīya sect who sides with the Śvetāmbaras (Jambūvijaya 1974, Shāntā 1985, 490ff.), whereas most other texts date from the eleventh century onward (references in Jambūvijaya 1974 and Jaini 1991). Let me summarize the main stages of the discussion.

Among the arguments expressed by Digambaras in favor of their position, a first group is based on pan-Indian beliefs (or prejudices) against women whose inborn nature is supposed to be bad. Birth as a woman can be due only to a great sin and to preeminence of wrong

belief. Women's nature is weak. Treacherousness is a woman's prerogative. Women are inferior to men with respect to glory and they
are not shown respect by men. In such cases the Śvetāmbaras answer by referring to counterexamples that invalidate the general
value of the thesis, quoting, for instance, names of women who
proved their energy, or saying that some of the criticisms leveled at
them could be leveled at men as well (Strīnirvāṇaprakaraṇa vss.
27ff.; Jaini 1991, 72ff.; Bhattacharya 1967, 610–13). In order to reply
to the Digambaras who contend that the inability of women to be
reborn in the lowest hell is a sign of their general lack of excellency
(prakarṣa), the Śvetāmbaras reply that since there is no adequation
(avyāpti) between this well-admitted inability and the inability for
emancipation, it cannot hold as a cause (Strī° vss. 5–6; Jaini 1991,
51ff.; Bhattacharya 1967, 607).

However, as stated earlier, the major discussion centers around
the question of clothing. According to the Digambaras, emancipation means total rejection of all belongings and giving up the satisfaction of physical needs (such as eating). But wearing clothes would
mean transgressing the fifth vow of nonattachment and an inapti-
tude to observe self-control (saṁyama). Because of her innate physical impurity, a woman needs clothes in any case. Hence, since she
cannot fulfill the precondition, she is not fit for emancipation. The
Śvetāmbaras say:

> If clothes are a reason for the impossibility of Emancipation,
> let them be given up. But it would not be conform to the rule
> to give them up. They are a component of Emancipation (for
> women) as a whisk broom is. Otherwise the Teacher would
> have erred. The Teacher thought that giving up clothes (would
> mean) giving up of all (good conduct), and that there was very
> little harm in accepting clothes. Therefore he prescribed them.
> As for attachment it can exist with respect to food and so on
> (viz. not only with the respect to clothes). . . . If implements
> are a tie for the nun, (they would be one also for a man). In
> that case a man could not be a nirgrantha either. Even some-
> body who is adorned with clothes, jewellery, etc., can be with-
> out attachment, provided he has no acquisitive egotism. If he
> has, he will be tied, even though he is naked. . . . Non attach-
> ment is absence of acquisitive egotism, nothing else. (Strī° vss.
> 10 –16; see Jaini 1991, 56ff.)

Thus they seem to favor a spiritual interpretation of the concept
of nonattachment rather than a literal understanding of the term.

This appears to be a general feature of theirs in the present debate, as can be seen by their clear statement that the only way toward emancipation is the combination of "right faith, right knowledge and right conduct" (the three *ratnas*), that nothing shows women's inability to behave accordingly and annihilate karmic matter (*Strī°* vss. 2ff.; Jaini 1991, 49; Bhattacharya 1967, 603): "(Suppose that) a karman leading to femininity is acquired. As a matter of fact both women and men are Emancipated when their individual karmans are destroyed. Since the ātman is exactly the same in both women and men, woman is fit for Emancipation." (*Pramāṇasāra* [15th century]: *Jaina Philosophical Tracts* [Ahmedabad 1973], 119).

Laywomen and Laymen. It has been seen above that the fundamental debate about woman's ability to gain salvation probably reached its climax in the middle ages. Once the question of man's and woman's inequality on the religious level was put through this specific application, it could be easily extended. Thus even those who always supported the equality of women (the Śvetāmbaras) could not just state it as self-evident. They had to try to *prove* it. This takes place for instance in the *śrāvakācāras*, starting with Hemacandra (twelfth century) onward when the concept of the "seven fields" in which a Jain should sow wealth is adduced: two of them are the laymen and the laywomen, but the fact that the two groups should be treated identically has to be discussed in the form of a fictitious logical argument.

Interestingly enough, the solution lies in refusing absoluteness (*ekānta*) and recognizing the manifoldness of reality (*anekānta*) as the Jains fundamentally do. Thus even if there are "two opposing poles of prejudice: the reverence shown to a few individual idealized women . . . and the contempt shown to women in general" (Leslie 1989, 272), the Śvetāmbaras at least consider the existence of a positive pole more important and sufficient to support extension to laywomanhood as a general concept:

Affection to be shown to laywomen should be inferred as being exactly the same as the one shown to laymen, not more and not less. Since they too are endowed with right knowledge, right faith and right conduct, since their chief characteristic is to be satisfied with chastity (*śīla*) whether they are widows or not, since their hearts are devoted to the Jain doctrine, they must be considered as co-religionists too.

Objection: But in the world as well as in the Teaching women are well known to be receptacles of bad points. They

are indeed poisonous flowers without earth, Indra's thunder-
bolts without being produced from the sky, diseases without
remedy, death without cause, prodigies without signs, female
snakes without hoods, tigresses without a cave, real ogresses,
destroyers of affection between relatives and elders, full of untruth and deceit (*māyā*). As it is said: "Untruth, violence, deceit, stupidity, excessive greed, impurity and cruelty are the
innate negative points of women." "When heaps of infinite
sins arise comes womanhood, know that well, Gotama." In
all treatises, almost at every step, they are criticized. Hence
they should be avoided from far. How then can the fact that
they should be objects of charity, respect and consideration
be justified?

Answer: There is no invariability (*ekānta*) in the fact that
women only are full of bad points: the same is true of men
too. They also are very often seen to be cruel, full of bad
points, unbelievers, ungrateful, perfidious against their masters, destroyers of trust, liars, attracted by women or others'
wealth, without pity, deceivers of their kings or their elders.
And all that does not justify that great men be despised. Similarly in the case of women. Even if some of them are found to
be full of bad points, there are also some who are full of good
points. As a matter of fact, even though they are women, the
Tīrthaṁkaras' mothers are worshipped even by the highest
gods and praised by the best sages because of the importance
of their qualities. . . . Thanks to the power of their chastity,
some of them change fire into water, water into earth, wild-
cats into jackals, a serpent into a rope, poison into nectar. In
the fourfold sangha, the fourth part is the laywoman indeed.
The fact that women are very often criticized in the treatises
is only meant for the Liberation of those who are strongly attached to them.

In the treatises we hear about (the following things): the
qualities of laywomen such as Sulasā and others are praised
even by Tīrthaṁkaras. In heavens they are eulogised even by
the best of gods as able to teach the Law. The right faith they
have cannot even be shaken by strong holders of wrong faith.
Some of them are in their last incarnation. Some others will
come to Emancipation after two-three births.

Thus, as mothers, sisters, or daughters, laywomen are ab-
solutely entitled to affection. That's all. (Ratnaśekhara's
Śrāddhavidhiprakaraṇa [14th century], fifth section, p. 21)

Women and Mythology. Now some instances can be considered which show how the views about women are echoed in the mythology of the two main Jain sects. In an atheistic movement like Jainism, the mythology mainly centers around the twenty-four Tīrthaṁkaras ("Ford-makers"), whose teaching enables everybody to know and practise the path, and around events connected with their biographies. However, partly under the influence of the general Indian context (the rise of bhakti, etc.), Jainism progressively developed a pantheon where female deities play an outstanding role.

The Twenty-fourth Jina, Mahāvīra. Representation of woman as a threat to the monk's chastity and complete renunciation of the world accounts for a discrepancy between Śvetāmbaras and Digambaras as far as the life of the twenty-fourth Jina, Mahāvīra, is concerned. According to the generally more rigorous tradition of the Digambaras, when reaching the age of thirty, he renounced the world, and, as some texts insist, though his physical structure was that of a handsome and strong young man, he overcame love. On the contrary, it is quite clear that women play a central part in this Jina's biography as told by the Śvetāmbaras. As far back as their canonical scriptures they state that Vardhamāna was married. But whereas the *Kalpasūtra* merely gives the information, the later biographies try to justify it, and, one must admit, they are obviously quite embarrassed. Therefore they feel the need to advocate instances taken from the past, saying that the first Jina Ṛṣabha married, or insistingly indicate that the would-be Jina accepted marriage reluctantly after many negotiations and only to comply with his parents' wishes, which when in his mother's womb he had already pledged never to disobey. Here the attitude toward women might symbolically serve to highlight a fundamental difference in the importance ascribed to the layman's and the mendicant's path by the two sects: renunciation (implying perfect chastity) is the only way to salvation and can be reached *directly* according to the Digambaras, whereas a passage through the state of a perfect householder is a preliminary condition for the Śvetāmbaras.

Other questions are raised by the place of women in Mahāvīra's genealogy. How to explain in the Indian context that Śvetāmbara literary sources *unanimously* show him as the father of a *girl*, and mention her name as well as the name of his granddaughter? Or was this meant specifically as symbolic since it was known that the Buddha had fathered a *son?* The question is of some importance if we consider that this girl married a certain Jamāli who in turn was

Mahāvīra's nephew through his (elder) *sister* and that the couple was responsible for the first schism in the church. Whatever the interpretation may be, I cannot imagine that this stress on feminine lineage was a matter of chance. Apart from depending on legal matters, it might also aim at emphasizing a sectarian individuality (Śvetāmbara versus Digambara; Mahāvīra versus Buddha). The problem should at any rate be examined more thoroughly than it has been until now.

The Nineteenth Jina, Malli. The debate about women's ability to gain salvation and the answers given by both sects are best evidenced by the narrative literature relating the human existence of the nineteenth Jina. According to the Śvetāmbaras who narrate this Jina's biography already in their canon (Roth 1983), Malli is the feminine rebirth of the ascetic Mahābala, who, in spite of the agreement made with six of his companions to observe fasts of identical lengths, observed longer fasts. This had a double effect: it explained the rebirth as a woman (because the ascetic resorted to perfidy and lie) *but also* the destiny as a future Jina since asceticism is recorded among the twenty causes leading to Jinahood.

According to the Digambara versions (Jaini 1979, 40 n. 93; Roth 1983, 49–57), Malli is born as a boy and thereafter lives the ordinary career of a Jina. Except for a perhaps doubtful and apparently unique gloss, which could lead us to think that even among them Malli could have been a woman before the time that salvation was denied to this sex (Roth 1983, 53–54), this represents a unanimous tradition.

The interesting question about Malli's femininity is raised for the first time by Bhāvasena, a Digambara writer of the fourteenth century (Jaini 1986) who cleverly adduces (indisputable) iconographic observations as support for his position that Malli could not have been female:

> For example, no one in the world has ever perceived the (alleged) femininity of the images of the Lord Malli; on the contrary, those images are always depicted in masculine gender. . . . The Lord under debate must be a man, because he is never portrayed as female in his images. This is like the images of Vardhamāna (Mahāvīra), which are well known to be male in the traditions of both parties. (Bhāvasena's *Muktivicāra* §20: trans. Jaini 1986, 217)

I have not had access to later Śvetāmbara answers to such an argument, but one could wonder whether discussing the depiction of sexual characteristics in Tīrthaṃkaras' images is of any meaning, since these stereotyped standing or sitting images are conceived as material aids for meditation, basically supposed to show emancipated souls and not their physical features.

The Mothers. The ambivalence of the Jain image of woman is best seen in the fairly high status ascribed to women as mothers or protective entities, and the development of a specific worship in connection with them *among both sects.*

A first instance of this trend is provided by the rather ancient respect shown to the parents of the Tīrthaṃkaras, and especially to their mothers (Shah 1987, 47ff.; *Śrāddhavidhi°* quoted above) as iconography proves. In the Śvetāmbara literary tradition a particular place is given to Marudevī, the mother of the first (legendary) Jina, Ṛṣabha, since she is said to have been the "first emancipated soul of the current descending era."

Canonical evidence is available to show that already at an early period learning could be identified with womanhood. Sarasvatī is revered as an embodiment of the Jinas' teaching that she protects (Cort 1987, 236). Thus her name is often quoted at the end of the fivefold homage-formula to the masters (*pancanamaskāra*). The same is true of the sixteen *vidyādevīs* (depicted in Mt. Abu) who were first seen as magical powers, the acquisition of which was disapproved, and then held in rather high esteem. I wonder if what the Jains name "the eight mothers of the teaching," an expression that includes basic terms of the doctrine (the five *samitis* and the three *guptis*), is not a conceptualization at an ethical level of the Hindu *mātṛkās*.

Even more important are the female attendants (*yakṣiṇī*) of the major Jinas (Cakreśvarī/Nemi; Padmāvatī/Pārśva; Ambikā (=mother)/Mahāvīra) who after a long process (described in Cort 1987, 241ff.) undoubtedly became the main Jain goddesses. Their worship does not yield the same results as the Jinas' worship. While the Jinas help the devotee along the path of emancipation, the goddesses are mostly "approached to assist [him] in worldly affairs" (Cort 1987, 248), on given occasions when a specific problem arises (illness, need to protect a pilgrimage place, need of assistance in a religious debate, etc.). Thus they appear as benevolent maternal figures connected with fertility.

CONCLUSION

Whatever the way we consider the problem of womanhood in Jainism, we see *two* irreconcilable theologies at work. The "theology of subordination" (Radford Ruether 1987, 207f.), based on the idea that woman is ontologically, intellectually, and morally inferior to man, which contends that she will never be able to reach emancipation—the main goal for which the teaching of the law is meant—is supported by the Digambaras. The "theology of equivalence," admitting that man and woman are human persons of equal value even if they are *different*, and thus that both are equally entitled to reach the final goal, is supported by the Śvetāmbaras.

There are, however, two types of limitation to this bipolarization.

The first one is the law of karma. If one's birth depends on one's own conduct, womanhood (which is due to specific karmic matters) will never be a permanent feature of the individual through the cycle of rebirths. Thus no one is excluded from emancipation for good. The "failure" will last as long as womanhood lasts.

Secondly, even if the theology of equivalence advocates *theoretical* equality of men and women, it in fact also shares the postulate of the theology of subordination regarding the inferiority of women, although it is expressed through insinuations and not given the same extension. This contradiction probably translates difficulties in solving the conflict between the general Indian environment, including the negative ideas it conveys about womanhood, and the attempt to go beyond them through religion. Thus whatever the theology espoused, nuns have had a less important position than monks in the religious hierarchy and have been mostly denied leadership roles in spite of their large numbers.

framework, I was an outsider. However, to the extent that religion encompasses beliefs and practices of the living faith, the worldview that translates these beliefs and practices into everyday experiences, I was an insider.

Having grown up as a member of the Parsi Zoroastrian community in India, I could bear witness to the totality of the experience that stresses the cultural aspect of religion. At the same time, I was not a representative of an uncritical insider's voice. I had always harbored some misgivings about the exclusivity and rigid boundaries that an ethnic religion feels compelled to impose upon its followers. Understanding of its vulnerable position as a minority religion did not persuade me of the necessity for absolute compliance on all counts. In this respect, Young's characterization of the phenomenology of religion methodology as emphasizing a "sympathetic but not submissive attitude toward the insider's view" seemed to fit my experiential preparation for undertaking this study (Young 1987, 2).

There was a point of departure, however, in my thinking from Young's definition. It centered on the extension of the phenomenological method to the study of women in world religions. She states that women scholars "begin from within their own feminine perspectives and so may have a good perception of what a woman's experience entails" (Young 1987, 2). I maintain that the "feminine" perspective is a necessary but not sufficient condition to understand the societal significance of religious traditions—what Lincoln calls the "darker side" of rituals (Lincoln 1981, 108). A "feminist" perspective is essential in order to grasp both the religious and sociopolitical implications of individual and systemic prescriptions that are part of the "women and religion" domain. In addition, a feminist analysis across religious boundaries needs to be blended with a cultural sensitivity in order to avoid a chauvinistic interpretation of data where one's religious/feminist framework becomes a model for the others. The blending, though, has to be approached with a conscious awareness that advocacy of a "cultural" viewpoint could also lead to a defensive posture by reacting in one of the following ways: (1) glossing over the adverse effects of certain religious precepts on women; and (2) coming repeatedly to the defense of these positions in the name of religious/cultural solidarity or sensitivity toward insiders' reactions. The limited amount of literature on women in Zoroastrianism is very much affected by both these tendencies, as will be shown later on in the chapter. In this respect, my feminist-cultural orientation might provide a critical balance to evaluate interpretations that reflect only one of these frameworks.

Finally, aside from the experiential base, I have done research on Parsi Zoroastrian communities that might help me to present more than my own views on the contributions of women in the social and economic spheres. The in-depth, demographic studies of Parsi Zoroastrian households reveal information on the actual lives, attitudes, and behavior of women. Although there is no necessary correlation between the status of women in the religious tradition and their participation in the societal domain, the latter information is helpful in providing a reality base to test if the gender differentiation embodied in the written word is part of daily practice.

On the other hand, a relatively egalitarian ideal that might govern societal sex role behavior is no defense in downplaying the significance of possible negative images of women in the texts and traditions. In other words, it is important to disentangle these various sets of information, and recognize the fact that societal changes in sex roles is not a precursor of _automatic_ changes in old sex role models that are endorsed by patriarchal religions. To construct a new social order that also seeks religious validation for the transformation of female and male roles, one has to deal with the politics of both religious and societal institutions. This argument does not deny the fact that at certain historical junctures, some religious leaders might have played a determining role in bringing about radical changes in societal views of appropriate sex roles. However, as Tong (1977, 339) has pointed out:

> Society has shaped religion much more than religion has shaped society. As soon as a religion adapts to its social _environ_, its critical or countercultural impact is weakened. Gradually, it loses any ability it may have had to transform society; and ultimately it becomes a mirror for the culture which has overpowered it.

In this chapter, I propose to survey the major periods in the history of Zoroastrianism from the perspective of the theology and the practice of female-male relations within the context of the religious tradition, as well as society. This is a very complex history, which encompasses a period from about 1500 B.C.E. to the present. It also involves the study of diverse cultural contexts. Zoroastrianism was a major religion in ancient and medieval Iran. After the Arab conquest of Iran by 651 C.E., it became a minority religion, and many Zoroastrians migrated to India. Today the Parsi Zoroastrians of India (Parsis or Persians, the name used by the Indians for anyone who was an inhabitant of Iran) are considered the most influential segment of this religious community. Zoroastrians continue to dwell in Iran although the exact number of adherents is uncertain. Besides these two major centers, Zoroastrians have settled in Pakistan, Britain, Canada, United States, Australia, Singapore, and Hong Kong, among other places. Thus, to talk about women in Zoroastrianism, particularly as it relates to the modern period, is to make overgeneralizations that cannot possibly apply to the total religious community. In addition, my experiential base in the Parsi Zoroastrian community limits my familiarity with the topic as it applies to women in other Zoroastrian concentrations to available literary sources.

This chapter, therefore, is based on the analysis of a chronological sequence of scriptural and secular writings, and the historical studies and demographic research that I have conducted among the Parsi Zoroastrians as a participant observer. Needless to say, the contemporary studies can only provide complementary data that might suggest possible connections between women's current roles and the gender role ideals that are espoused in the texts that stand for past traditions. This methodology does not solve the inherent problem in dealing with the scriptural and secular writings on this topic—namely, that what passes for evidence is men's views about women that are often presented in a highly polemical fashion. It is in this context that a feminist-cultural lens might prove to be a valuable tool when it is brought to bear on textual materials to provide an understanding of the past, and link it to contemporary studies of women's lives to know the living faith.

ANCIENT PERIOD

The religious culture of Zoroastrian Iran originated perhaps thirty-five hundred years ago, but clearly many of the traditions associated with the prophet Zarathushtra (or Zoroaster as he was known to the ancient Greeks) must reach back much further. Because of its antiquity, the chain of evidence that can be used to trace the history of the Zoroastrians to Indo-European times is a mixture of "fact, legend, and myth" (Pangborn 1982, 1).

In all probability, the Iranians and the Indo-Aryans originally formed one complex of people who were a branch of the Indo-European family of nations. The linguistic evidence suggests that these people lived on the south Russian steppes, to the east of the

Volga. It is generally believed that sometime during the third millennium B.C.E. one group of these people, the Indo-Aryans, moved across northeast Iran and settled in northwest India, taking over the Indus Valley civilization. A further wave moved into Iran later in the second millennium B.C.E. Before these two groups drifted apart, they forged a religious tradition whose elements are preserved to this day in the ancient scriptures of the two countries—the Hindu Vedas and the Zoroastrian Avesta.

Indo-Iranian Heritage

The fragmentary evidence regarding the Indo-Iranian society in this nomadic stage points in the direction of a kingship system that concentrated power in the hands of high kings. The division of society into three classes—warriors, priests, and herdsmen—reflects an orientation that stressed wars and conquest, pastoralism, and the hope of salvation for those who had the means to win the favor of the gods. The patriarchal hierarchy mounting up to a position of great power for its head was based on a kingship system that supported the extreme male dominance through a fourfold grouping: the family, settlement, tribe, and country.

Boyce (1975, 5) supports the traditional explanations for this social structure on the grounds that it was a necessary stage in the establishment of kingdoms since the "uncertain conditions of a wandering life" and a societal pattern of conquests required "good leadership." This functional explanation for the creation of patriarchy is as much a *total* rationale for societal arrangements in archaic times as sociobiology is a *total* explanation for gender arrangements in today's society. In Lerner's words (1986, 19), both explanations might be interpreted as a "political defense of the status quo in scientific language."

The previous discussion of societal arrangements is significant in view of the fact that "this pattern of society appears to have become reflected in that of the gods" (Boyce 1975, 4). Boyce comments on the kingship imagery in the Mihr Yašt (one of the oldest of the Avestan hymns) as mirroring the societal patterns of the day. She also believes that the aristocratic and priestly traditions of the times might have been responsible for denying ascent to paradise to the humblest members of the community, "with women and slaves," and consigning them to the kingdom of shadows beneath the earth (Boyce 1975, 251). Again, a feminist perspective suggests that the aristocratic and priestly frameworks are not sufficient to explain the consignment of all women, even those of noble class, to the subterranean kingdom of the dead. A conscious applications of the feminist framework might provide the missing perspective to understand why women as a *class* of people were excluded from full participation in the religious experience.

The ancient Iranians did relate to feminine imagery on the divine level. The links with traditional feminine attributes are obvious. There is an old coupling between Father sky and Mother earth—the god Asman and the goddess Zam. The goddess is viewed positively with her name interpreted as "bounteous beneficient earth" or "bounteous devoted earth," referring very probably to the nurturing qualities attributed to a female diety as well as earth. Boyce (1975, 207) also points out that the connection between devotion and earth is an old link, since peasantry, low in the social order, is expected to display submissiveness. Another divinity is the pagan goddess of fortune—Aši—who is described as "great gifted" or "treasure laden." Her yašt (scripture devoted to the worship of divine beings) (versus 6–14) describes what she is able to bestow: "values of the good things of this world . . . frank pleasure in . . . earthly riches . . . in a world of which man is the center and wherein the woman, like the cattle, the gold, and the silver, minister to man's enjoyment." Indeed, this is a perfect depiction of patriarchal heaven. A water deity, Ardavi Sūrā Anāhitā, is identified with the life-giving power of rivers that nurtures crops and herds. The Avestan hymn dedicated to her (Yašt 5.2) reveals that she is worshiped as goddess of fertility, who purifies the seeds of all males, the wombs of all females, and makes the milk flow, which nourishes the young.

It is also interesting that while mortal women were thought unworthy of attaining paradise, the soul of a dead man on its departure from earth at the end of the third day after death is seen as meeting a female figure on its upward journey—the maiden of the bridge. Those souls who had acquired merit in the eyes of the gods could hope to ascend to heaven by crossing safely over the "bridge of the separator." The undeserving fell from this bridge to live in the dark shadows of the underworld under the rule of the lord of the dead. If the pleasures of paradise were visualized as being reserved solely for the delight of men, the apparition of the welcoming maiden makes sense since woman's role was perceived as ministering to men's needs. Another version of the feminine quality—the guiding hand—seems to be manifested in the depiction of Cistā, the goddess of the way, the one instructed in the paths to be followed. Apparently, she is a source of energy; "she inspires with the power to continue on the way" (Boyce 1975, 62). The sustaining power of feminine energy as a source for *others* rather than self is a common theme in patriarchal religions as well as society.

The Indo-Iranian views about the world also included beliefs in spirits, some kindly and some malevolent. Some of these spirits were conceived as female beings. The benevolent *fravartis*, the guiding spirits of the dead, are winged creatures who inhabit the air and could be persuaded, through offerings, to come to the aid of humans. The evil supernatural beings, *parikās* (Yašt I.10), could beguile men to their harm by taking on human form of extraordinary beauty. They were capable of harming humans physically, by undermining their moral character, or damaging the material world around them. The recognition of feminine power as a symbol for good or evil has been mythically expressed in many religious beliefs (O'Flaherty 1976). It often goes hand in hand with a deep ambivalence regarding women—a natural consequence of the general misogyny of patriarchal societies that spawned these religious traditions.

Zoroastrian Religious Inheritance

The revelations of the prophet Zarathushtra or Zoroaster (lived 1500–1200 B.C.E.) relating to the religious status of women contain some of the Indo-Iranian elements mentioned previously that became blended with the prophet's own teachings. But it is safe to say that despite the fact that the religion retained the patriarchal characteristics that were part of its pagan past and its own male-dominated society, it also challenged the status quo by introducing a more gender-inclusive philosophy—even if it still reflected a male worldview. The most significant departure from the pagan tradition was that Zoroaster promised the hope of salvation to both women and men. Paradise was no longer the exclusive domain of men who had the means to achieve it. From the Gāthās (hymns or songs believed to be composed by the prophet himself), it is clear that Zoroaster's conception of the morally good life went beyond a design for ethical human behavior; it implied an eschatology. Paradise was now attainable by all those who had chosen to live the righteous life—whose good thoughts, words, and deeds outnumbered the bad. Thus, the prophet proclaimed: "Man or woman . . . whomever I shall impel to your invocation, with all these shall I cross the Bridge of the Separator" (Yasña 46:10). In fact, the prophet's handling of the belief in the maiden of the bridge illustrates how some pagan ideas were accepted and harmonized with his own teachings.

The stress on righteous living as the passport to paradise is emphasized by the fact that the maiden is now seen as personification of an individual's conscience (daēnā). If the person has led a good moral life, then the soul is guided over the bridge to paradise by its own daēnā in the form of a lovely young damsel. But if the soul is that of a wicked person, it is met by its conscience, a hideous hag, who plunges with it off the bridge down into hell (Pavry 1929). The break from past traditions is evident in the prophet's attempt to provide an ethical connotation to a previously amoral figure of the welcoming maiden. The imagery, however, of a damsel and a hag to personify goodness and wickedness, seems to be an acceptable vehicle to introduce radical ideas in traditionally understood sex-linked stereotypes.

The Avestan texts provide further elaboration of the fact that on some counts the prophet did provide a vision of equality between women and men in the religious experience. Even when the transcendent was imaged as a supreme male being (the wise lord—Ahuramazdā, often referred to in the texts as the "father"), his first creative act of bringing into being six lesser beneficient divinities in the struggle against evil (the Ameša Spentas) included three female yazatas. The scriptures (Yasna 39.3) talk about worshiping the "bounteous immortals" (Ameša Spentas), both females and males. Each of them protects one part of the total creation in the material world against the onslaught of evil from the evil spirit (Angra Mainyu). The assignment of female yazatas to guard over earth, water, and plants can be explained easily as a reference to the females' capacity for nurturance and growth.

What is more interesting, however, is that in the later, more conservative, era, the Pahlavi literature fully sets out the association of Spendārmad—the Ameša Spenta who protects the "lowly submissive, and fecund" earth (Boyce 1975, 204)—with that of protector of "virtuous woman." And Ohrmazd (wise lord) is said to preside over "just man," which seems to divide up the protection of women and men between female and male immortals.

It is also worth noting that the sex-linked attributes—virtuous and just—might be the appropriate role models that the religious world considered worthy to be singled out for attention. Moreover, the guardian of earth (and by association, peasants) and virtuous woman is known by her characteristic—devotion—that must have been prized among those who are low in the social gradation, since "women like peasants, were expected to be devoted and submissive" (Boyce 1975, 207). Again, the degree of correspondence between the societal arrangements of the day and religious imagery gives us a chance to understand how far the prophet went in presenting new ideas, to what extent these beliefs retained the patriarchal structure, and how the combination might have helped followers to accept his message.

The sacred liturgy reveals another area where the prophet included women in the religious tradition. Veneration is offered to the *fravašis* (the Indo-Iranian *fravartis* referred to earlier) of the just women as well as men (Yasňa 37.3). The inclusion of the former seems to be a specifically Zoroastrian conception. Fravardīn Yašt (Yašt 13), which preserves the names of those who upheld the faith at its inception, lists the names of a group of women whose *fravašis* are worthy of worship. In fact, Ahura Mazdā is said to have created women to aid him in the vanquishing of corporeal and spiritual evil through following the path of righteousness. In this sense, Ahura Mazdā needs the women along with men to be his allies in seeking salvation for the world—to defeat Angra Mainyu and the onslaught of evil—and restore the world to its pristine state. Thus, in the initial stages of the spread of Zoroastrianism, women and men were ideally considered to be equal partners in the struggle against evil.

These egalitarian ideals, however, were not completely translated into religious doctrine or everyday practice, since Iran was basically a male-dominated society. It is true that according to the Avestan texts, both women and men were entitled to be initiated into the religion by the investiture of the sacred shirt and girdle (Vendidad 18.54, 58). Women as well as men were asked to fulfill their duty to proclaim and teach what is true and good (Yasňa 35.6). In fact, there is some evidence that besides taking part in the holy ceremonies and solemn offerings, women were considered fit, under certain circumstances, to officiate for the minor priestly duties (Dhalla 1922, 74).

At the same time, it has to be recognized that the language of the sacred texts reflects a patriarchal worldview. For example, the conception of woman "advanced in her holy thoughts, and words, and deeds," who is considered worthy of being invited to an offering ceremony, includes the requirement that she also be "well subordinated, whose ruler is her lord" (Visperad 3.4). The conception of the righteous man in the same invocation is not qualified by his sex-role definition.

In this sense, the texts symbolize the sacralization of the social order. Throughout the scriptures, there is a subtle differentiation between the sexes that seems to reinforce the traditional patriarchal system. And this is true despite the fact that there is enough evidence that the duty to marry and procreate is thought to be not only desirable, but a holy pursuit for both women and men. The Zoroastrian strong ethnic self-consciousness made the begetting of children for the propogation of the race and the spreading of the faith a religious function—to further the kingdom of Ahura Mazdā and cripple the power of Angra Mainyu. Hence, the Avesta declares that a married man is far above him who is unmarried; he who has children is far above him who has no offspring (Vendidad 4.47). Thus, to be without children is the greatest calamity that can befall a family. Moreover, childlessness is perceived as being a curse visited upon the impious by the good spirits (Yasña 11.3). Undoubtedly, within a patriarchal framework, this "blaming the victim" philosophy must have weighed more heavily on the woman who must have wondered how she had sinned to deserve such a punishment.

A further pressure on the Zoroastrian wife in fulfilling her religious destiny was not only to bear children, but specifically bear "male children," "a troop of male children" (Yašt 8.15). Having a son is a blessing bestowed by the benevolent spirits upon the righteous (Yašt 10.65), and again, the gift is denied to a woman who does not follow the proper rituals (Yasña 10.15). Moreover, sons were necessary to have the proper ceremonies performed after death to aid the departed family members' souls on the upward journey to paradise. In fact, the importance of the cult of ancestral dead required that provision be made for the adoption of a son in case a man had none borne to him. Interestingly, although the texts are silent on the issue of praying for female children, or receiving the blessings of female children from the good spirits, some authors seem to display the defensive cultural attitude discussed earlier by interpreting the *omission* as a "lack of displeasure" at the birth of daughters (Sanjana 1892, 16). The ethnic self-consciousness of the Zoroastrian community about their past accomplishments, plus the protective tendencies of scholars who might be overidentified with their subjects, tend at times to present a somewhat idealized picture of the laudable manner in which women were treated in this religious tradition.

Perhaps, a more accurate description of the status of women in the religion and everyday life might be that the Zoroastrian religion represented a significant step up in the recognition and appreciation of the *traditional* roles of women—an improvement on patriarchy in the Indo-Iranian context. Furthermore, the religion emphasized the *mutual* responsibilities of husband and wife, albeit within a patriarchal structure. This is illustrated by the language used to denote the status of the wife (nm̃ano-pathni, "the mistress of the house"), while the husband is addressed as nm̃ano-paiti ("the master of the house"). Zoroaster's advice to the bride and bridegroom sets forth the injunction to "let each one cherish the other in righteousness; thus alone unto each shall the home life be happy" (Yasña 53.5). Thus, marriage and the family unit become part of the divine order of the world and the begetting of children contributes more hands to do battle against the evil spirit and achieve the renovation promised to humanity.

In this context, the traditional duties of woman as wife and mother become an important instrument to achieve religious objectives. Moreover, her involvement in the family and the rituals plays a pivotal role in the cosmic battle against evil. The co-participation of husband and wife in the daily prayers to the wise lord and her co-presence in the domestic and public rituals lends credence to the importance of the housewife's role in the total religious experience. Besides, in certain aspects, the housewife's contribution must have been paramount in the preservation of the religion such as the religious instruction to children, and fulfilling the requirements of the performance of rituals. Because the religion, which catered to the well-being of the family, was centered in the home, it must have provided a degree of recognition plus sustenance for many women's faith that their home-centered work was part of the larger cosmic picture. In fact, the texts specifically mention the fact that although the housewife is encouraged to pray with her husband, her work in the home is so valuable that it may itself serve as prayer if her duties preclude her reciting the required Nyāyašes (Simmons 1987, 1). Furthermore, in the daily cleaning of the home, the housewife is thought to sweep away the dirt and decay that are part of the weapons the evil spirit uses to spoil Ahura Mazdā's good creation (Hinnells 1981, 37).

The reinforcement of women's traditional roles and the emphasis on the "cult of domesticity" is understandable in the historical context of a male-dominated society. What is surprising, however, is that even in today's academic environment where women's issues are part of scholarly consciousness, no one in the area of women in Zoroastrianism has commented on the negative impact of these belief systems in confining women's activity to the private sphere. Even in the home environment, there is enough evidence (Dhalla 1922, 75) illustrating that the woman might have been the "minor partner of man in the religious life of the family." For example, the domestic hearth was also the family altar around which the family gathered for its devotions. Although the woman had to tend to the fire as part of her household work (and see to it that it was never allowed to go out), it is said that the fire awoke the master of the house and not the mistress at night, when it sought fuel for its nourishment (Vendidad, 18.18–21). This is because as the head of the family the man was the "chief of all family worship" (Dhalla 1922, 75). Dhalla continues to make his point about the low status of women in the hierarchy of the household by showing that the texts mention that a physician shall "heal the master of the house for the value of an ox of low value . . . he shall heal the wife of the master of the house for the value of a she-ass" (Vendidad 7.41, 42).

Other evidence about the ideal role of a woman can be gleaned from the developmental highlights that are singled out for attention in the sacred liturgy. The Avesta contain direct allusions to the status of a maiden in the "father's" house (the patrilineal and patrilocal family). She was given training in the religious schools after the age of seven so she could be initiated into her faith. Other than that, education consisted of preparation for the housewifely role:

> General training in moral and religious precepts, the elementary rules of sanitation, the art of tending domestic animals, of spinning and weaving the sacred girdle as well as garments, of superintending the labourers in the field and the milking of the cows . . . in short she aspired to be the delight of her husband in the future. (Sanjana 1892, 17–19)

This concern for building a stable family life and begetting children led to the early marriage of girls at about the age of fifteen—"at the age of puberty, with earrings in her ears . . . whom no man has known" (Vendidad 14.15). Obviously, chastity is considered to be the most essential quality in a bride, although no mention is made about the value of the same quality in a groom. Other characteristics that are praised besides a "mind absorbed in piety" (Yašt 11.4) is "receiving her instruction well, having her husband as her lord" (Gā 4.9).

The texts also provide an instructive view of the ideal images of the maiden and her phantasies of the prospective bridegroom. These passages display not only an interest in physical beauty, but a connection between youthfulness and virility, and the child-bearing capacity of the maiden. In her daily prayers, the maiden is said to ask for a boon of "a husband, young and beautiful of body, who will treat us well, all life long, and give us offspring; a wise, learned, ready-tongued husband" (Yašt 15.40). And what is the ideal of female beauty? The ideal is personified in the description of the maiden of the bridge discussed earlier: "beautiful maiden, brilliant, white-armed, strong, well-grown, erect, tall, high-bosomed, graceful, noble, with a dazzling fall, of fifteen years" (Haug 1878, 220).

The parents or guardians generally arranged the marriage, although the girl was consulted in the choice of the husband. The ideal union was considered to be based on mutual affection. There is some evidence, however, that under certain circumstances, there was some room for love marriages. Moreover, in this context, women were described as being capable of stepping outside the societal constraints of role definition and display the "force of character" to "go straight to [their] objective without hesitation" (Vacha 1950, 169). Thus, we read in the Shāhnāma, book of kings (the Persian epic), that women like Manijeh, Rudābeh, and Tahmina were "transported by love into making active advances," while at the same time protecting themselves and soothing their beloved's male ego by disclaimers about their "immodesty": "No one has ever seen me outside the purdah nor has any man ever heard my voice" (Vacha 1950, 169–70)

The fact that there were at least a few Zoroastrian women who gave themselves permission to act in an unconventional manner through using conventional excuses (transported by love) cannot be seriously doubted. Nor can it be denied that the stories display a certain amount of grudging respect for women who are the responsible parties in consummating the union. There is no reason, however, to believe as some authors have done (Sanjana 1892), that these scattered instances of alliances between aristocratic lovers can be generalized as proof of the "high" status of women in the Zoroastrian tradition.

The general Zoroastrian view of sexual love is that within marriage, sex and procreation are virtuous acts, since the begetting of children brings more people into the world to do battle against the evil spirit. Every new birth is seen as sending a thrill through the whole creation of Ahura Mazdā and casting a shadow of gloom over the wicked world of Angra Mainyu. In this sense, sexuality is viewed in the context of a religious duty, and as such, it is a pious act only within the confines of marriage. However, within this narrow definition, there is no downgrading of the physical needs of the human body compared to the higher status of the spiritual sphere. Hence, the celibate state is discouraged. In fact, the Avesta recognizes the joy that the sexual encounter can bring to both husband

and wife, although the language and imagery reflect a male world-view: "The men whom thou dost attend . . . have their ladies that sit on their beds, waiting for them: they lie on the cushions, adorning themselves. . . . 'When will our lord come? When shall we enjoy in our bodies the joys of love'?" (Yašt 17.10).

The patriarchal nature of the family and society during the ancient period is evident from the fact that conjugal infidelity as a sin and an offense is spelled out very carefully in the case of a woman, but the texts are silent on how adultery is perceived among men. The infringement of chastity on the part of woman grieves Aši (feminine personification of piety), who is pictured as fleeing to the heavens or sinking into the earth at the sight of an unchaste female: "the courtezan who destroys her fruit" and the "courtezan who brings forth a child conceived of a stranger and presents it to her husband" (Yašt 17.54). Such a woman is unfit to offer any prayers (Yašt 17.54). The *yazata* Haoma is entreated to hurl her mace "against the body of the harlot, with her magic minds o'erthrowing with (intoxicating) pleasures" (Yasňa 9.32). Whether she gives her body to the faithful or unfaithful, there is no difference (Vendidad 18.62). Furthermore, the male control of the family, especially the "ownership" of the female, is demonstrated by the fact that once the woman has borne children, she cannot be divorced for any other reason except adultery (Choksy 1989, 90).

Other taboos on sexual intercourse are centered on the Zoroastrian belief that menstruation results in a woman losing her ritual purity and becoming capable of spreading the impurity to all those who have contact with her. Thus, husband and wife were strictly forbidden to have intercourse during this period, and for three days after she had performed her postmenstrual ablutions. Ignoring this taboo is listed as the fourth of the five sins that render one a *Peshô-tanu* (a high level of sin requiring a punishment of up to ninety lashes) (Vendidad 15.7, 13–16). The Vendidad goes even further by declaring that such a man does not act better than "if he should burn the corpse of his own son, born of his own body . . . and drop its fat into the fire" (16.17).

Obviously, the Zoroastrian conception of menstruation and its relationship with the status of women is a far broader subject that the taboos associated with marital relations. The notion that menstrual blood is dangerous is widespread among many cultures and religions. (See, for example, Carmody 1987, and Hays 1964.) In Zoroastrianism, all substances leaving the body are considered ritually impure and polluting. Such substances include hair, nails, skin, feces, saliva, breath, blood, semen, and menstrual blood.

These substances are open to grave pollution by the corpse demoness, since any flow of blood out of the body is a breach of the ideal physical state of human beings. Boyce (1975, 306) attributes this phenomenon to the fact that these substances are "associated with change and mortality rather than with the static state of perfection." Douglas (1966, 121), in analyzing the concept of pollution, states that any matter that traverses the boundaries of the body tends to be considered "marginal stuff." Thus, it is understandable that the Zoroastrian doctrine linked the origin of menstruation to a blight caused by the evil spirit—a "counter-creation" of Angra Mainju who "by his witchcraft" produced "abnormal issues in women" (Vendidad 16.18–19). Therefore, the flow of blood from the body is perceived as an attack by the demons on the perfect creation of Ahura Mazdā. As Choksy (1989 94) has noted, this conception allowed the primitive beliefs and fears surrounding blood and its power to be reinforced by demonology, and elaborate rules then had to be evolved to combat the ritual impurity resulting from this dreaded pollution.

Thus, at the onset of menstruation, very rigid precautions were called for to prevent contamination of the good creation of Ahura Mazdā. The texts specify that a menstruant should withdraw fifteen paces from fire, water, and barsom twigs and three paces from other Zoroastrians (Vendidad 16.4). During menstruation, the woman is supposed to withdraw from the family, sitting apart in a designated place. Boyce (1971) describes the original practice of having the woman pass these days in a tiny windowless hut that had only one entrance. She had to wear old clothes that were set apart for this purpose. Any Zoroastrian who had physical contact with her was required to purify himself or herself with unconsecrated bull's urine and water. The menstruant was supposed to abstain from performing any household duties, since everything she touched became polluted. She was required to eat sparingly, and food had to be served to her at a distance on a metal plate to stop the spread of impurity. The detailed nature of these precautions betray the need to control this powerful source of energy "lest she should gather strength" because "the fiend is in her, any strength she may gain accrues to Ahriman" (Vendidad 16.7).

After the end of menstruation, a woman had to purify her entire body three times with unconsecretaed bull's urine and water while saying the required prayers. Other prayers that specifically ask for expiation from sins were also recited. At menopause a woman was required to have priests perform a solemn purification ceremony, which marked her rejoicing in "being wholly and perpetually clean at last, and able thus to prepare herself for eternity" (Boyce 1975, 308).

Although pregnancy gave a woman respite from the restrictions attendant on menstruation, the texts specify that childbirth also results in ritual impurity to both the mother and the child. All taboos that apply to the menstruant are to be enforced during this period. It would seem logical to assume that childbirth might have been conceived as an act of purity, since it increased the ranks of the faithful who could do battle against the evil spirit and his pandemonium. In fact, all Zoroastrians are thought to be polluted by impurities associated with the birth process and their mother's milk, which is believed to be derived from blood (Choksy 1989, 100). Moreover, birth had no place in the perfect world created by Ahura Mazdā, and will have no place in the universe after the final renovation. Birth belongs, therefore, only to this world of mixture—to fight the evil spirit—and so can logically be considered as partly a result of demonic forces (Boyce 1975, 308).

Zoroastrians considered miscarriages and stillbirths as even greater sources of contamination, since it meant that the woman had borne carrion within her womb. The rituals of purification enjoined for this extensive impurity were prolonged and rigorous. In addition to the period of seclusion, a woman was not permitted to drink the pure creation of water during the first three days of seclusion unless lack of it threatened her life. Instead, she had to consume "*gomez* [unconsecrated bull's urine] mixed with ashes . . . to wash over the grave within her womb" (Vendidad 5.51). Abortion was prohibited since the Zoroastrians regarded it as murder and prosecuted people for this crime (Sanjana 1892.46). The Vendidad admonishes the woman not to "produce in herself the menses against the course of nature" (15.9). If the woman receives help in getting an abortion from the "man" or another person in the form of drugs, all three are considered equally guilty (Vendidad 15.14). The man is exorted to take care of the woman and child, and bring up the child until the age of seven.

The Zoroastrian beliefs regarding menstruation, childbirth, and miscarriage probably represent elaborations of ancient restrictions inherited from the Indo-Iranian period. Most authors seem to view the phenomenon within the general context of the Zoroastrian emphasis on fighting the spread of impurity (the creation of the evil spirit), and prescribing the required purification rituals in order to reintegrate the person into ordinary life (Boyce 1971; 1975; 1977; 1979; 1982; Choksy 1988; 1989). There are disagreements, however, regarding the elaborations of the legend on the origin of menstruation, and these arguments will be covered later on in the chapter since they involve the medieval period.

In addition, the interpretations of how much the religious practices (including menstruation taboos) contributed to the negative self-concept of Zoroastrian women will be dealt with in the discussion on the modern period. Here, it is worth noting though, that the literature on women in Zoroastrianism is remarkably lacking in presenting a feminist-cultural perspective, which recognizes that cosmic claims—however logical they may seem within the confines of the faith—reflect the views of the dominant class and religious institutions. Viewed thus, it is obvious that the belief systems would function to preserve male hegemony rather than worry about representing the female voice in religious doctrines. On the other hand, a "standard" feminist analysis like Culpepper's (1974) on Zoroastrian menustruation taboos (to be discussed later), which reveals "an unfamiliarity with the religion as a living faith, [and] an overreliance on texts" (Simmons 1987, 2) lacks credibility because it mistakes the "dark side for the total phenomenon" (Lincoln 1981, 108). Still, Culpepper deserves credit for recognizing the need for examining these menstrual rituals as a *separate* topic of significance to religion and feminism, rather than including it in a general treatise on misinterpretations of the text regarding the position of women.

The texts present *indirect* evidence on some other subjects that are very relevant in terms of their impact on women. No literature (sacred or secular), however, is available that deals with these important topics—monogamy/polygyny and consanguineous marriages—in terms of recording the effects on women. After all, women had no voice in establishing the religious or societal decrees that governed the most intimate aspects of their lives. What is more pertinent from the methodological point of view is that none of the authors writing in the area of women in Zoroastrianism have covered these topics from a feminist perspective. The concern seems to be highly focused on either the existence or morality of these practices, with the writings reflecting a lot of cultural defensiveness that adds to the complications of sorting out the facts from fiction.

Regarding the question whether polygyny prevailed in Iran during the ancient period, there is no passage in the texts that provides direct evidence on this subject. Buch (1919, 128–29) points to a stanza in the Vendidad (3.3)—"in the house of the righteous, women and children are present in rich abundance"—as the one that has given rise to speculation that polygyny prevailed in Zoroastrian Iran. Sanjana (1892) and Katrak (1965) concur with Buch on this point and agree with his interpretation that the stanza might not imply the practices of polygyny. All three authors seem to believe that in a joint family situation that prevailed in ancient Iran, the plural "women" may also refer to sons' wives.

However, there is contradictory evidence on this subject, which seems to stress the testimony of Greek writers that "every Persian marries many lawful wives" (Choksy 1989, 89). The disagreement on this subject seems to hinge on the point whether some kings or noblemen flaunted custom and practiced polygyny, or whether the sacred texts endorsed the practice and it was the customary marriage pattern in ancient Iran. Both Sanjana (1892) and Katrak (1965) take great pains to go through the Avesta and point out every passage that refers to the wife in the singular form, which leads them to conclude that monogamy was the preferred system of marital union.

Similarly, there is even more of a debate whether the original meaning of the Avestan word *xvaētvadatha* referred to consanguineous marriage as defined by incestuous relationships or as marriage between first cousins—a practice that is still very prevalent among Zoroastrians in Iran (Fischer 1978) and in India (Karkal 1984; Gould 1985; 1988). Choksy (1989, 153) cites the work of Richard N. Frye on Zoroastrian incest to demonstrate that there is no evidence for the widespread practice of incestuous marriages among Zoroastrians in the ancient period. Boyce (1975, 53–54; 1982, 75–77) is a little more tentative. She does refer to the testimony of Greek writers to raise the possibility that the practice might have prevailed among certain Achamenian kings and their subjects. Again, Sanjana (1932) and Katrak (1965) question the credibility of the evidence presented by Greek writers. They claim that the foreign writers misunderstood the cultural practices; that among many traditional communities, the designation "sister," "daughter," or "mother" is a honorific term that is applied to other close relatives. Therefore, the marriages that were assumed to be incestuous (within the close family circle) were in fact unions between first cousins.

Both Boyce (1975) and Choksy (1989) have analyzed one passage in the ancient texts that refers to consanguineous marriages: "I pledge myself to the Mazdean religion . . . which upholds consanguineous marriage" (Yasna 12.9). Both, however, seem to lean in the direction of believing that the original meaning of the word *xvaētvadatha* is unclear. Moreover, Boyce (1975, 53) also thinks that the passage in question is "oddly placed . . . appearing towards the end in a section otherwise concerned with noble generalities, and so may well be interpolated." Whatever the practices may have been, one thing is perfectly clear: in the debate over the existence of polygyny and consanguineous marriages, women are nonexistent.

Before concluding the section on the ancient period, it is important to note that although Zoroastrian women were far from equal to men in the sphere of religious activities, they did enjoy some independence. Dhalla (1922, 74) provides evidence to demonstrate that Zoroastrian women did not veil themselves, and attended social and religions gatherings in the company of men. They owned and managed property. They could act as the guardian of a son who was disinherited by his father. They could legally conduct a plea on the husband's behalf, and manage his affairs in his name. If they were being mistreated, they could seek redress in a court of law against a cruel husband and secure his punishment. They could give evidence in cases involving litigation and they could serve as judges. Therefore, when it was a question of social, economic, and legal rights, women seemed to enjoy some degree of benefits, even though it might have occurred within the boundaries of a patriarchal society.

MEDIEVAL PERIOD

The previous section has demonstrated that the Zoroastrian religion represented a significant step up in the recognition of the traditional roles of women as compared to the patriarchy in the Indo-Iranian context. At the same time, it is quite evident that the growing elaboration of beliefs and practices that regulated ritual purity and pollution must have affected women more disproportionately than men because of the impurity associated with menstruation, parturition, and abortion. Choksy (1988) believes that this elaboration occurred between the tenth to the third centuries B.C.E. and was codified in the Vendidad ("the law against the demons").

However, it is very clear that it was the medieval period, which encompasses the Sasanian and Islamic centuries (third to sixteenth century C.E.), that witnessed the most dramatic change in the perceptions of women's religious and secular roles. In reaching this conclusion, it has to be acknowledged, as Simmons (1987) has charged, that there is a tendency to place an overreliance on texts, most of which are concerned with matters of ritual purity. Undoubtedly, the scriptures during this period reflect the most conservative view-points since the Sasanians institutionalized the Zoroastrian faith as the official religion of the kingdom. The establishing of temple worship created a powerful elite of chief priests who wielded considerable power—hereditary offices that were an exclusive male domain (Boyce 1982, 229–30). Furthermore, Pangborn (1982) and Dhalla (1938) maintain that under the Sasanians, the priesthood spent an inordinate amount of time dealing with cultic and theological issues, which "descended to rigid formalism, stifled independent inquiry, stigmatized honest doubt as Ahrimanian, and sought to overrule original thinking by dogmatic assertions" (Dhalla 1938, 324).

The post-Sasanian period, with the stress involved in change of status of Zoroastrianism from state to minority religion (under the dominance of Islam) must have played its part in driving the religion to adopt a very patriarchal worldview. The stress of survival has often been correlated with the rise in male patterns of dominance toward women—an easy target since females are the most powerless members of a victimized group. Moreover, Zoroastrian fear of an alien religion and culture, especially when it was tied to their status of being the subjugated sect (Boyce [1977, 12] refers to many "stories" of rape and abduction of Zoroastrian women—a common fate suffered by many conquered populations) must have encouraged the surfacing of extremely punitive attitudes toward women. In addition, Dhalla (1938, 442–43) demonstrates that religious dissensions, especially the growth of sects "had racked the Zoroastrian world" during this period. One of these sects, Zurvanism, is known to have held a very perverse view of women (Zaehner 1955).

Given these circumstances, it might be too simplistic to conclude that the negative images of women in Zoroastrianism are due to the fact that the scriptural views of women during the medieval period have been misunderstood because of a "misrepresentation of certain fragmentary texts" (Simmons 1987, 2). In other words, the misrepresentations, although important to clarify, cannot explain away the fact that the texts are part of a more complex social and historical reality whose patriarchal structure is undeniable. Furthermore, the disputed passages are only a small part of the elaboration on many religious decrees that were designed to affect women's private and public lives.

In examining this period, it is instructive to note some similarities between different world religions in their treatment of women. Swidler (1974, 167–68) hypothesizes that one of the attractive forces of certain world religions (e.g., Christianity, Islam) is the fact that the "initial burst of human liberation extended to women as well as men in a very high degree. . . . To the degree women later do not participate in full measure . . . that religion is unfaithful to its initial insight."

I would tend to modify Swidler's thesis slightly and state that the ambivalence toward women's full religious participation is present in all patriarchal religions, although it is true that the initial vision does provide a sense of possibilities for women. If the societal forces change in the direction of conservation, these forces usually dictate the course of religious response. The ambivalence toward women then gains religious validation, plus endorsement from all the dominant structures in society. Therefore, as stated before, transcending this phase requires ability on the part of women to have enough of a power base to deal with the politics of both the religious and societal institutions. This thesis can be easily supported by Choksy's observation (1988, 81) that the "medieval images and functions of women . . . underwent little change within the Zoroastrian religious tradition until the modern period. The socioeconomic independence of women increased during the nineteenth and twentieth centuries," providing the necessary critical mass to force society and religion to reevaluate their official stance on women's full partnership in these institutions.

Legends

The convergence of patriarchal religious and societal forces with Zoroastrian conceptions of purity and pollution produced some elaborate legends that display strong ambivalence toward women. The association of menstruation with the evil spirit (Pahlavi Ahreman) led to the following legend that is preserved in the Bundahishn (3.7): "the original creation." After the initial attack on Ohrmazd's perfect creation, Ahreman had been in a three-thousand year swoon caused by the wise lord's recital of a sacred prayer and by the vision of righteous man (Gayōmard). Although his demons were powerless to wake him, the task was accomplished by the whore demoness (Jēh). She succeeded by promising to let loose affliction on the righteous man and the primordial bull and all the creations of Ohrmazd. "And she so recounted those evil deeds a second time that the evil spirit was delighted and started up from that confusion; and he kissed Gêh (or Jēh) upon the head, and the pollution which they call menstruation became apparent in Gêh."

Menstruation, then, comes from the kiss of Ahreman, and it was created in order to render human beings unfit to do battle against evil (Choksy 1989, 96). The question arises as to how this original affliction was going to be transmitted to human beings. According to the Zādspram (34.30–31), the evil spirit joined himself to the whore demoness. "For the defilement of females he joined himself to her, that she might defile females, and the females, because they were defiled, might defile the males, and cause [the males] to turn away from their proper function." Here, the female as the *source* of impurity, pollution, and temptation is portrayed vividly. Therefore, I maintain, that despite the misrepresentations that will be described presently, the *structure* of the legend itself conveys a negative image of woman that is very similar to some medieval Christian beliefs (Power 1975). The connection is explicated further in a statement in the Dēnkard that "menstruation, which is from that orifice through the satiety of that demoness, was in the entire body and from its flow her own stench, coporeal and spiritual, also come forth" (Choksy 1989, 96). Moreover, the Zoroastrian doctrine claims that since human beings are in a state of mixture of good and evil in the material world, they are open to pollution created by the evil spirit and his pandemonium. Therefore, menstruation caused in the whore demoness is replicated as a pollutant in all mortal women (Choksy 1988, 78).

The previous passages from the Bundahishn and the Zādspram are the primary sources for the criticisms that Simmons (1987) and Choksy (1988) have leveled at Zaehner for his interpretations of the status of women in Zoroastrianism (1955; 1956; 1961). Zaehner concluded that Jēh is primal woman; that woman was created good by Ohrmazd but fled to Ahreman, rather than being a part of the evil counter creation. She, in fact, then joined with righteous man, and from this union arose the first human couple, Māshyā and Māshyāne. Thus, menstruation is transmitted by this process to all women, who were regarded by the faith as polluted, sinful, and capable of defiling future males (Zaehner 1955, 1956).

Both Simmons (1987) and Choksy (1988) provide evidence to show that the whore demoness is not identical with woman. The passage in the Zādspram (34.30) clearly states that "when the Evil Spirit scuttled into creation, he had as (his) partner the irrelgious brood of the Whore Demoness, just as a man has women of good stature. For indeed, the whore is a demoness." Choksy (1988, 79) also relates another passage in the Bundahishn that refers to the fact that "the Whore came against women."

Furthermore, Simmons (1987) believes that Zaehner is mistaken in his interpretation that the first human couple were born from the union of Gayōmard and Jēh. According to the Bundahishn, Gayōmard died after Ahreman, Jēh and other demons invaded the material world. But in passing, "he let fall his seed . . . and one part was received by Spandārmad (the Earth, his mother). For forty years it remained in the earth. When the forty years had elapsed, Māshyā and Māshyāne grew out of the earth in the form of a rhubarb plant" (Zaehner 1956, 75). Simmons, in fact, goes back to the original coupling; that Spendārmad, the bounteous immortal, is the guardian of both the earth and virtuous woman. Therefore, the virtuous woman is the protégé of Spendārmad, and not Jēh. Jēh can be perceived in the context of dualism as the demonic antithesis of Spendārmad, and thus, the antithesis of good woman. Thus, Jēh and Spendārmad are two opposing points on a continuum, both of which affect women, at least as long as the material world is in a mixture of good and evil. Jēh defiles women and Spendārmad blesses them. Simmons concludes this argument by suggesting that until the final renovation when Ahreman and Jēh will cease to exist, the purity codes are needed to protect women and the rest of the good creation from the evil of Ahreman. In this sense, a woman is not inherently evil; she is always a part of the good creation.

Choksy (1988, 79) is more convinced that the medieval period does represent a real change in the perceptions regarding women; that "women were, in time perceived as easily corrupted and beguiled by the forces of evil . . . women were believed to be inferior to men, who although also susceptible to pollution and deception by the forces of evil, are not afflicted by a pollution which periodically manifests itself." These attitudes pervade the historical and religions texts, and the best that can be said is that at times the attitudes reflect an ambivalence rather than outright negativism toward women. Thus, in the story of creation, the legend of Māshyā and Māshyāne's fall from grace holds both of them culpable for their sins: they blaspheme, they worship the demons, and they devour their own children. At the same time, the ambivalence toward women is reflected in the fact that Māshyāne is portrayed as "ever-ready to worship demons. . . . This haste in worshipping . . . was attributed to Māshyāne's feminine inability to obey the laws and will of Ahura Mazdā" (Choksy 1988, 80).

Other Texts

Other passages in the texts are directly pertinent to the subject of women since they present Ohrmazd himself addressing women:

I created thee, whose adversary is the whore species, and thou
was created with a mouth close to thy buttocks, and coition
seems to thee even as the taste of the sweetest food [is] to the
mouth; for thou art a helper to me, for from thee is man born
but thou dost grieve me who am Ohrmazd. But had I found
another vessel from which to make man, never would I have
created thee, whose adversary is the whore species. (Zaehner
1956, 43)

The ambivalence toward women and sexuality, as well as a
grudging recognition of the necessity of having women around in order to produce children, is quite striking. Obviously, the theological
position had to be reinforced that it is the duty of righteous woman
to produce righteous man. At the same time, as in the ancient period, it is also clear that the religion exhibited some flexibility in
prescribing women's religious roles, albeit at a very peripheral level.
The Sāyest nē Sāyest (10.35), a compilation of "the proper and im-
proper," specifies some limited conditions under which a woman
can perform a few sacerdotal functions. She is "fit for priestly duty
among women," having the right to consecrate the barsom and perform liturgies. Still these functions by no means should leave the
impression as some writers have claimed (Shahzadi 1990, 39) that
"so sacred a work as that of . . . the chief priest . . . at a ritual was
not denied to their sex (women)." Here we are faced with some varying views about the status of women in Zoroastrianism, and the difference in interpretation might well be the influence of a feminist
worldview. It recognizes that a few alternatives, which might have
existed within the religion for women's active participation, did not
mean that women were regarded as the religious equals and partners of men.

In fact, the Pahlavi writers of the period were quite explicit in
delineating the fact that women were expected to be silent partners
in the religious experience. A post-Sasanian work, the Sad Dar
(59.1–2,5), a treatise on "a hundred subjects," expounds:

In the good and pure religion of the Mazda-worshippers, they
have not commanded the women to perform the Nyayises.
And their Nyayises are these, that three times everyday, at
dawn, mid-day prayer, and evening prayer, they stand back in
the presence of their own husbands, and fold their arms and
speak thus: "What are thy thoughts, so that I may think
them; what is necessary for thee, so that I may speak it; and

what is necessary for thee, so that I may do it?" . . . For the satisfaction of the sacred being is in a reverence for the satisfaction of the husband.

Besides the religious texts, it is also instructive to examine the wisdom literature, because the folk wisdom provides a clue to the kind of milieu that spawned the patriarchal religious perceptions of the day. In this context, statements attributed to Adurbād, the son of Māraspand (a high priest who lived during the reign of Shāpur II [307–3790 C.E.]) can serve as excellent examples: "Put not your trust in women lest you have cause to be ashamed and to repent; do not tell your secrets to women lest your toilings be fruitless" (Zaehner 1956, 114).

Dhalla (1922, 309–10) refers to other sources that echo the same sentiments: woman has no wisdom, and therefore a man can thank his creator that he has made him a man and not a woman; a woman's first and last duty is to obey her husband, and she is to be condemned to suffering in hell if she is wanting in obedience to her lord; and Viraj pictures the soul of a woman wending its way toward the infernal regions, reminding the pious soul of her husband that as her lord upon earth, it was his duty to have guided her on the path of righteousness and not allowed her to lapse into wickedness so that now after death she could have accompanied him to heaven instead of going to hell.

Choksy (1989, 97) believes that "perhaps the influence of Nestorian Christianity on Iranian society during the medieval period reinforced Zoroastrian misogyny," since "the view of woman as an instrument of the devil, both inferior and evil, also developed during the earliest period of the Christian Church, originating in the writings of St. Paul."

In describing the societal milieu, the Pahlavi texts mention five different kinds of marriages. The prevailing theme in this categorization seems to be the woman's primary role as the provider of children. A woman who is given in marriage through an arrangement made by the parents (the most common type of marriage) is called "privileged wife." A woman who marries against the wishes of the parents is called "self-disposing wife." A woman who is the only child of her parents, agreeing to give the first child to her parents is called the "one wife." A woman who is chosen to be the "adopted wife" of a youth who has died is then married to another youth with full dowry but is considered to be the wife of the dead man as far as it pertains to the life of her soul after death. In return, half her children belong to the dead man and half belong to the husband. A childless widow who remarries ("serving wife"), for purposes of the afterlife and the respective ceremonies, her name continues to be tied to her first husband. Half her children by the second marriage belong to the first husband in the other world (Dhalla 1922; Katrak 1965). Choksy (1989, 89) also provides references to various Pahlavi texts to show that they contain discussions of the practice of consanguineous marriages, and there are attempts to sanctify this practice by attributing it to Ohrmazd himself.

Both incestuous marriages and polygyny are said to have persisted during the medieval period among all classes of Zoroastrian society in both Iran and India. Again, as in the ancient period, there is no way to assess the effects of these practices on women, since it is impossible to circumvent the problem of women's "silent history."

The texts mention the fact that marriage could be dissolved at the initiation of either the husband or the wife, but the way the laws were formulated and practiced is quite revealing. Usually both parties had to agree to a divorce, but the wife's agreement was not required if she was infertile or guilty of adultery. Once the wife had borne children, she could only be divorced on the grounds of adultery. Generally, there were four reasons for which a man could divorce his wife: adultery, concealment of the fact that she was menstruating, practice of sorcery, and sterility (Choksy 1989, 90). A wife did have the right to seek redress in a court of law if the husband was seeking a divorce under wrongful circumstances. Dhalla (1922, 303) adds an interesting footnote to this topic by pointing out that the Rivāyat states that in order to have a male successor, a husband may take a second wife if the first wife is infertile, provided he is willing to continue to support the previous wife. The wife, however, was not allowed to divorce the husband if he turned out to be impotent.

Moreover, the same double standard is revealed in the texts on the subject of adultery. When a woman married, she literally accepted the husband as her lord and master. She was, in effect, her husband's property. Thus, the Zoroastrian pronouncements in the medieval period on the subject of adultery can be understood only in the context of male property rights. Buch (1919, 125) refers to various texts which can be interpreted in this manner: one should avoid adultery since "everyone who beguiles the wife of another . . . that woman becomes, in a moment, unlawful as regards her husband"; and "one should abstain from rape on another's wife and from causing a woman to occupy a separate bed from her husband." However, the greatest fear with adultery is the disturbance of woman's main function: the production of rightful male heirs. Thus, the texts claim, "and by it all lineage is disturbed, control is put an end to, and without the authority of the husband an intermingling of son with son occurs" (Buch 1919, 124).

It appears that all these negative views of women seemed to ultimately find their justification in the fact that women were the physical source of menstrual pollution—a major source of impurity—that is, evil—in the material world. Women, by extension then, became inferior, sinful, and evil. The medieval period witnessed a significant elaboration of taboos and rituals associated with menstruation and parturition. The texts lay out the exact number of steps that a menstruant must distance herself from the "righteous man" as well as other sacred elements. The period of confinement after miscarriage or childbirth was extended to forty days. During the period of menstruation, even her gaze and voice were believed to be capable of polluting all of Ohrmazd's good creation. The main effect of these misogynist views was that by the medieval period:

> Women came to be regarded, in religious doctrine, as dual faceted: god-created, yet periodically polluted, easily tempted, and untrustworthy. Although essential for the victory of good over evil, and the direct antagonists of the Whore Demoness, women were believed to have been afflicted with this demoness's characteristics: menstrual pollution and carnal temptation. (Choksy 1988, 80)

It is in this sense that I believe that the subject of women in Zoroastrianism has to be approached much more critically than it has been up to now.

Maybe part of the problem in evaluating the role of women in Zoroastrianism has been that the authors have felt the need to present a unidimensional view—positive or negative. The reality seems to point toward ambivalence—a much more understandable stance since the male ecclesiastical authorities must have realized that the initial equality preached by the prophet was at great odds with the male control of religions institutions, congregations, and households in the medieval period. Hence, the dilemma had to be resolved by providing women some opportunities for flexibility in their religious and societal roles. Dhalla (1922, 300) gives examples of these alternatives: women officiated at minor ceremonies; they owned property and acted as a guardian of the family when no male relative was living to guard its interest; women could succeed to the throne if the king had no male issues; and women were not subject to the harsh restrictions in public that the coming of the Arab hegemony imposed on the Zoroastrian minority.

Parsi Settlements in India

Although the early history of the Parsi Zoroastrian refugees' flight to India in about 936 C.E. and the settlement in Sanjan is shrouded in legend, the story itself makes some references to women that are instructive. The *Kissah-i-Sanjan* was written in 1600 C.E. by a learned priest whose sources were old books, plus oral history. It claims that when the refugees came ashore, the local ruler was afraid of the large body of armed strangers, and asked the priest who had come as the group spokesperson to explain their religion and customs. The priest answered in sixteen Sanskrit *shlokas* (stanzas). Interestingly, the references in these stanzas to women stress their traditional roles—"(a community) whose married females are not (looked upon as) pure if devoid of husband"—or the fact that females observed the menstrual taboos: "Pure-hearted men, whose females in menstrual period, become pure on the seventh night; (and when) delivered of child pure in body after a month from the day of delivery; (whose females) are noble on account of their graceful conduct . . . are powerful and strong and have always laughing faces" (Paymaster 1954, 10–13).

The Rivāyats ("traditions"—a compilation of instructions provided by the Zoroastrian priests of Iran to inquiries raised by the Parsi priests in India about ritual practices; Parsi emissaries brought back twenty-six Rivāyats between 1478 and 1773) reveal that the Zoroastrian doctrines regulating women's behavior during menstruation and childbirth were conveyed in elaborate detail to the early settlers in India. In fact, it might be interesting to speculate if the Parsi priests' fear of not remembering the details of ritual practices, and the Iranian priests' stress on describing the most exact routines might not have resulted in even more conservative traditions being preserved during this period. For example, Choksy (1989, 91–93) describes how the Persian Rivāyats and Parsi writings in Gujarati cover such topics as the number of times the married couple were supposed to have intercourse per month if the wife was not pregnant, and the rituals that both parties had to follow after each act to cleanse themselves of ritual impurity.

Scattered references to topics pertaining to Parsi women are also available in other sources such as foreign travelers' accounts of what they observed in India. The Rev. Edward Terry, chaplain in the service of the East India Company, 1616–1619, noted about his visit to Surat that the "Parsis took only one wife who was chosen with priestly guidance" (Hinnells 1978, 24). Thus, the practice of polygyny must have been on the decline, although Zoroastrian men were still permitted to take a second wife if the first was infertile. Another priest, Rev. Henry Lord, who was in Surat between 1615 and 1623, described the five forms of marriage that were prevalent among the Parsis, and the types match the medieval period marriages among the Zoroastrians in Iran (Paymaster 1954, 40–41).

The remaining citation relating to women's activities again falls in the area of traditional lore. The incident is supposed to have happened about the end of the eleventh century. It describes the valor with which Parsi women, dressed as men, defended the settlement of Variav from hostile troops who were there to collect tribute. Apparently, the Parsi men were away partaking in a feast—a fact that reveals that women, indeed, did not participate in all public functions. As victory was at hand for the valiant women, their disguise was discovered at the drop of a helmet. Realizing that they were fighting women and not men, the hostile troops rallied again. The women could not fight off this assault and knowing that they would be defeated, they preferred death to dishonor and drowned themselves (Paymaster 1954, 23–24). The legend does convey the impression that women were capable of taking independent action, albeit under unusual circumstances. However, the reason for the action is protection—not some unfeminine cause like power, and in the end the women are revered for their sacrifice, not triumph through slaughter on a battlefield. In other words, the legend symbolically tries to solve the patriarchal society's ambivalence toward women.

MODERN PERIOD

Choksy (1988, 81) makes a categorical statement about the present-day status of women in Zoroastrianism after discussing their precarious position during the medieval period. He believes that the increase in the socio-economic independence of women and the decrease in the observance of practices relating to purity and pollution led to a point where "women gradually came to be regarded as the religious equals and partners of men." In this section, I will demonstrate that although Choksy is on the right track, the conclusion is by no means as clear-cut as Choksy maintains, in both the religious and societal arenas; that despite the recognition of options for women, the dream of equality is still mired in the context of the male control of the sacraments and ecclesiastical functions, as well as community leadership. This conclusion is based primarily on data relating to the Parsi Zoroastrians of India—the most influential segment of this religious community and the main source of Choksy's statement about the present-day status of Zoroastrian women.

The socio-economic independence of women has often been pointed out as an outstanding characteristic of the Parsi Zoroastrian community (Kulke 1974; Visaria 1972; Karkal 1984). However, the checkered history of this phenomenon has usually been glossed over in an effort to glorify the past. The move to India lead to the adoption of certain Hindu customs like infant marriages that did not show a decline until the last part of the nineteenth century (Sahiar 1955). Polygyny also prevailed during this time period, with the Parsi Panchayat (a quasi-judicial-cum social body) forbidding bigamy, but dispensing permission to remarry if the first wife was unable to bear children. At the same time, however, the patriarchal structure of society was gradually being eroded by the fact that by the middle of the seventeenth century the Parsis had made the transition from villages to towns, and had branched out from agriculture to become artisans, merchants, traders, and bankers. By the end of the eighteenth century, there was an exodus from the hinterlands to the port of Bombay, where the Parsis assumed the mercantile role, which became a source of their wealth and power. They established a mutually beneficial relationship with the British as "mediators and pace-setters of social change" (Kulke, 1974, 9)—a role that would expose them to what must have seemed like a very liberal Western system of sex-role relations. Gradually, the Parsis abandoned the system of purdah (seclusion of women), and the female members of the families of prominent reformers and some *shethias* (business magnates) mixed socially with outsiders at private and public functions. By 1884 this "innovation" had grown into a popular custom among the Parsis (Shahiar 1955, 168).

The changeover though was not as smooth as Kulke (1974, 104) maintains—that Parsi reformers interested in "purifying the religion" were successful in eliminating such customs as infant marriages, polygyny, or the prohibition of widow remarriages, since these practices were only assimilated superficially from the Indian environment. In fact, the tenacity with which these customs hung on for a few generations attests to the fact that the priests, who were the spokespersons of the community during the early years of the Parsi settlement in India, gave it their tacit stamp of approval. However, when Bombay became the new stronghold of Parsi immigrants, it was evident that the strength of the clergy in the new city was weak. The Bombay Panchayat, which sought to carry on the leadership function of the community, became an organ for heriditary membership for leading merchant families.

This change from priest to laity in leadership positions was a mixed blessing for rulings affecting the status of women. For example, the Panchayat passed regulations against bigamy, but tolerated it among its own members. It tried to control the free movement of females by interjecting an interesting religious twist in one of its ordinances. In 1819 the Panchayat ruled that no woman could stir out of the house before sunrise and after sunset, and no woman could visit Hindu temples or Muslim tombs or perform any related ceremonies in their own home.

The accompanying charge that "superstition and pernicious practices had taken root among Parsi women" (Mody 1959) turned out to be a very clever ploy on the part of Panchayat leaders, because it ended up appealing to both the orthodox and reformist wings of the community. The conservatives were looking for an acceptable way to turn the tide of alien influences, which they blamed for ruining the traditional sex-role structure of the community. They were afraid that the newfound freedom of Parsi women would lead to "numerous cases of divorce and domestic trouble reported in England which were attributed to mutual intercourse between the sexes" (Murzban 1917, 322). The reformists worried about how the community would "abjure priestcraft . . . organize a new national church founded on simple tradition of good thought, good word, good deed . . . weed scriptures of its verbiage" (Malabari 1884, 160).

The turmoil over the religious/ethnic community identity was also fanned by the introduction of Christian mission school education that the Parsi middle class recognized as an avenue of upward mobility, but also feared for its ability to convey Christian teachings. The 1839 conversion of two Parsi boys in Rev. John Wilson's school stirred up the community to a state of frenzy, especially since Wilson attacked the validity of Zoroastrian teachings. The community realized that the double-edged effect of education, both in helping the community and undermining the religion, could only be dealt with if the Parsis themselves became knowledgeable about their own religious traditions (Hinnells 1978).

There were, however, other changes that were taking place in the educational arena in the mid-nineteenth century where the outcry was no less bitter. The first schools for female education were being established, originally by missionaries, and later by organizations like the Students' Literary and Scientific Society. At first, the schools provided education in the vernacular language (Gujarati), although education in English was provided by Parsi schools after 1860. Of course, the females could have attended the girls' schools established by missionaries between 1824 and 1830. But the Parsis, like other respectable families, were opposed to breaking purdah and sending girls out of the homes to acquire English schooling that might lead women "to make slaves of their husbands" (Masani 1939, 47).

The first Indian girl who was sent to such a missionary school through the efforts of a very unusual, strong mother happened to be a Parsi Zoroastrian. She has written a feminist document that presents what it was like in 1842 to encounter the ire of the community in acquiring English education. Jessawalla's autobiography (1911) is the only piece of literature that drives home the point that although the male Parsi reformers, who are lauded for their pioneering efforts on behalf of female education deserve all the credit, the girls themselves—the real heroines—are a forgotten page in history.

Ultimately, the *shethias* themselves, and then the government, decided that the idea of female education had gained enough public support to risk their participation in establishing such schools. By 1881 the census recorded that "over fifteen years of age, the smallest proportion of illiterate, either male or female, is found in the Parsi population" (Census of India 1883, 51–52). This fact did not exactly overjoy the majority of the community. Newspaper articles expounded the theory that "education would spoil the health and delicate bodies of the females. They need education in English, but they need sufficient education, nothing beyond that" (Kaiser-E-Hind 1902, 5).

The 1880s saw the beginning of yet another radical trend that was not so obvious in terms of its consequences for the future of the community. Visaria (1972) has demonstrated that as early as 1881 the marital fertility of the Parsis was only 46 percent of the maximum potential. Obviously, this finding indicates that even before the introduction of modern contraception, resort was sought to some form of control of fertility within marriage. The continuing demographic decline of the Parsi community during the twentieth century with its pattern of late marriage, nonmarriage, and low fertility has led to a few studies (some sponsored by the Bombay

Panchayat) to understand and possibly deal with this critical phenomenon. (See, for example, Visaria 1972; 1974; Gould 1972; 1980; 1982; 1987; 1988; Karkal 1984.) The 1981 census reveals that the Parsi population of India was 71,630, with 62,478 or 87.2 percent of them living in greater Bombay (Census of India 1981, 58; Karkal 1984, 17). The 21.5 percent decline in population in the 1971–1981 decade (some of it due to emigration) is disastrous for the survival of an endogamous ethnic minority community that sees itself facing extinction if these trends continue unabated (Gould, in press).

Although an involved discussion of the above subject is beyond the scope of this chapter, the topic itself has great significance for understanding the bitter religious controversy regarding conversion and intermarriage, and the ambivalent attitude toward the status of women in Zoroastrianism. In fact, an understanding of this issue is essential in comprehending one of the reasons why I contend that Choksy's statement that women in Zoroastrianism are regarded as the religious equals and partners of men is misleading. Among the Parsis, a marriage is recognized as a "Parsi marriage" when both parties are Parsi Zoroastrians, and the priest consecrates the marriage by the *ashirvad* (blessings) in the presence of two Parsi witnesses. Despite this regulation, it has been shown that many Parsi men took non-Parsi wives, especially during the early years of their settlement in India (Sahiar 1955). It is also evident that these non-Parsi wives, as well as some other adults like personal servants, were initiated into the Zoroastrian religion (Sahiar 1955). The children of these intermarriages between Parsi men and non-Parsi women, as well as the illegitimate children of Parsi men had also been accepted into the religion by having an initiation ceremony that is reserved for children of both Parsi Zoroastrian parents.

The occurrence of these phenomena are attested to by the fact that from time to time there were public outcries about admitting such persons to the fire-temples, and consigning their bodies to the towers of silence. In fact, in 1770, this matter was referred for clarification to the Zoroastrian authorities in Iran, who saw nothing objectionable in admitting converts. In 1818 the Panchayat decreed that the initiation ceremonies of children of Parsi fathers and "alien" mothers could not be performed without its sanction. Notice that in the patriarchal religion there is no record of Parsi women marrying non-Parsi men, and the consideration that children of such unions can be initited into the religion.

In 1903 a member of a prominent industrialist family in Bombay married a French woman while he was abroad. When he returned to India, he had her converted to Zoroastrianism and married her in a

Zoroastrian ceremony. An *anjuman* (community) meeting passed a resolution that she could not enter a fire-temple, use Parsi trust funds, or have her remains consigned to the towers of silence. The resulting court case, popularly known as "the Parsi Punchayet case of 1908," set the standard on conversion (an undoubtedly important topic for a dwindling community) that has not been challenged to this day. The Bombay high court ruled that even if a non-Parsi is duly admitted into the Zoroastrian religion, such an individual is not entitled to the uses and benefits of the funds and institutions that are under the Panchayet's control, since these privileges are traditionally reserved for only those individuals who are Parsi Zoroastrians (a caste). Thus, the ruling spelled out that a Zoroastrian could not be automatically considered a Parsi. The judgment upheld the customary definition of the Parsi community as follows:

> Parsis who are descended from the original Persian emigrants, and who are born of both Zoroastrian parents, and who profess the Zoroastrian religion, the Iranis from Persia professing the Zoroastrian religion, who come to India, either temporarily or permanently, and the children of Parsi fathers by alien mothers, who have been duly and properly admitted into the religion. (Desai 1977, 25–26)

A related case, Saklat vs. Bella 1925, did involve a child of a Parsi mother and a non-Parsi father. This child (a girl) was the "orphan" daughter of a Goanese Christian father and a Parsi mother who was brought up in a Zoroastrian household of Rangoon from early infancy. After her initiation ceremony was performed, Bella was taken by her adoptive father (a Parsi) to the Rangoon fire-temple on March 21, 1915. Ten days later, three members of the Parsi community of Rangoon filed a suit against Bella and the adoptive father, claiming that they had "not only wounded the religious feelings entertained by religiously inclined Parsis, but also caused the desecration of the said sacred temple" (Privy Council Judgement 1990, 18). The case was thrown out in the preliminary judgment, and the chief court of lower Burma agreed with the initial judgment. But on appeal to the privy council, they ruled that Bella was "not entitled as of right to use the temple, or to attend or to participate in any of the religions ceremonies performed therein" (Privy Council Judgement 1990, 28). But the judges also noted that while the trustees "can treat her as a trespasser . . . it does not follow that they are bound so to treat her" (Privy Council Judgement 1990, 28). Thus, the right of admission to converts could be decided by the trustees of the fire-temple. This particular point in the ruling, however, is only a salve at this point, since nearly all the community trusts governing fire-temples and towers of silence require the beneficiaries to be both Parsis and Zoroastrians (Paymaster and Gorimar 1976, 32).

The succeeding years saw the conflict over these religions/societal issues translate itself into questions regarding the literal meaning of Zoroastrian scriptures, tenents, doctrines, and tradition. The orthodox and reformist camps battled it out at several Zoroastrian conferences, with some elite reformists, trained at Western universities, pushing for a more rational, less ritualistic view of the religious tradition. The early 1940s saw at least two major events that shook the orthodox foundation of the community: the mass initiation ceremonies of children of Parsi men and non-Parsi women in the village of Vansda, and the "wrongful" consecration of the Fasli free temple in Bombay (Doctor 1988). The furor resulted in the reformist group suggesting a round table conference to settle various religious issues, but the orthodox wing refused on the grounds that further discussions would snuff out "whatever faith that Zoroastrians had in their scriptures" (Doctor 1988, 97). The attacks and counterattacks between the two camps were played out in the Parsi newspapers over the next decades, with clear lines being drawn at times between those who supported the reformist and those who supported the orthodox cause, and a turnaround in editorial support at other times that infuriated supporters. Doctor (1988, 98) mourns the effect of all these factors on community identity today, since he views with alarm the fact that "fissiparous tendencies and internecine squabbles and wrangles have done far more damage to the orthodox cause than the attacks of all the heterodox thinkers put together."

The previous discussion should clarify the point that the history of such strong dissensions in the community on religious matters are tied significantly to a patriarchal religious and societal structure. An examination of some other laws might provide further proof of the ambivalent attitudes toward women in Zoroastrianism. In 1868 the Legislative Council, Calcutta, had introduced a bill to legalize marriages between members of communities who were not Christians. The Parsis, afraid of the implications of such a bill for interreligious marriages, prevailed on the government to pass the Special Marriage Act, commonly known as the Civil Marriage Act of 1872, making the contracting parties renounce their Zoroastrian religion. However, in 1918 a Parsi woman married a Christian not under this act, but under the Indian Christian Marriage Act of 1872. She continued to practice her religion, and on her death, her relatives wanted her body consigned to the towers of silence. After consultation, her body was consigned to the *chotra* where "doubtful" bodies are assigned. The decision was still based on the belief (supported by the advocate general) that even if she remained a Zoroastrian, she went out of the community by having married a non-Parsi.

During the intervening years, the question again surfaced in 1948 when the trustees of the Panchayat were concerned about the "large number" of Parsis marrying outside the community (Desai 1977, 97). The trustees drew up a case for opinion, and they were advised that if the woman continued to be a Zoroastrian, the only way they could deprive a Parsi woman marrying a non-Parsi from enjoying the benefits of Parsi institutions was to prove one thing: that there was a prevalent custom that such a marriage meant that she left the community automatically. However, the opinion stated that legally, it was not possible to prove such a custom. As a result of this opinion, the Bombay Prevention of Excommunication Act, 1949, was passed.

The issue of how the Parsi community should respond to intermarriages of Parsi females was complicated further by the passage of the Special Marriage Act of 1954, which nullified the necessity of renouncing one's faith in the case of a civil marriage (required by the Civil Marriage Act of 1872). The 1954 law strengthened the argument that a Parsi woman does not leave the community automatically when she marries a non-Parsi, as long as she continues to profess the Zoroastrian religion. Again, the trustees asked for legal advice, and were told that the Bombay Prevention of Excommunication Act, 1949, had already established the rights of Parsi women who married non-Parsis but continued to practice the Zoroastrian faith.

The roadblocks, however, to establishing and maintaining the religious rights of these Parsi women are numerous. The main problem are some orthodox high priests who exert their authority in their own "territories" (Toddywalla 1987a), and influence their *anjumans* to support their decisions to prevent such women from entering fire-temples, attending religious ceremonies, and having their remains disposed of in the customary Zoroastrian traditions of the community. In fact, they also refuse to accept the 1908 Parsi Panchayat case decision by not performing the initiation ceremonies of children of *any* mixed marriages, or offering the sacred elements that are required at such ceremonies so that other nonlocal priests could perform the *navjote* (initiation) (Toddywalla 1987a). Thus, there is a checkered pattern of compliance with the special marriage act of 1954, with different *anjumans*/Panchayats following their own individually defined rules or practices.

Recently, the question of conversion has assumed a new urgency (see, for example, *Readers' Forum* 1990, 3–6) because there is sentiment in some liberal quarters that part of the solution of the demographic decline might be to accept the children of Parsi women married to non-Parsis as Parsi Zoroastrians—an issue that has not been dealt with at all since the prior question of the Parsi woman remaining a Parsi Zoroastrian has not been established in practice. The supporters of the idea of initiating the children of Parsi women married to non-Parsis men into the Zoroastrian faith point out the fact that the 1908 judgment in the Parsi Panchayat case was clearly discriminatory against females; that Parsi males married to non-Parsi women were provided an option that was never even considered for females—the right to decide whether they wanted their children to be initiated into their religion. They argue that a new legal precedent needs to be established, which gives equal religious standing to both females and males (Gae 1977).

These divisive issues have been exacerbated by the disputes over the locus of authority in terms of making final decisions regarding community matters. As mentioned previously, the Zoroastrians (both Parsis and Iranians) have emigrated to various parts of the world. Hinnells (1985), in his study of what he calls the "diaspora communities," has found that for the older Parsi diaspora, particularly in Hong Kong and until recently London, the "center" is still Bombay. In this context, it is very important to point out that the rules of the Bombay Parsi Panchayat go so far as to decree that only three of the seven trustees at any given time can be women—not a very positive venue to decide issues of concern to Parsi women. No wonder the Zoroastrian communities in the United States and Canada, and now London, seem to harbor the thinking that the Bombay branch is out of touch with current community concerns (Hinnells 1985).

Hinnells also reports that the belief that overseas communities have to determine their own fate has led to the decision to "quietly" initiate the non-Zoroastrian spouses and children of Zoroastrians married to "outsiders" into the faith—a practice that the communities do not view as wholesale conversion. In Iran itself, the Tehran Zoroastrian *anjunan*, after "stormy sessions," has decided that spouses and children of interfaith marriages should be accepted into the religion if both partners agree (Shahzadi 1990). In fact, the Iranians are increasing their numbers by accepting back into the religion those Zoroastrians who had converted to Islam, but have maintained their religious fervor and now wish to rejoin the community. Their initiation ceremonies are carried out publicly, and have also been sanctioned by the Zoroastrian *anjuman* of Tehran. Thus, the 1986 Iran census lists the Zoroastrian population of Iran as 90,891—a figure that is considered to be inflated in view of past reports on community numbers (Khullar 1990). However, the Iranian Zoroastrians resent unfounded speculation on the census figures, and the fifth world Zoroastrian congress held in Bombay in January 1990 witnessed an open confrontation between the Parsis and the Iranian Zoroastrians on this and other issues—disputes that have also erupted in some cities on the American continent (Irani 1990).

Despite the heat that the subject of intermarriage and conversion has generated, there are no reliable data to judge whether statistically this is a significant problem (Gould 1985). Hinnells (1985) found that 15 percent of his population of "overseas" Zoroastrians had married non-Zoroastrians. Khullar (1990) reports that out of a small Parsi population of 219 families in Delhi in 1978, sixty-nine families (approximately one-third) were "mixed." Moreover, the number of Parsi females marrying out of the community was more than double the number of males (49 versus 20). However, a 1980 update of the survey found that the ratio of males marrying outside had increased considerably: out of forty-nine "mixed" marriages, twenty were males.

These scattered statistics in these two studies are only representative of a very specialized universe—hardly the basis for deciding the extent of the "problem." Unfortunately, the orthodox sentiments of the community prevent it from recognizing the benefits of keeping or collecting reliable data on intermarriages that would help in making rational decisions regarding this sensitive issue.

The ambivalent attitude toward women is also evident in the fact that although the recent Hindu code puts the daughter on the same footing as the widow and the son in the matter of inheritance, the latest Parsi code (Indian Succession [Amendment] Act, 1962) decrees that a daughter gets half the share of the son and widow. This is an improvement over the Parsi succession act of 1865 where the son got double the share of the widow, and the daughter received half the share of the widow. In the interim years, organizations like the Women's Association were very active about changing the law and giving an equal share to the daughter when the father died intestate. The effort was particularly strong during the 1930s when a new law—act no. 17 of 1939—was about to be passed to update the 1865 law. It is safe to say that the discriminatory attitudes toward women in matters of inheritance have also had a long, checkered history like the issue of intermarriage and conversion.

Up to the early part of the nineteenth century, the Parsis had no special law that applied to them, as was true of some other communities. In 1835 when a Parsi male, who was the eldest son of an intestate Parsi, instituted a suit to be declared the sole heir on the basis of English common law, the community petitioned the legislative council for relief. The resulting Chattles Real Act (act 9) of 1837 declared that the property was to be divided according to the English statute of distribution: a third would go to the widow and the residue was to be divided equally among the children. The *moffusil* Parsis were exempted from this law. They continued to be governed by the regulation of 1827 by which the usage of the place or the law of the defendant would govern the decision.

At this point, it is interesting that it was the Parsis of Bombay—the urbane community—who showed their displeasure with the law, especially the fact that the wife was allowed to exercise independent control to dispose of any property she wished. They wanted to control this right on the wife's part during the lifetime of the husband, including the right to dispose of any property she might have inherited from her own family. They appealed these regulations, pointing out that "if a son and a daughter got equal shares, it was invidious as the son had to carry on the name of the father" (Desai 1963, 3).

In 1855 the Parsi Law Association was formed to draft a uniform code that would apply in all communities. The *moffusil* Parsis were unhappy at this venture, since they objected to women inheriting property, and the recommendation that the widow get half the share of the son and the daughter get half the share of the widow. They also wanted to eliminate the recommendation that married women could hold and dispose of property. However, the Parsi succession act, 1865, incorporated these points, and established a uniform law for the community.

Although the present law has tried to minimize the distinction along sex lines, the Parsi association has not eliminated the problem. The share of widow and son is still double of each daughter. If there is no widow, the son gets double the share of the daughter. If a females dies, the widower and each child get equal shares. It used to be that the widower got double the share of a child. If a widow re-marries, she loses her share. Some reformers have also pointed out that the latter clause is not supportive of the claim that the Parsis do not put any roadblocks to widow remarriages. Recently, there has been some sentiment to "gauge whether the community today favors granting equal rights to women" (Toddywalla 1987b, 24). The Federation of Parsi Zoroastrian Anjumans was asked to make recommendations on this issue—a long way from changing the law itself.

Aside from examining these various laws and regulations affecting women in Zoroastrianism and the Zoroastrian communities, it is also instructive to examine some demographic data to see if the stereotypes regarding the socio-economic independence of Parsi women are correct. For example, the high proportion of never-married Parsi females has been blamed on the fact that these women do not think that Parsi males measure up to their standards, because of their own achievements—high education, employment, and personal income. My demographic studies of 551 households in the rural and urban areas of Gujarat, India, revealed that these fac-tors were not significant in differentiating between never-married women who rated themselves "likely" and "unlikely" to get mar-ried. Moreover, in complete contrast to the theory that education is a "sterilizing factor" for women (Desai 1948, 65), it was the females who considered themselves "likely" to get married who happened to be the most educated group rather than those who rated them-selves unlikely to get married. Furthermore, contrary even to my expectations, an utterly traditional resource, household income, turned out to be the most significant factor in differentiating "likely" from "unlikely" females in terms of their prospects for marriage—which indicates how slowly old customs die (Gould 1980; 1982).

A small footnote on this finding might help stress the point even further that the position of women in the Zoroastrian community is still shaky. When the results of this study (that it was not the edu-cated women who were the "cause" of the community's demo-graphic downfall [nonmarriage] was presented to the secretary of the Bombay Parsi *panchayat*), his only comment was that he did not be-lieve the findings. The so-called tiger women's reputation was in-tact, at least in the mind of the community's leading proponent of demographic studies.

Since the educational achievement of Parsi women has generated so much discussion (especially in comparison to Parsi males), it is worthwhile to examine data from the previous demographic study to check the following: (1) if there were sex differences among school-age persons in enrollments at different levels of age and education; and (2) if families of current students provided equal educational opportunities to their daughters and sons.

The respondents' definition of "educational opportunity" was based on two factors: receiving education in schools that had the English medium of instruction, and for best results, being sent to elite English medium boarding schools, since these tracks were the accepted avenues for upward mobility. The results of this study indicated that in the rural areas, 26.9 percent of the women who studied in the Gujarati medium (the vernacular language) dropped out of school after four to seven years, compared with 8 percent of the males—a sex differential that did not show up statistically for any other group. When parental characteristics were considered, it was revealed that even in a patriarchal framework, the mothers' medium of instruction was the *strongest* variable in the rural areas in predicting whether the daughter went to English medium schools: 60 percent of the female children in families where the mother was educated in the English language received that extra boost to be sent to English medium schools. Moreover, when these female children received the opportunity of studying in the English medium, they also got the added advantage (even more than the boys) to attend the elite boarding schools—63.6 percent of them were sent outside the rural areas, versus 46.2 percent of the boys to attend these prestigious schools.

The urban picture was more encouraging in closing disparities between the education of girls and boys. Yet it is worth noting, that only 10 percent of the urban females who had completed their education in the Gujarati medium had some college compared to 30.2 percent of the males (Gould 1983). In general, the comparison of all of the subgroups revealed that conditions had to be perfect before females received equal educational opportunities as males, while men received these opportunities regardless of external factors.

Finally, the discussion about the status of women in Zoroastrianism during the modern period has to consider Choksy's last point for claiming religious equality between women and men: the decline in observance of beliefs and practices relating to purity and pollution. Undoubtedly, the elaborate, scripturally prescribed *ritu-*

als connected with women's status—menstruation and parturition—are not adhered to as strictly today, and the practice of
complete seclusion of women during these periods is definitely on
the decline. But Choksy is mistaken when he asserts that "only a
few orthodox *elderly* women still maintain the practice of staying at
home" (1989, 99; italics added). Here he is underestimating the
strength and numbers of orthodox Parsis—both among priests and
laity—who believe in the power of menstrucation in endangering
the purity of all beings. Thus, sitting separately during menstruation, albeit not in a dark secluded corner, is a phenomenon that involves more than *elderly* women in orthodox households, as I found
in my demographic studies (Gould 1988). Moreover, even the educated, urban working women from orthodox families might leave
the house during menstrual periods to conduct their "public" working lives, but will come home and observe the practice in "private"
of sitting separately from other family members.

Rudolph and Rudolph (1967) and others have commented on
many of these traditional practices in the Indian setting that are
adapted to modern circumstances, which they have labeled the
"modernity of tradition." In addition, Choksy is wrong in claiming
that "strict abstinence from sexual intercourse during menses was
practiced by the Parsis up to the 1930s" (1989, 92). I have statistical
data from my demographic studies of urban and rural Parsis that
demonstrate that the beliefs about menstruation are so deeply and
so unconsciously ingrained that even today, none of my respondents
had sexual intercourse during menstruation (Gould 1988). Here I
might suggest that Choksy's idea that only "a few devotees abstain
from intercourse during menses" (1989, 92) might be based on a
nonprobability sample study that dealt with qualitative, rather than
quantitative, data. In Iran, Boyce (1977) and Simmons (personal
communication) found the same pattern that I observed in India—
that segregation of women during menstruation is still practiced,
and abstinence during menstruation is a common pattern (Simmons, personal communication).

The question then arises whether any of these beliefs and practices regarding purity and pollution have consequences for the status of women in Zoroastrianism. Unfortunately, it prevents the
consideration of women to be ordained as priests since they are afflicted by the "pollution" of menstruation, which manifests itself
regularly. Thus, even if there is an effort to remove the restriction
that priests have to belong to the hereditary, priestly caste (in Iran
they accept the young *laymen* as assistant priests [Shahzadi 1990]),

women would not qualify, because of the misogynystic beliefs about menstruation. Boyce (1977, 106) does report that in Iran women who had passed menopause and had undergone the proper ritual ceremonies to purify themselves could be "appointed the guardians of lesser shrines" and play an active part in the religious life of the community.

The remaining question has to deal with the effects of such patriarchal religious attitudes on the personal and spiritual identity of women in Zoroastrianism. Boyce (1971; 1975; 1977; 1979; 1982) has maintained all along that although Zoroastrian women have suffered under these menstruation taboos (more so in past generations), the orthodox observe them voluntarily. "The rules are stern, to observe them is often a struggle, but they are part of the fight against evil, and so to be strictly kept" (Boyce 1975, 308). Boyce (1977, 106–7) believes that Zoroastrian women are not "warped by a sense of physical degradation" because of these scriptural definitions of women's being, and are "stoic" about the rigors involved in following the rituals. Culpepper (1974, 207), on the other hand, asserts that "to feel one's self so primordially unclean . . . is severely damaging to one's self concept." It must have left Zoroastrian women feeling "vaguely in league with evil."

In fact, Boyce (1977, 107) goes a step further and puts forth the arguments used by many priests and orthodox laity—that the enforced rest involved in seclusion during menstruation is beneficial to health. Moreover, she argues, if women suffer a "monthly eclipse," they also reemerge every month to enjoy the freedom that was taken away from them for a few days. As a Parsi Zoroastrian, who has an experiential understanding of the problem, I can only reiterate that both Boyce and Culpepper present an undimensional view. On the one hand, the notion that the women *actively feel* that by suffering passively they are helping positively to restrict the infection of evil (Boyce 1977, 107) is a projection on the part of a scholar who is very strongly identified with the religious tradition and the living faith.

On the other hand, Culpepper's (1974) *theoretical* interpretation of the dire effects of menstruation taboos on women's self-concept comes from a complete unfamiliarity with the experiential base of the living faith. This is an equal and opposite problem from Boyce, since Zoroastrian women are not so naive that they would suffer severe damage to their self-concept by buying some priestly assertions that women are carriers of the "sin" of menstruation. Ultimately, however, important as it is to consider the *personal* beliefs or practices of Zoroastrian women, the religious quest for true sexual equality and partnership cannot be based on individual opinions. The focus in Zoroastrianism has to be the same as in all patriarchal religions: to examine and analyze the *systemic* problems in religious thinking and practice, and deal with the *structural* problems and politics that have allowed generations to victimize women. Zoroastrianism, like all religions, needs to write a new script whereby the religious and societal lives of *all* individuals can take on meaning.

Rajkumari Shanker

WOMEN IN SIKHISM

This investigation of women in Sikhism begins by indicating some of the limitations that fetter the scope of the present research, mainly due to lack of available literature on the subject; overlapping of religious categories; and the various competing subcodes within Sikhism. It then provides a brief overview of women in Hinduism, based on the article by Katherine Young, and also discusses how the bhakti (devotional) movement emerged to give hope to women's religiosity. A short presentation of the life of Guru Nānak, the founder of Sikhism in the fifteenth century follows, and prepares the ground for a discussion of Sikh beliefs.

The second section analyzes the attitudes toward women and ideals of femininity in the primary and secondary Sikh scriptures. Beginning with the portrayal of women in the Ādi Granth (c. 1600–1700), the primary Sikh scripture, the discussion moves on to shed light on women from the perspective of the Sikh gurus and models of femininity in the secondary sources of Sikh religion—that is, the Janam-Sākhīs (1580), the traditional narratives of the life of Guru Nānak and the Rāhat Maryādā (finalized in 1945), the Khalsa code of discipline.

After the textual passages of the Sikh scriptures have been examined, the third section surveys some the chronicles of the Sikhs in the eighteenth and nineteenth centuries, and endeavors to assess the actual fortunes of women in this historical period, with special reference to prevalence of sati and polygamy among the Sikh elites. The fourth section examines the aftermath of Operation Blue Star in 1984 and the involvement, extent, quality, and limits of the Akali-led women's movement in the Punjab.

LIMITATIONS OF THE ANALYSIS

Paucity of Research

Although the contemporary period has witnessed a surge of publications on Sikhism, to date there is little scholarly research available on the subject of women in Sikhism. Apart from references that are few and far apart, no significant or systematic work has been undertaken on the position of women in the Sikh religion. The ensuing analysis is perforce primarily based on the Ādi Granth and the secondary Sikh scriptures. The various sources of Sikh history, religion, culture, and literature reflect androcentric biases, making it difficult to retrieve images of the feminine. This is compounded by the fact that little is known of the ordinary Sikh women, and the limited material that we do possess reflects an androcentric perspective.

Fusion of Traditions

This analysis becomes even more complex, for until recently Sikhs had displayed little collective concern in distinguishing themselves from the predominant Hindu culture and religion. Consequently, the fortunes of Sikh women have been inextricably associated with that of Hindu women:

> Sikh notions of time, space, corporeality, holiness, kinship, societal distinctions, purity and pollution, and commensality were hardly different from those of the Hindus. Also the two shared the same territory, language, rites of passage, dietary taboos, festivals, ritual and key theological concepts. The construction of personhood within the two traditions and their solutions for existential problems were quite alike. Despite having specified their religious orientation, the semeiotic, cultural, affective and territorial universe of the Sikhs and the Hindus virtually remained the same. (Oberoi 1987, 136–37)

These subjective and objective affinities were so striking that the colonial authorities until the end of the nineteenth century found it very hard to differentiate between their Hindu and Sikh subjects. In the 1855 census in the Punjab, the Sikhs and Hindus were often confused in many districts of the province. Denzil Ibbetson, a census commissioner for the Punjab, registered in his report:

But on the border land where these great faiths meet, and especially among the peasantry whose creed, by whatever name it may be known, is seldom more than a superstition and a ritual, the various observances and beliefs which distinguish the followers of the several faiths in their purity are so strangely blended and intermingled, that it is often impossible to say that one prevails rather than the other, or to decide in what category the people shall be classed. (Ibbetson 1883, 101)

This excerpt sums up the colonial understanding of the subcontinent's religious realities. As the religions of India grew and evolved from a variety of cults and beliefs, the citizenry did not perceive of themselves as belonging to any "one" religion; the categories of religions extended, intermingled, and coexisted in the region, and most people continued their daily lives without bothering to label their religious beliefs. The following extracts, drawn from diverse sources, illustrate this point:

In the Indian religious Tradition, unlike the Judeo-Christian, there was no notion of a well demarcated religious community possessing a centralized ecclesiastical hierarchy. People did not conceive of themselves as "Hindus" or "Sikhs." These categories overlapped and it is historically more precise to speak in terms of a continuum or simultaneity of religious identities rather than of distinct religious collectivities. An "either-or" dichotomy is often of very little value in conceptualizing Indian religious traditions. (Oberoi 1988, 140)

Religion was primarily a localized affair, often even a matter of individual conduct and individual salvation. For much of their history the people of the subcontinent went on with their rituals, pilgrimages and acts of religious piety without objectifying religion into an exclusive entity. Religious traditions were based on local traditions and not on a pan-regional organization of communities. Islam may have been the only exception to this, but then, Indian Islam, heavily coloured by Sufism, is of a radically different genre from its counter part elsewhere. (Kinsley 1986, 197–211)

Pluralistic Framework

Another component that complicates this study considerably is the pluralistic framework within which Sikhism has operated. Initially, there were at least eleven known traditions,[1] of which very little historical literature is available, except for the Khalsa, Udasis, and Kukas. Much of Sikh history is chronicled and comprehended exclusively as the history of the Khalsa, which was only one of several competing cultural codes within the polyphonic complex of Sikhism. The question as to how the Khalsa came to establish its predominance over other traditions, remains unresolved to date:

> In absence of a centralized church and an attendant religious hierarchy, heterogeneity in religious beliefs, plurality of rituals, and diversity of life styles were freely acknowledged. Far from being a single "Sikh" identity, most Sikhs moved in and out of multiple identities. . . . The boundaries between what could be seen as the centre of the Sikh tradition and its periphery were highly blurred. There simply was no single source of authority within the Sikh tradition and thus several competing definitions of what constituted a "Sikh" were possible. (Oberoi 1988, 137)

It is important to recognize these limitations at the very outset of the analysis, for collectively, they make it difficult to understand sex roles and project a pattern on the lives of women in the Sikh tradition. However, before we go on to examine the textual materials at hand, it is important to examine the images of Hindu women, which remains the basis for understanding women in Sikhism.

Women in the Hindu Religious Tradition

The early Hindu tradition was patriarchal, life-affirming, and demonstrated, to a certain degree, respect and appreciation of women. The complementary of male and female roles for the well-being of the family, society, and cosmos was perceived and reflected in the religious symbols such as the concept of a divine couple. However, by the classical time (c. 500–1500 A.D.), disparity between men and women intensified. Women were prohibited to move about in public alone, were considered ignorant, and were denied inheritance. Chastity and purity became a substitute for knowledge. Since scriptural knowledge was deemed essential for enlightenment, most women were excluded from the possibility of attaining salvation, and as a result they were oriented toward rebirth (Young 1987, 75). The following extracts from Katherine Young's account of Hindu women are relevant in the present context:

> For the ascetic, the Hindu woman represented sexuality, reproduction and the family, the very obstacles to liberation. (1987, 70)

> If a woman became a widow, theoretically she had the extreme option either to perform satī, self immolation, on the funeral pyre of her husband, or more commonly to undergo the rites of passage to widowhood. (1987, 83)

> The segregation of sexes became more severe after the twelfth century C.E. in those areas of the subcontinent that were under the Muslim rule. . . . Hindu women, already carefully controlled by or segregated from men, imitated the *purdah* of the Muslim women. The consequence was that many upper caste Hindu women, already bound to the home, were further restricted that they rarely left their residence. (1987, 87)

> The Hindu woman was to focus on her husband, he was to be her "god". . . . The apotheosis of the husband . . . was not a simple exaggeration of androcentrism, but part of Hinduism. The Brahmins considered themselves as gods and so did the gurus and kings upon occasion. . . . Hindu theism became increasingly monotheistic in the sense of involving a primary if not exclusive devotion to either Viṣṇu or Śiva as supreme deities, a similar tendency may have developed in the domestic sphere so that the husband too became the "supreme and only" one. This tendency helps us account for the ideal woman's "exclusive" devotion to her husband. (1987, 73–74)

> The patriarchal organization of the family and a woman's rebirth orientation led her to desire to be with her husband for

lives to come. . . . A woman's appreciation of her husband as pati or god was central to her daily life. (1987, 75)

The most explicit form of feminine self-sacrifice was in the form of a *vrata* (vow) . . . in which a woman voluntarily denied something to herself; for example, she fasted (*upavāsa*) in exchange for a favour for her husband (such as good health or a son). Despite the focus on her husband and limitation to the domestic sphere, the Hindu woman took pride in her powerful religious role. (1987, 75)

In the late fifteenth century, when Guru Nānak started preaching his message, both Hindus and Muslims considered women to be inferior to men, an impediment in the way of spiritual progress, and the cause of man's moral degradation. Polygamy was rampant, and widows were denied remarriage and social recognition. *Satī*, child marriage, and female infanticide were widespread. Women were economically, socially, and psychologically dependent on men. Redemption surfaced in the form of the bhakti (devotional) movement:

It is in the context of bhakti that the woman's private and public religion intersected . . . and gave a universal soteriology to Hinduism just at the moment when Brahmanical sacerdotalism and asceticism encouraged extreme androcentrism. . . . Popularity of Bhakti resulted in no small measure from its inclusion of such marginal groups as women and Śūdras. . . . Being female was generally no bar to Bhakti. Marriage mysticism was common in Bhakti literature. The lady devotee (*bhakta*) was none other than the woman in love who lamented any separation from her beloved and ecstatically rejoiced in union with him. . . . Concentration on the pati for a female saint meant exclusive devotion to the deity understood as supreme husband, whereas for an ordinary woman devotion was expressed both to her human husband as pati and deity as pati (assuming the chosen deity was a male). (Young, 1987, 76–77)

Bhakti

The bhaktas (devotees) believed that God, though known by many names and beyond human comprehension, is the one and only reality; all else is illusion (*māyā*). Singing hymns of praise, meditation under the guidance of a guru, and repetition of the name of God was deemed by the bhaktas the means par excellence to achieve salvation. The bhakti movement opposed the monopoly of Hindu priests and the caste system. It succeeded in inspiring a group of men and women who have left a profound influence on the religious traditions of the subcontinent. Foremost of these were two near contemporaries: Kabīr (1440–1518), and Nānak (1469–1539), the founder of Sikhism. Kabīr was the link between Hindu bhakti and Muslim Sufism, which had gained considerable following among Indian Muslims. Kabīr and Nānak preached that the conflict between Hindus and Muslims was mistaken, because God was one.

By the time Sikhism arrived on the Indian scene, the Hindu tradition had seen at least twenty-five centuries of religious, philosophical, and social beliefs and practices, along with a substantial corpus of literature, various modes of attaining salvation, and all conceivable concepts of God. The Sikhs inherited not only some of the theological concepts of the Hindus, but also the established social and cultural norms of the society within which it took birth.

Since the fundamental religious concepts of Sikhism may not be familiar to many and, since a cursory knowledge at the very least is essential to the understanding of the role of women in the religious tradition of the Sikhs, we begin our study with a brief overview of Sikhism.

Sikhism, an Overview

The Sikhs are disciples of their ten gurus or teachers beginning with Guru Nānak and ending with Gobind Singh (1666–1708). Nānak may have founded a new religious community or path within the larger Hindu fold, but he neither violated nor abandoned the Hindu tradition. Born a Hindu, he remained one until the day he died, and so too did his successors. The doctrines that he preached were already popular in north India, and accepted by many of his Hindu audience (McLeod 1989, 16).

Sikhism is the evolved product of subsequent centuries, a complex system of beliefs and practices. Nānak had preached a vision, the organizations and institutions came later (Smith 1962, 67). A monotheistic tradition, Sikhism believes that God can be known only through personal experience of mystical union. Repudiating ritualism, Sikhs aspire to realize the experience of God through devotion (bhakti) under the guidance of a guru. They reject the Hindu caste system and the religious authority of the Brahmins.

The religious beliefs of the Sikhs, greatly influenced by the contemporary devotional (bhakti) movement, are contained in the Ādi Granth.[2] Emphasis is given to the unity of God, complete devotion of the worshiper, and the paramount role of the guru (teacher). Sikhism believes that liberation can be achieved by devotion directed to Akāl Purukh, the "timeless being," or Sat-Kartār, the "true creator." In addition, and of vital importance, is the fact that followers are given specific tenets that could be converted into daily practice: *nām* (the word), *dān* (charity), *ishnān* (cleanliness), *sevā* (service), and *simran* (worship).

The nine successors of Nānak[3] continued to preach the message of the founder. They molded the followers of the emerging group into a significant religious and political community. The last guru, Gobind Singh, externalized the religion by providing it with a definite form and creating the khālsā (the pure) community. The khālsās, both men and women, were henceforth identified by five marks: *kes* (uncut hair), *kanghā* (comb), *kach* (shorts), *karā* (steel bracelet), and *kirpān* (a saber). In addition, they were to follow the Khālsā code of conduct (Rāhat Maryādā), abstain from intoxicants and narcotics, respect women, follow the teaching of the guru, reject caste differences, and take up arms, if necessary, for a just cause.

The Sikh religion, like many religions of the world, constructed its identity around a male mentor and his teachings. Both men and women were among the earliest followers of the emerging religion. Initially, identification with the new religion was based on choice rather than birth; access to soteriology was individual. Women could belong to the new organization and were granted the possibility of attaining salvation. Despite this universalism, in subsequent Sikh history there was not a single woman guru, and no woman held a significant position in the religious community. Moreover, very few are mentioned in the chronicles of the Sikhs.

WOMEN IN THE SIKH SACRED LITERATURE

The Ādi Granth: Composition and Beliefs

The Ādi Granth (or the Guru Granth), the sacred scripture of the Sikhs, is a collection of nearly six thousand hymns of the Sikh gurus and various medieval saints of different religious denominations. The book was first compiled in 1604 by the fifth guru (Arjan Singh). In 1704, the tenth and the last guru, Gobind Singh, added the hymns of his predecessors, and enjoined that after his own death the Granth would take the place of the guru. The Ādi Granth is the basis and not the object of worship in the *gurudwārās* (Sikh temples), and looked upon as the inspired word of God, which none may question. It contains neither history nor mythology nor incantations. The hymns are exhortations to spiritual life, arranged according to the musical modes (*rāgas*) in which they are meant to be sung, and not in any logical sequence. The Ādi Granth, in its original form, is written without separating words; as a result, words may often become incomprehensible upon erroneous reading.

The Sikh doctrines, as laid down in the Ādi Granth, combine elements from Muslim, Hindu, and the bhakti traditions. Importance is given to personal awareness of God. The divine-human relationship is that of the lover and the beloved, the anguish and ecstasy that ensues with separation and union of the two. Though the imagery and symbols are not to be taken literally, language of a tradition is symptomatic of the psyche of that culture. In light of this statement, we can anticipate stereotypical portraits emerging from the Ādi Granth that could prove to be important to our study. Cultural stereotypes about women often confirm what may be primarily part of the men's religion, and sometimes they may be part of a general religious outlook (Gross 1987, 40).

Women in the Ādi Granth

Most Sikhs[4] believe Sikhism is an egalitarian religion, more supportive of women than Hinduism, Islam, or other religions. However, contrary to the opinion of the majority, the Sikh canonical text does not always endorse this idea. The Ādi Granth reveals a wide spectrum of views on women, most of which reflect male attitudes of the enlightened religious gentry, whose attitudes seldom, if ever, reflect sexual equality.

Analogous to other religions, the Sikh religious tradition has been dominated by a patriarchal power structure. The Sikh gurus authenticated a normative modus vivendi for women by formulating ideals of femininity and by including them in the Ādi Granth. There is a range of views—positive, negative, and ambivalent—suggesting a tension between an inward psychological struggle and an outward social decorum.

Consistent with the bhakti tradition, the Ādi Granth is replete with mystical imagery in which the devotee assumes the role of the female lover, whereas God is the male beloved. The following texts, a small sampling of hymns from the Ādi Granth, offer a survey of sexual role patterns in Sikhism and reveal men's perception of, and stereotypes about, women's ideal behavior. Effort has been made to compile first the positive representation of the feminine; this is followed by more negative images in the Ādi Granth. However, before we proceed with the analysis of women in the Ādi Granth, certain methodological assumptions must be noted. The fundamental assumption is that a religious phenomenon is best comprehended on its own measure of reference. This is necessary, for every religious phenomenon is irrevocably social, historical, psychological, and existential. Consequently, for a better appreciation of a religious tradition, understanding of the milieu and cultural perspicacity is crucial. This often means going beyond and behind the manifest phenomenon to grasp the sacred; the sacred thus perceived, epitomizes fundamental religious and philosophical truths. The excerpts from the Ādi Granth are quoted extensively[5] to substantiate and refute prevalent arguments and conclusions.

The Sikh claim of the equal worth of the two sexes and their share in human dignity, surfaces in the frequently quoted verse:

Women and men, all by God Himself are created
All this is His own play
Saith Nānak: All thy creation is good, holy. (AG: 304)

The importance of women as procreators of new generations and those responsible for the preservation of norms is expressed in the following verse by Nānak:

From woman is man born, inside her is he conceived;
To woman is man engaged, and woman he marries,
With woman is man's companionship,
From woman originate new generations.
Should woman die, is another sought;
By woman's help is man kept in restraint,
Why revile her of whom are born great ones of the earth?
From woman is born man, no human being without woman
   is born.
Saith Nānak: The holy eternal alone with woman can dispense,
The tongue by which is the Lord praised. (AG: 473)

Maternal love remains a significant metaphor in the subcontinent's literature, both sacred and profane. On the religious plane, the Ādi Granth sanctifies motherhood, especially procreation of sons. On the temporal level, the status of a woman is enhanced when she becomes a mother of sons. The mother-son relationship manifests reciprocity of love and dependency; it is a model for the devotee's love for God:

> As does the mother cherish her pregnancy, in her son pinning her hope; That grown up, would he give her wherewithal, And bring joy and pleasure; Even such is the love of God's devotee to the Lord. (AG: 165)

God, in the Ādi Granth, is coerced to assume the role of an indulgent mother:

> Any misbehaviour by the child made
> The mother remembers not.
> Lord, Thy child am I
> Why my faults dost Thou not annul?
> Should the child in extreme anger even run off,
> The mother still in mind bears not that. (AG: 478)

The concept of mother is hallowed and held in high esteem: "Make holy thinking thy mother, thy very life" (AG: 172).

The apotheosis of the husband, a legacy of Hindu Brahmanic and bhakti traditions (in which the devotee enters into "marriage mysticism" with a male deity and assumes the psychology of a woman in love [Young, 1987, 77]) forms an integral part of the Ādi Granth. In the following passages, the devotee appropriates the role of an exemplary wife:

> The devotee is like the wife enjoying wedded bliss,
> With her lord ever in her heart;
> Ever sweet-spoken and modest,
> Blessed in her lord's arms:
> Of noble repute and wedded bliss,
> Is she whose love for the Lord knows no bounds. (AG 31)

> The wife that wins her Lord's pleasure, is in His eyes truly beautiful.
> Saith Nānak: Those united by the holy Word never again are parted. (AG 56)

However, in order to win the master's grace, an ideal woman must possess "perfection of conduct," indicating uncompromising subordination and self-abnegation to male domination:

> Possessed of thirty-two merits, holy truth is her progeny,
> Obedient, of noble mien
> To her husband's wishes compliant. (AG 371)

> What is the mark of the blessed?
> Pure of heart, radiant her face, in her Lord absorbed.
> (AG 785)

> Discarding pride, in joy she disports.
> Dedicating body and mind, no distance from him she keeps,
> Neither casting eyes on strangers nor listening to them, nor
> discoursing with them. (AG 793)

> The female that effaces lust, wrath, avarice and attachment,
> And self-acquired foul thinking casts off
> And in humility serves the holy,
> The Beloved's favour shall win. (AG 377)

> The seeker-female, decking herself with the Master's Word
> Of her egoism is rid. (AG 61)

The divine-human relationship in the Ādi Granth is occasionally portrayed as that between a master and his servant, and sometimes as that between a husband and wife. The nature of devotion is generally sedate and sanctimonious, channeled through discipline and sacrifice. Passages indicating women's subservient status are not wanting. Although the language of the Ādi Granth is considered to be allegorical, it no doubt reflects social reality:

> The Lord is my husband, I his wife
> The Lord is immensely great, I so small. (AG: 483)

> A wife faithful to her Lord must devote
> herself body and soul to him
> And must behave in all respects as the faithful wedded-
> wives. (AG: 31)

The wife at the

sight of her spouse is in bloom of joy
Thus does God's devotee live by contemplation of His name.
(AG: 198)

As at the sight of the calf is the cow pleased;
As is the woman pleased at the husband's return home
God's devotees are pleased, as is sung the Lord's praise.
(AG: 164)

From her very childhood, the career of a woman is oriented toward securing a spouse on whom she will depend and around whom her life will revolve:

The wife in the husband's absence decking herself,
Only makes waste of her charm in ignominy.
Never shall she enjoy the couch of bliss—
Without her husband is all her decking wasted. (AG: 58)

The wife without her Lord cannot live,
In the dark night, terribly long.
In love for the Lord finds she no rest. . . .
Without the Beloved, has she none to care. (AG: 243)

The mark of a good woman is,
She surrenders herself body and soul to her Lord. (AG: 89)

One that surrenders to her Lord her self, mind, home and body,
Saith Kabir, is truly the blessed wife. (AG: 328)

Now is my home my own, and this woman turned my wife,
She the servant: I the exalted Master to be one of the nobles.
(AG: 371)

Blessed is the happily-wedded wife who her Lord venerates,
His command obeys and casts-off pride. (AG: 737)

The feminine is perceived to represent attachment, the profane, a barrier to salvation and the material possession of a man:

Attachment to progeny, wife is poison
None of these at the end is of any avail. (AG: 41)

Maya afflicts one who by egoistic thinking is intoxicated;
It afflicts one involved with progeny and wife,
It afflicts too one attached to elephants,
horses and material objects. (AG: 182)

This wealth, beauty, progeny and wife which for test to man
  have been granted,
Man in these remains entangled, by his senses attracted.
(AG: 336)

Progeny, wife, home, all objects—false is attachment to
them. (AG: 401)

The female that effaces lust, wrath, avarice and attachment,
And self-acquired foul thinking casts-off
And in humility serves the holy,
The beloved's favour shall win. (AG: 377)

But:

The unlucky wife, who to the Lord has not offered constant
devotion,
Both worlds loses. (AG: 793)

The female of cursed matrimony cast-off from His love . . .
Devoid of the Lord's glance, in sighing she suffers
Deluded by her great pride. (AG: 928)

Cursed is the life of the woman abandoned, by duality
  deluded:
Like a wall of alkaline sand, day and night is she crumbling
  to fall . . .
deluded woman! what good decking thyself without thy
Lord. (AG: 18)

And again:

A woman full of unapproved qualities shall be cast-off from
the sight of the spouse. (AG: 37)

A woman not having bliss with her Lord,
Her youth has wasted
Thou ignorant woman without merit! what joy for thee?

With beloved gone to strange lands, the lonely wife pines
Like a fish in shallow water she wails . . .
The woman of false mind, of bad ways is found of little
merit;
In her father's home and in the husband's
With her false and bad ways is she ever in torment. (AG: 54)

The egoist is like a woman, doing make-up
with her husband gone to strange lands. (AG: 127)

Whereas subservience, obedience, docility, and dedication by
women were cherished and rewarded, such activities by men
are not:

Men obedient to their womenfolk
Are impure, filthy, stupid,
Man lustful, impure, their womenfolk counsel follow.
(AG: 304)

Negative images of women are also found throughout the Ādi
Granth:

The egoist is like a woman foul of mind, given to duality
(AG: 639)

From door to door with evil minds they wander
Like a woman of ill repute. (AG: 651)

The ten sources of senses which are to be controlled are
like ten females. (AG: 693)

Maya attachment is like a loose woman,
A bad woman, given to casting spells. (AG: 796)

And:

Whoever worships the Great Mother
Shall though man, be incarnate as woman. (AG: 874)

The total rejection of goddess worship can be explained in part
by the fact that Sikhism is a strict monotheism. Acceptance of one
God is assumed to be an essential factor in the quest for liberation.

It is interesting that the most recurrent name for the monotheistic God in the Ādi Granth is Akāl Purakh, often translated as the "Timeless Being," but the word *purakh*, which means "man," is used. This is perhaps incidental as men held virtual monopoly over all the intellectual, cultural, and religious functions of society. The worship of a goddess is not only repudiated ideationally, but being born as a woman is perceived as a catastrophe of cosmic dimension, to be fled like a plague. The very birth as woman is said to be the result of bad karma (in this case worship of the mother goddess) and a curse. One might thus deduce that a woman by nature is inferior; she is subservient and dependent on a man.

The present investigation displays conflicting images of the feminine: from the hallowed image of the mother to the harlot, a woman without a husband. These images were sanctioned in the popular literature of the subcontinent and were instrumental in influencing preachers and proletariat alike.

WOMEN: FROM THE GURUS' PERSPECTIVE

In the formative years of Sikhism, the gurus pronounced doctrines for the new social and religious order, and subscribed equal religious status for both men and women. The same teachings were dispensed, the same spiritual path was open to all, the same goal pointed out. The gurus (from Guru Nānak to Guru Gobind Singh) even succeeded in giving the same conceptual message. The gurus, in other words, advanced the same basic convictions and formulated practical responses as circumstances required.

Guru Amar Das (1479–1574) and Guru Ram Das (1534–1581), encouraged widows to remarry. Guru Amardas condemned the practice of purdah and urged women to come to the *sangat* (assembly) without veiling their faces. He also delegated women to go forth and preach the new religion, calling them *peerahs*, from the Punjabi word for chair. Guru Amardas introduced many innovations, advocated monogamy, encouraged intercaste alliances and remarriage of widows, and strictly forbade the practice of sati. Guru Hargobind (1595–1644) called women the conscience of man, gave importance to household life, condemned asceticism and the belief that marriage was a barrier to achievement of self-realization. Guru Gobind Singh (1666–1708) made the Sikh *khālsā* baptism compulsory for both men and women.

The precepts of the gurus concerning the amelioration of the situation of women remained just that: precepts. The reason for this shortcoming might be attributed to historical and cultural circumstances. The Sikhs and Muslims during the time of the gurus were too embroiled fighting wars, which were a combination of guile, regional ambitions, feudalism, and later on survival. Another justification for not implementing the professed reforms could be attributed to the deep-rooted traditional and cultural attitudes toward women, which proved to be too powerful for the Sikh leaders to eradicate. Or it could have been that some gurus themselves accepted the status quo and endorsed the male-dominated religious system, which relegated women to oblivion. In other words, there existed an enormous incongruity between Sikh precept and practice.

Images of Sikh Women in Later Centuries

History books contain little information about women; and the few glimpses of women that are provided are for the most part about those who rose to prominence or fell to disgrace. Portraits of these women certainly cannot be said to be typical of women in Sikhism. However, the excerpts that follow do give us a fragmentary picture of the attitudes toward women in Sikhism, acknowledging the fact that stereotypes do incorporate an element of authenticity.

On the military front, Sikh women demonstrated exceptional determination and valor. During the period of persecution of Sikhs in 1748–1763 by Mir Manoo, the governor of Lahore, Sikh women reportedly stood by the side of their men. Thousands of women were tortured and imprisoned, but not a single one is said to have relinquished her faith despite atrocities. George Thomas states in his memoirs:

> Instances have not infrequently occurred in which Sikh women have actually taken up arms to defend their habitation from the desultory attacks of the enemy, and throughout the contest behaved themselves with an intrepidity of spirit, highly praiseworthy. (Singh, 1965: 15)

These were exceptional women; the routine behavior for women revolved around the house, husband, and children.

Sati and Polygamy

The gurus had consistently condemned ills that plagued society such as polygamy, sati, and female infanticide. As often the case, the elites of society did not concede to the reforms of the new religion. Polygamy, sati, and female infanticide remained rampant.

Ranjit Singh (1780–1839), the only maharajah of the Sikh kingdom, which endured for no more than fifty years, is said to have had twenty-two wives. When the maharajah died on June 21, 1839, Rani Guddun (Singh 1966; I-140) is said to have "placed the head of the deceased on her lap, while the other ranis with seven slave girls seated themselves around, with every mark of satisfaction on their countenances" (*Lahore Akhbar*, June 1839).

Dr. Honigberger (1852) takes up the tale: "The Brahmins performed their prayers from the Sastras, the priests of the Sikhs did the same from their holy scriptures called Granth Sahib. . . . Along with the ruler of Punjab, four of his wives and seven slave girls were reduced to ashes."

This was not an isolated instance of sati among the Sikhs. When Maharajah Kharak Singh died on November 5, 1840, two of his wives are also said to have committed sati. When Chand Kaur, one of Kharak Singh's widows, proclaimed herself Maharanee (Singh 1966:II-14–15):

> The Punjabis were unable to reconcile themselves to being ruled by a woman who could not leave the veiled seclusion of the zenana. And Chand Kaur proved to be singularly inept in the art of diplomacy; she was vain, ill-tempered and given to using language that became a bazaar woman more than a Maharanee.
>
> Bedi Bikram Singh of Una, who had come to Lahore to carry out the investiture ceremony, stated categorically that he had come to give the Tikka (saffron mark) to Kanwar Sher Singh and not to a woman, for no woman had or could ever reign at Lahore.

The short reign of a month and a half ended, and she was obliged to relinquish her claim to the throne.

L. J. Trotter (1880:I-197, 206) in his *Life of Lord Lawrence*, records:

> Female infanticide was not only practiced by the Rajputs, but was universal among Sikhs. . . . They had never allowed a single female child to live. John Lawrence, when renewing the leases on the land holders made them repeat, "Beva mat jalao" (do not burn widows), "Beti mat maro" (do not kill daughters).

This occurred despite the fact that Guru Gobind Singh had prohibited female infanticide and said he would excommunicate those who killed female children. Guru Gobind Singh's prohibition can still be seen printed in large characters at the entry of the Akal Takht alongside the Golden Temple. Sati was legally outlawed in 1829 in British India; remarriage of widows was authorized under the government act of 1856. In 1853 the code of rules limiting the extent of dowries, one of the primary reasons for not wanting female children, was drawn up. And yet:

> By the turn of the century, one of the places in Punjab where you might fancy buying pornographic literature, or bedding a prostitute, or perhaps gambling, was the Sikh temple, the gurudwara. This was not an isolated scourge. And this astonishing decadence had touched even the noblest of places, the Golden Temple at Amritsar. Innocent women coming to pray in the temples were not safe: the mahants or priests used to boast about this, rather than feel embarrassed, announced to those who felt too concerned about the morality of their women should avoid sending them to the gurudwaras. Women from the "best" families often got pregnant after a bout of "worship." The Mahant at Guru ka Bag, for instance, used to keep two mistresses . . . in addition to a regular harem of prostitutes. (Akbar 1985, 134)

Beginning of a New Sikh Identity

The Sikhs had lost their independence, their symbols, their temples, and their fortunes by the end of the nineteenth century. "Notwithstanding the Sikh Gurus' powerful denunciation of Brahmans, secular Sikhs now rarely do anything without their assistance. Brahmans help them to be born, help them to wed, help them to die, and help their souls after death to obtain a state of bliss" (Macauliffe 1909, lvii).

Hinduism seemed to be assimilating Sikhism. The *gurudwaras* were becoming either Hindu temples or haunts of depravity, or both. If Sikhs were to exist as an independent religious community, they had to understand their religion. Day-to-day life was influenced by a network of kinship and caste relations. Consequently, the religious groupings of "Hindu" and "Sikh" remained fluid and frail. There was hardly any difference between the way Hindus and Sikhs received a child into this world, contracted a marriage alliance, or performed funeral rites. These commonalities tied them together into a common symbolic universe. The result of all this was that the two were integrated into a common cultural universe. They shared the same grammar of social relations based on vertical ties of kinship and caste rather than the horizontal solidarity of religion and community:

> However, the Khalsa sub-tradition that did not blend very well with the amorphous state of the Sikh faith. The Khalsa Sikhs had their own notion of what constituted the Sikh past and more importantly they possessed a distinct life-cycle ritual in the form of "khande da pahul" or baptism rites. Those who maintained this rite had to maintain the well known symbols of the Khalsa and in addition strictly observe the injunctions laid down in the Rahit Maryada. (Oberoi 1988, 147)

Identity formation is inevitably a dual process. It is not sufficient for a group of people to think that they constitute a separate entity; those among whom they interact must also recognize this claim. Therefore the khālsā self-perception of being distinct from the rest of the civil population in the province did not automatically mean that they were accepted as such by others who belonged to the Sikh tradition or by the Hindus. The khālsā urge to strike a separate identity was further diluted by the fact that it was not mandatory for all Sikhs to undergo khande da pahul (rite of sword-baptism as initiation to the khālsā). Secondly, the different subtraditions constituting the Sikh movement had their own distinct rites of initiation:[6] "of all the competing entities, symbols and norms that went into constituting the Sikh movement, it was the Khalsa subtradition that came to imprint its image on the 'new' community" (Oberoi 1988, 150).

The khālsā condemnation of existing rites was based on three major factors: they were Hindu in origin, intent, and purpose. Sikh Gurus were opposed to these practices and had developed separate rites for their followers. Finally, many elements within the prevalent rites were considered to be unprogressive.

The prenatal and postnatal practices described as Hindu rites were simply discarded. All Sikhs—Jats, Khatris, Mazhbis—were required to perform the same rituals without any reference to their caste or birādarī traditions. A comparable change was effected in marriage arrangements. How and why this happened has been discussed by Oberoi (1988). What initially were changes introduced by a minority imperceptibly came to be accepted by the Sikh public at large. The khālsā transformation of these rituals, however, turned them into powerful bearers of the "new" Sikh consciousness. They came to dramatize the distinction between "us" (Sikhs) and "them" (Hindus).[7]

In sum, the khālsā gave identity, a particular vision of history, and an exclusive communal solidarity to the Sikhs. While the roots of the drive for this cultural autonomy may be traced by some scholars back to Guru Nānak, the reasons for its consolidation certainly lie entangled in the social history of the late nineteenth-century Punjab. The oft-repeated rhetorical statement *Ham Hindu Nahin,* "we are not Hindus," now had a real basis. Innovations in the spheres of language, history, theology, sacred places, religious calendar and territory enhanced the sense of a separate identity.

The khālsās not only defined a distinct identity for the Sikhs, they also incorporated changes for women in the Rāhat Maryādā.

Women in the Rāhat Maryādā

The Rāhat Maryādā, guide to the Sikh way of life, spells out the basic beliefs, principles, and practices of an ideal Sikh existence. The passages that follow demonstrate a certain deference toward women, indicating an improvement:

> Sikhism condemns infanticide outright, particularly female infanticide, and Sikhs should have no dealings with any who condone it.
> Sikhs must not commit adultery.
> A Sikh should respect another man's wife as his own mother, and another man's daughter as his own daughter;
> a man should enjoy his wife's company and women should be loyal to their husbands.
> It is contrary to Sikhism for women to veil themselves.
> A Sikh daughter should marry a Sikh.
> Child marriages are not permitted. A girl should marry only when she has attained physical and mental maturity; neither a girl nor a boy should be married for money.
> There is no prohibition against widows or widowers remarrying if they wish. The ceremony should be the same as that of the first marriage.[8]

Modern Age

The Sikhs, however, were still unable to bring about any significant change in the position or participation of women in the community, mainly because their primary concern was to consolidate Sikh authority rather than engender change for women. Nevertheless, change did surface after the tragedy of Jallianwala Bagh in 1919, when R. E. H. Dyer ordered the massacre of a primarily Sikh congregation of unarmed men, women, and children. Punjab rose against the British after this incident. The members of the Akali (a political party created to reform the Sikh temple) formally committed themselves to the cause of freedom by passing resolution supporting Gandhi's call for noncooperation with the British:

> The British Raj went so far as to add the reason of social concern for Hindu [Indian?] women to its rationale for ruling India. Hindu leaders appropriated this criticism of Hindu women on political and domestic fronts and sought reforms. Hence, it is no surprise to find the cause of Indian Independence was simultaneously the cause for women's liberation from more oppressive aspects of the domestic situation. Significantly, it was a cause that both Hindu men and women joined. (Young 1987, 93)

Mahatma Gandhi had been a source of inspiration to the women of India. He realized how women could become the leaders in national movement of satyagraha (nonviolence): "which does not require the learning that books give but does require the stout heart that comes from suffering and faith" (*Harijan*, February 24, 1940).

Women knew well the language of self-denial, suffering, self-control, and patience. They could redirect that orientation from the domestic arena to the national front. When their traditional religious psychology became a tool for changing a situation rather than coping with it, they experienced a new freedom. Gandhi helped women break out of their domestic prisons by redirecting their traditional self-sacrifice and service from husband to nation (Young 1987, 96–97).

With India's independence (1947), women were granted social, political, and economic rights along with men. Forty-four years later, despite attempting to improve the general situation of women problems such as bride burning, dowry, and the abortion of female fetuses remain.

Participation of Women in the Akali Movement

The fate of Sikh women centered primarily around the Akalis who believed that it was inconceivable to defend their faith without political power. The Akali-led movement in Punjab was dramatically enhanced during the emergency in the late 1970s and 80s. The participation of women was striking; they began to come out in large numbers in response to the call of Longowal, their leader, for help.

The women dedicated themselves to the cause even though the movement had nothing to offer them as women. The repression unleashed by the Indian government on their men was a more important causal factor for their participation than any of the political demands. They repeatedly said that they had joined the movement to do sewā or service, to give rather than to take. "You take whatever sewā you want from me" was their general attitude. An unquestioning obedience to leadership in a do-or-die spirit was conspicuous during the agitation:

> The Akali women were able to become a significant presence in the movement despite the fact that in normal times the political participation of women in rural Punjab is particularly low. Women normally live extremely secluded and restricted lives and are not allowed political participation event at the gurudwara or village level. The participation of this movement became possible because the men of the community were willing to release them from domestic responsibilities so that they could strengthen the movement. (Kishwar 1988, 2755)

In fact the bravery and steadfastness of these simple, illiterate women has been the main strength of the whole movement (*Manushi*, no. 40, 1987, 6). Often, it has been noted that women are deliberately put in the front line to face repression. This has been justified on the grounds that police would show restraint in the presence of women protesters, and even if they do not, women would face the attacks more valiantly than men. In many instances, women were manipulated and used as a means by the men. When villages were raided, men would flee to the woods, abandoning women, children, and the elderly. Some men openly admitted that they had to hold off the police by putting women in the front. The reasons they offered were: "Women do not lose their cool as easily as men do, and are able to resist without unnecessary violence; if the police start using force, women do not run away as men tend to do; they often fight to the last to protect their men and children" (*Manushi*, 1987:6).

While female victims of aggression were often projected as heroines and martyrs, their own husbands and communities often rejected and ostracized them, particularly if they suffered sexual assault while defending the community. They would be denied family protection and were not allowed to participate in any rituals.

Since women by and large participated in the movement more out of a desire to support their men in a crisis than out of determination to acquire any clout as women, there are hardly any instances of women pressuring the leadership to improve the lives of women. Women's fronts remained auxiliaries. They seldom became involved in power struggles. While women competed with each other, they did not offer any competition to male leadership.

The initiative to organize a women's front came at the initiative of male leadership. Most activists confirm that the few women who are able to take an active part in movements are wives of men already involved. Women who come against the wishes of the male members of the family are seldom able to sustain their involvement over a long period of time.

Linked to the crucial need for family permission is the age factor. In most movements, while a number of male activists are unmarried youth, young unmarried girls are seldom allowed to participate. An important reason is that parents fear a girl's reputation will be ruined is she mixes with men in a public domain, and their chances of marriage would be ruined. For older women, this was a lesser problem, but they faced the double disadvantage of being heavily weighed by work and of being illiterate. However, young married women may more easily get permission from their families to join in movement activities if respected older women of the village are already involved and can act as escorts.

Women did not determine agenda. The Stree Akali Dal did not raise the question of oppression of women, because this was not on the agenda of Akali leadership. Sant Longowal's message to women as reported by Harwant Kaur was: "Do not harm anyone. Live in peace and love with all. When you go to your in-laws' house, love everyone there. Serve your husband. Have no relationship with any man other than your husband."

The Akali leadership even proposed to curtail women's rights by introducing a personal law for Sikhs which would have deprived women of whatever legal inheritance rights they had, and legally legitimized the practice of levirate. Despite rural women's militant contribution to the movement, no protest against this move emerged from the Stree Akali Dal. Whatever protest was voiced came from urban women's groups in Chandigarh and Delhi, even though the question of land inheritance primarily affects rural women:

> On the whole, men were more interested in women participating in large numbers in action programmes, but were less interested in their developing an independent identity. As a result, while women came and participated in a big way in demonstrations, and were often in the forefront, they did not have any decision making, or leadership roles. (*Manushi*, no. 14, pg. 11)

There is no doubt that despite the auxiliary role they play, women who are mobilized for different actions gain significantly in terms of self-confidence, mobility, and a chance to see the world outside the village, and to interact with other women.

The knowledge that they played an indispensable role in the movement's success helps women build a more positive self-image. Women's heroic actions become part of the movement lore and some individual women may emerge as role models different from the more normal model of woman as server and giver within the family. Even if they get pushed back into the domestic sphere once the crisis is over, each phase of participation represents an irrevocable step of some kind, and does change somewhat the collective consciousness of women. They become at least conscious of their ability to emerge and act in the public and political domain.

A necessary precondition for women's mobilization is the general and usually prior mobilization of the men in the rural community. Movement leaders have seldom, almost never, begun by mobilizing women as an integral part of their rural organizations. In almost all cases, their organizing efforts have initially focused primarily on men—whether the organization is of peasantry or of the landless poor. However, as soon as the organization undertakes mass actions and gets into a state of confrontation for getting its demands met, women often come out spontaneously to lend support to the movement, especially at moments of crisis. This is true of the Akali Dal, besides other movements in India.

Even though women tend spontaneously to join rural and urban movements during the phases of militant action, it has been found that in most cases the leadership begins to make a special appeal to women to join when the movement is facing a crisis like government and police repression or a backlash from oppressive forces. At such times, leaders call on women more easily because the community is compelled to suspend the normal rules of behavior in order to cope with the emergency and the men become more willing to encourage women's participation. At such times of crisis, women too tend to perceive their participation as a duty to family and community.

CONCLUSION

The present investigation of portraits of women and the feminine demonstrate the extreme views of misogynist attitudes, on the one hand, and the religious ideals of wisdom and universal salvation, on the other. These views were upheld in varying degrees throughout a wide range of Sikh literature and history. The traditional attitudes toward women tended to relegate the feminine to the sensual realm as opposed to the spiritual realm. The imminent seductive powers of the feminine suggest that men perceived women as potential threats to their spiritual welfare. The evil power of sexuality was associated with women and household life. Possible notions of pollution or contamination through any interaction with women remained implicit. Women were viewed as the cause of mental anguish and pain, and as threats to familial stability because of women's adulterous behavior.

Woman as mother was also tied to the sensual realm, to a state of attachment to home and children. Although woman as mother does not threaten the family structure, being almost synonymous with household life, woman as mother cannot move out of that domestic sphere to the religious. She is respected as a paragon of womanhood through her procreative function as the bearer of children, but she is also inextricably entwined with a world of suffering—namely, a world of children and attachment to them. The path to salvation represents the compromising efforts of reconciling the tensions between ingrained prejudices and religious goals to universal salvation. Limitations which the Gurus imposed on women were primarily due to fear of losing their own spiritual position; recognition that women were constrained by society, particularly by their close association with familial responsibilities, which were more demanding for women than for men; the association and imposition of inordinate sexual powers to the feminine, generalized to all women as inherently sensual and destructive beings.

Textual descriptions in the Guru Granth, reflected the concern for the disintegration of the family structure, if women were to leave their homes. Accounts of happily wedded wives and other women also implied, in some instances, dependence and subordination. The happily wedded wives were capable of teaching and respecting the *gurumatā*, through their daily activities. The familial associations with a husband, father, or child is constantly mentioned, suggesting that it was through her familial responsibilities that she could attain God. God is undoubtedly a male figure, exemplified as all-loving, spiritually perfect, desireless, and omniscient, frequently described as both the mother and father of all living beings. Certain texts go on to suggest that the female sex was weaker both physically and mentally, more vulnerable to ignorance, and perhaps even somewhat defective, both in terms of spiritual weakness and physical handicaps.

The Sikh scriptures affirm that women ought to take an active part in social, cultural, and religious pursuits. The idea that woman is evil, unclean, an impediment is not rejected, as we are often made to think, but endorsed in the Guru Granth. The episodes from the Janam-Sākhīs (stories about the birth and life of the gurus)[9] often suggest that Guru Nānak was a reformer speaking and acting against the caste system and working to improve the situation of women.

However we do see conflicting images in the Guru Granth, one affirming equivalence, the other defining women as subordinate to men, socially and even ontologically.

Granted the subordinate status she inherited from the Hindus, the Sikh woman did not fare horribly. If she were a good wife and mother, specially of sons, she could expect praise. Marriage continues to be the normal state for both men and women. The goal and purpose is to bring under control all the unruly potentialities of sexuality. Overall, the female domain of home and family was considered material. The spiritual religious domain belonged to men. It is, however, fair to say the women were usually cherished in private and treated with respect in public, but considered ignorant.

The prevailing societal restrictions on women also undoubtedly influenced descriptions of women and the feminine. Portraits of women frequently focused on the woman's important functions within the household life. Women were expected to bear the majority of familial responsibilities. If women were to leave the domestic sphere of activities, social institutions would collapse with the expected breakdown of the family. However, there are sympathetic portraits of women and the feminine. The predominant tendency was undoubtedly to promote the welfare of all beings and to alleviate their suffering without prejudice or favor.

Susan S. Maneck

WOMEN IN THE BAHA'I FAITH

The Baha'i faith is the youngest of the world's religions. Baha'u'-
llah, the prophet-founder of the Baha'i faith, was born in Iran in
1817. He claimed to be the latest messenger sent by God, an asser-
tion that irremediably separated the Baha'is from their Islamic
background. Baha'is believe that while all religions have been ordained by God, the social teachings of religions have varied according to the needs of the age in which a prophet appears. The central
theme of the Baha'i message is the establishment of the unity of humankind in a single global society. This necessitates the establishment of a world government, the achievement of universal
education, the elimination of all forms of prejudice, and the attainment of full equality of men and women.

No other world religion has been quite as explicit as the Baha'i
faith in its support of the principle of the equality of men and
women. Baha'is themselves proudly assert it as one of the distinguishing features of the new revelation. This equality does not refer
solely to the spiritual plane, for Baha'i scriptures explicitly state
that there should be "no difference in the education of male and female in order that womankind may develop equal capacity and importance with man in the social and economic equation."[1] They
further assert that "women will enter all the department of
politics."[2]

Yet the understanding of this principle varies considerably
among Baha'is. Many support a higher evaluation of women's traditional roles, particularly in family life, but foresee little change in
the roles themselves. Others call for a fundamental transformation
of the very structure of relations in community life, which would

incorporate values that have been viewed as feminine. Support for both stances can be drawn from Baha'i scriptures. Regarding family life, the secretary of the Guardian of the Baha'i faith wrote on his behalf: "The task of bringing up a Baha'i child, as emphasized time and again in Baha'i Writings, is the chief responsibility of the mother."[3] The Universal House of Justice, the supreme governing body for the Baha'i world, asserts that the corollary to this is that the financial responsibility for supporting the family rests with the husband. The exclusion of women from the Universal House of Justice (which will be discussed later) has tended to perpetuate arguments for "separate but equal spheres" in other realms as well.

At the same time, Baha'i ideals for a new world order cannot be attained without a change in societal structures, with women playing a leading role:

> The world in the past has been ruled by force, and man has dominated over woman by reason of his more forceful and aggressive qualities both of body and mind. But the balance is already shifting—force is losing its weight and mental alertness, intuition, and the spiritual qualities of love and service, in which woman is strong, are gaining ascendancy. Hence the new age will be an age less masculine, and more permeated with the feminine ideals—or, to speak more exactly, will be an age in which the masculine and feminine elements of civilization will be more evenly balanced.[4]

Many Baha'i women today have tried to hold together all of these statements in the writings by exhibiting the "supermom" syndrome: fulfilling their roles as wives and mothers while attempting to excel in their chosen careers. Needless to say, this doubling of duties creates tremendous stress for these women.

Baha'is are often unaware of the historical contexts in which various pronouncements regarding women were made, and this creates great confusion regarding their proper understanding. This issue is confounded by the fact that the development of the Baha'i faith in its early formative period took place in two radically disparate cultures and continents. Originating in Iran in the middle of the nineteenth century, the religion spread to North America in the 1890s. While Baha'i theology was born in the context of a nearly homogeneous Islamic Shi'ite culture, its administrative structure developed in the United States.

In the course of this chapter I will trace the role of women within the Baha'i faith from the time of its inception as the Babi movement, through its introduction to the West, until the present time. I will examine both the scriptural status of women as well as the reality of their position within the Baha'i community. While Baha'i communities exist in nearly all countries, I will restrict my discussion to Iran and North America, since sufficient documentation exists only for those two areas, and developments in those religions have largely determined the direction taken by the rest of the Baha'i world.

TAHIRIH: A BAHA'I PARADIGM OF WOMANHOOD

Nearly every religion has its paradigm of the "ideal" woman. In Hinduism this has been Sita, the perfect wife who remains faithful to her husband at all costs. In Christianity the most eminent woman is the Virgin Mary, symbol of motherhood. Islam has Fatimih, daughter of Muhammad, who models the roles of mother, wife, and daughter together. Tahirih, the most well-known woman in Babi-Baha'i history, presents a startling contrast to the former models.[5] This gifted poet of nineteenth-century Iran, far from being a dutiful daughter, continually opposed the theological positions of her father, Mulla Salih, a prominent Muslim cleric of Qazvin. Neither is she admired for her success as a wife and mother, since her estrangement from her husband resulted in her forced separation from her children as well.

In 1844 A.C.E. (1260 A.H.) Siyyid Ali Muhammad al-Bab secretly revealed himself to be the Qa'im, the messianic figure expected by the Shi'ite Muslims. He selected eighteen followers as his chief disciples and entitled them, along with himself, the Nineteen Letters of the Living.[6] At the time, Tahirih was a leading figure within the Shaykhi[7] sect. Although she had never met the Bab, she immediately embraced his religion and was appointed a "Letter."

Tahirih, whose given name was Fatimih Bigum Baraghani, was the daughter of the leading clerical family of Qazvin. She had received an excellent education in all the traditional Islamic sciences and was able to translate many of the Bab's writings from Arabic into Persian. Despite her background, Tahirih's writings were fiercely anticlerical. Basing her authority on her claim to an inner awareness of God's purpose, she instituted a number of innovations within the Babi community. Claiming that much of Islamic law was no longer binding upon Babis, she refused to perform the daily ritual prayers. But her most audacious act was occasionally to appear unveiled in gatherings of believers.

According to Abbas Amanat, this was probably the first time an Iranian woman had considered unveiling at her own initiative . The circle of women who gathered around Tahirih in Karbila, and later Qazvin, Hamadan, Baghdad, and Teheran, were perhaps the first group of women in those regions to have attained an awareness of their deprivations as women.[8] Yet Tahirih's activities did not represent a woman's liberation movement in the modern sense. For Tahirih, removing the veil was primarily an act of religious innovation. Neither the writings of Tahirih nor the Bab concern themselves with the issue of women's rights as such.[9] Apparently Tahirih experienced the Bab's revelation as liberating, whether or not it addressed itself to the status of women per se.

Tahirih's activities created much controversy within the Babi community itself. Many Babis did not view the Bab's revelation as requiring a total break with the past or with Islamic law. They regarded Tahirih's behavior as scandalous and unchaste. For this reason, the Bab gave her the title by which she is now known, Tahirih, meaning the "pure." The opposition of the non-Babi ulama (Islamic clergymen) went much deeper. During the month of Muharram, 1847, Tahirih deliberately excited their reaction by dressing in gay colors and appearing unveiled instead of donning the customary mourning clothes to commemorate the martyrdom of Imam Husayn. She urged the Babis, instead, to celebrate the birthday of the Bab, which fell on the first day of that month. The enraged clergy incited a mob to attack the house where she was staying. Finally the governor intervened and had Tahirih placed under house arrest before having her sent to Baghdad.

Accompanied by the leading Babi women of Karbila, along with a number of devoted male followers, Tahirih set out for Baghdad, where she continued her activities, offering public lectures from behind a curtain.[10] This aroused further opposition and caused her to be imprisoned in the house of the mufti, or leading Sunni cleric of Baghdad. But she was not tried for apostasy, since the usual penalty for that crime (death) could not be applied to women. Meanwhile, her family in Qazvin was quite disturbed by her activities. Her unveiling, in particular, led to rumors of immorality. Tahirih's father dispatched a relative to Iraq who induced the governor to order her return to Iran. Wherever she traveled en route, more excitement was raised. In the village of Krand some twelve hundred people immediately offered her their allegiance. In Kirmanshah her presence caused such an uproar that the Babis were attacked by a mob and driven out of the city, but not before Tahirih had expounded the teachings before its leading women, including the governor's wife. In Hamadan Tahirih met with both the leading ulama and the most notable women of the city, as well as members of the royal family.

On the arrival in Qazvin, her husband, Mulla Muhammad, from whom she had been long estranged, urged her to return to his household. She told him:

> If your desire had really been to be a faithful mate and companion to me, you would have hastened to meet me in Karbila and would on foot have guided my howdah all the way to Qazvin. I would, while journeying with you, have aroused you from your sleep of heedlessness and would have shown you the way of truth. But this was not to be. Three years have lapsed since our separation. Neither in this world nor in the next can I ever be associated with you. I have cast you out of my life forever.[11]

Tahirih's uncle and father-in-law, Muhammad Taqi, had a reputation for being virulently opposed to both the Babis and the Shaykhis. On numerous occasions he incited mob violence against them. After one of these incidents, Mulla Abdu'llah, a Shaykhi and a Babi sympathizer, decided to retaliate. When Mulla Taqi appeared in the local mosque to offer his dawn prayers, Mulla Abdu'llah fatally stabbed him and fled.[12] This led to the arrest and torture of many of the Babis in Qazvin. Tahirih was implicated as well. In order to stop this orgy of violence, Mulla Abdu'llah turned himself in. Despite this the other Babis were not released and many were executed. Tahirih escaped with the assistance of Baha'u'llah, who hid her in his home in Teheran.[13]

Later, following a general call to Babis to gather in Khurasan, Tahirih and Baha'u'llah traveled to a place called Badasht, where some eighty-one Babi leaders met to consider how they might effect the release of the Bab, who was then imprisoned, and to discuss the future direction of the Babi community in the face of growing persecution. At the meeting tension developed between Tahirih—who headed the more radical Babis advocating a complete break with Islam as well as militant defense of their community—and the more conservative Quddus—who initially advocated policies aimed at the rejuvenation of Islam and prudent accommodation with religious and secular power. Babis generally accepted Quddus as the chief of the Bab's disciples, but Tahirih reportedly said in regards to him. "I deem him a pupil whom the Bab has sent me to edify and instruct. I regard him in no other light." Quddus denounced Tahirih as "the author of heresy."[14] At one time when Quddus was rapt in his devotions, Tahirih rushed out of her tent brandishing a sword. "Now is not the time for prayers and prostrations." she declared, "rather on to the battle field of love and sacrifice."[15]

Her most startling act was to appear before the assembled believers unveiled. Shoghi Effendi vividly describes that scene:

> Tahirih, regarded as the fair and spotless emblem of chastity and the incarnation of the holy Fatimih, appeared suddenly, adorned yet unveiled, before the assembled companions, seated herself on the right-hand of the affrighted and infuriated Quddus, and, tearing through her fiery words the veils guarding the sanctity of the ordinances of Islam, sounded the clarion-call and proclaimed the inauguration of a new Dispensation. The effect was instantaneous. She, of such stainless purity, so reverenced that even to gaze at her shadow was deemed an improper act, appeared for a moment in the eyes of her scandalized beholders, to have defamed herself, shamed the Faith she espoused, and sullied the immortal Countenance she symbolized. Fear, anger, bewilderment swept their inmost souls, and stunned their faculties. Abdu'l-Khaliq-i-Isfahani, aghast and deranged at the sight, cut his throat with his own hands. Spattered with blood, and frantic with excitement, he fled away from her face.[16]

Unperturbed, Tahirih declared, "I am the Word which the Qa'im is to utter, the Word which shall put to flight the chiefs and nobles of the earth!"[17]

Tahirih, much to the dismay of many Babis, finally won Quddus over to her point of view.[18] He conceded that Islamic law had been abrogated. So complete was their reconciliation that the two departed from Badasht riding in the same howdah. When they neared the village of Niyala, the local mulla, outraged at seeing an unveiled woman sitting next to a man and chanting poems aloud, led a mob against them. Several people died in the resulting clash and the Babis dispersed in different directions.

Pitched battles raged between the Babis and government forces between 1848 and 1850 in the Iranian province of Mazandaran, and in the cities of Zanjan and Nayriz. Tahirih remained in hiding, moving from village to village for about a year. Around 1849 authorities arrested her on charges of complicity in the assassination of her uncle. They brought her to Teheran where they imprisoned her in the house of the *kalantar* (mayor). The kalantar's wife soon became very attached to Tahirih and women again flocked to hear her discourses.

On July 9, 1850, the Bab was executed in Tabriz by order of the shah. Two years later a small group of Babis sought to take revenge by assassinating the shah. The attempt failed and a general massacre of Babis ensued. The government decided to execute Tahirih as well. She was taken to a garden and strangled to death.[19] Her body was thrown down a well. Her last words (perhaps apocryphal) are reported to be. "You can kill me as soon as you like, but you cannot stop the emancipation of women."[20]

BAHA'I WOMEN IN IRAN 1868–1892

I have dwelt at length on the figure of Tahirih, for she has become the most widespread model of the ideal woman within the Baha'i community. As such she represents a marked departure from the typical norm found in other world religions. Yet, except for her, in the years preceding the introduction of the Baha'i faith in the West, women are most notable by their absence. During the Babi upheavals a few women donned male clothing in order to participate in armed conflicts, earning the admiration of men. Others, not surprisingly, were protégées of Tahirih's. More commonly Persian Baha'i hagiographies mention women as the wives and mothers of martyrs, spurring on their men to sacrifice.

Peter Smith, in his admirable overview of Babi-Baha'i history, suggests that both religions tended to have been originally male preserves and that generally women learned of the faith from their menfolk. The significance of women, he holds, increased during the Baha'i period, but men were the primary carriers of religion; women were important in ensuring the religious socialization of their children.[21] This assessment appears premature and based on an uncritical use of written sources. Baha'i historians, particularly in Iran, have been overwhelmingly male. Where women have found their way into the biographical literature, they did so because they managed to make their mark within the male sphere of activity, which in nineteenth-century Iran was virtually any function outside the home. Such women functioned essentially as "honorary men." Given the very separate spheres imposed by Iranian society, that any women would have been able to function publicly is, in itself, extraordinary. But the few biographies of Iranian Baha'i women that do exist indicate women had their own networks, self-sustaining and self-led, within which religious ideas could be disseminated and promulgated, apart from the observation of men. These networks, outside the observation of men, never were recognized as important factors in historical works written by men.

Recent but unpublished research conducted by Anthony A. Lee suggests that women played a significant role in the dissemination of the Baha'i faith at least among the Jewish community. Women's networks must be painstakingly reconstructed on the basis of oral histories. Literary sources will not, by themselves, enable us to obtain a full picture of the role of women in early Babi-Baha'i history. However, even given that women may have played a larger role in promulgating the new religion than they have usually been given credit for, it still must be admitted that with the notable exception of Tahirih, women played virtually no public role in the development of the initial administrative organization of the Baha'i community within Iran.

WOMEN IN THE WRITINGS OF BAHA'U'LLAH

The writings of Baha'u'llah unequivocally proclaim the equality of men and women, ásserting that "in this Day the Hand of divine grace hath removed all distinction. The Servants of God and His handmaidens are regarded on the same plane."[22] Elsewhere he suggests that differences between the sexes are the result of "vain imaginings" and "idle fancies," which by the power of his might had been destroyed.[23] He further insists on the education of girls. Yet Baha'u'llah's writings do present some problems from a feminist standpoint.

The *Kitab-i-Aqdas*,[24] the book that contains Baha'i sacred law was written in Arabic, a language that by its nature requires the male gender to be used for collectives. Most of its admonitions and laws are addressed to men. A literal reading of its text would suggest that divorce was solely the male's prerogative. Bigamy appears to be permissible, although monogamy is preferred. Should a marriage be contracted on the basis of a woman's virginity, and the man subsequently discover she was not a virgin, the marriage could be repudiated and the dowry forfeited, although Baha'u'llah states that it would be preferable to conceal the matter and forgive.

In certain contexts, women are given special treatment. They are exempt from the obligation to perform pilgrimage. They are also exempt from the daily ritual prayers and fasting during their menses. Other exemptions exist for pregnancy and nursing. Most problematic is Baha'u'llah's reference to "the men of the House of Justice." which has been interpreted as excluding women from the highest administrative body in the faith.

This androcentric view, which a cursory reading of the text gives, is not, it should be recognized, the manner in which Baha'is have typically understood the *Aqdas*. Baha'u'llah's son, Abdu'l-Baha, whom Baha'is recognize as the authorized interpreter[25] of the sacred writings, stated that since bigamy was conditioned upon equal treatment of both wives, which is impossible, monogamy alone is permissible. Shoghi Effendi further states that women have the same rights as men to sue for divorce and that the requirement for virginity can certainly be applied to either sex. Only in the case of membership in the Universal House of Justice has the male-oriented language been taken literally.

When read within the context of nineteenth-century Iran, the *Kitab-i Aqdas* presents some startling contrasts to the norms of male-female relations. While the *Aqdas* makes it optional for women to perform the obligatory prayers or fast during their menses, within Islam they are not permitted to do so at all, since they are regarded as ritually unclean at such times. Many of the laws contained in the *Aqdas* were addressed to specific concerns raised by individuals, usually male, within the community. For instance, Baha'u'llah made parental consent a prerequisite to marriage. The question immediately arose as to whether this was binding on men as well as women, and if it were binding on women who had been previously married. Baha'u'llah refused to make any distinction between male and female in this regard, insisting that this regulation existed solely for the unity of the family and had nothing to do with the status of women.

Most startling is Baha'u'llah's treatment of sexual issues. The sexuality of women, in both Judaism and Islam, has been seen as a potentially dangerous force that threatens the honor of the family and, indeed, the whole social fabric. The duty of male relatives to defend that honor historically has led to the strict seclusion of women. Women who violated sexual mores were commonly killed, whereas men received the death penalty only if they had intercourse with a married women, thus violating another man's rights. But according to the *Aqdas*, adulterers are subject to a fine, not the death penalty. Baha'is are even discouraged from divorcing on the grounds of adultery. Control of sexuality in the *Aqdas* is a matter of great spiritual significance, with important social implications, but it is not treated as the glue of community life.[26]

Baha'u'llah's treatment of certain economic issues in regards to women is somewhat more problematic and has raised a certain amount of controversy lately. The inheritance laws presume a situation where the male is the primary breadwinner of the family. These laws are quite complex, but generally speaking, in the case of intestacy, female heirs are awarded only half of what their male counterparts receive. In this they are similar to Islamic inheritance laws, which are, however, binding on all with or without a will. This led some Baha'is to assert that the law of intestacy represents what ought to be normative among Baha'is. Men retain their position as the primary breadwinners of the family, with certain rights and responsibilities. A patrilineal, though not patriarchal, society is thus maintained. Such an arrangement is necessary to insure the participation of the male in family life.[27]

Others, including this author, have argued that since Baha'u'llah requires all believers to write a will, what he has written in regards to intestacy is exceptional, not normative.[28] The *Aqdas* describes an equitable distribution of property within the context of nineteenth-century Iran and is thus more descriptive than prescriptive. The *Aqdas* also excludes non-Baha'is from inheritance entirely, a provision made in a situation of oppression and persecution where Baha'is were commonly disowned by non-Baha'i relatives. Shoghi Effendi states that under normal circumstances it is only fair for Baha'is to provide for non-Baha'i relatives, and emphasizes the need for all Baha'is to write wills to do so. The Baha'i claim to equality of sexes, many hold, would be meaningless if it did not embrace the economic sphere.[29]

Perhaps the key issue in this debate revolves around the yet unresolved issue of the treatment of scripture. The more conservative believers interpret the sacred writings in an absolute, timeless sense, minimizing their cultural context. They therefore draw essential principles from all parts of scripture equally. The more liberal understanding regards the historical situation within which such writings were revealed to be essential for meaningful exegesis. It holds that the most meaningful portions of scripture are those that depart radically from the cultural context in which they were written. In regards to gender relations, the conservative approach leads to a situation where equality is enjoined in the spiritual realm but social inequalities are allowed to persist.

Another issue that might be raised with regard to Baha'u'llah's writings is the use of gender in connection with the deity. It has been argued, with good reason, that the exclusive use of male gender in referring to God leads to a perpetuation of male dominance. Baha'u'llah's legal writings were composed in Arabic, a language which necessitated the use of the male gender when referring to God. In order to preserve the integrity of the text, Shoghi Effendi has stated that it is impermissible to change the gender of the writings even in the use of prayers. Baha'u'llah's more mystical writings, however, are in Persian, which has no gender. Nevertheless, these writings have, without exception, been translated into English using the male gender. The mystical-erotic language employed in many of these texts, which refer to God as the beloved, might suggest that the female gender would be more appropriate. Sufi mysticism often depicts God as a beautiful woman and Baha'u'llah's Persian writings utilize much Sufi imagery.

FROM EAST TO WEST

In 1892 Baha'u'llah passed away, leaving the leadership of the Baha'i community in the hands of his eldest son, Abdu'l'Baha. The following year, a Baha'i convert of Lebanese Christian background, Ibrahim Kheiralia, introduced the religion to the West. As was the case in nearly all religious groups in nineteenth-century America, women played a prominent role. Female converts generally outnumbered men by two to one. The August 20, 1910, issue or *Baha'i News* stated "nine-tenths of the active workers in the Cause in the West are women." Not all Baha'i men were delighted with this state of affairs. The same issue of *Baha'i News* contained a letter from Charles Mason Remey complaining that in most Baha'i localities women performed the bulk of the work, holding Baha'i meetings in the early afternoons when men were unable to attend. Women, he held, were content simply to attend meetings, but men needed to do work and very few localities were organized for "efficient work."

The belief existed among many American Baha'i men that women ought to confine their activities to the teaching work, leaving administrative activities to men. This opinion was apparently reinforced by many of the Iranian Baha'i teachers sent to America by Abdu'l-Baha. In the fall of 1899 Edward Getsinger organized a "Board of Counsel" for the Baha'is of northern New Jersey. Isabella Brittingham was appointed corresponding secretary but was not a voting member of that body. In March 1900 Thornton Chase reported that Chicago had formed a "Board of Counsel" consisting of ten men. Later that year Abdu'l-Karim Tihrani reorganized the board, expanding its membership to nineteen and including women. The following year Mirza Assadu'llah Isfahani again reorganized the governing body, insisting only men could be elected. At that time the board began calling itself the House of Justice.[30] Some Baha'i women expressed dissatisfaction with this arrangement, complaining that "Mirza Assad'ullah ignored us, although they were all invited to meet with us, and he established a House of Justice of men only."[31]

Perhaps most distressed with these developments was Corinne True, who appealed to Abdu'l-Baha to rescind the directive confining membership on the House of Justice to men. She received a reply from Abdu'l-Baha in June 1902 but refrained from sharing it with the Chicago Baha'is until the fall of that year. The letter read:

> Know thou, O handmaid, that in the sight of Baha, women are accounted the same as men, and God hath created all humankind in his own image, and after His own likeness. That is, men and women alike are the revealers of His names and attributes, and from the spiritual viewpoint there is no difference between them. . . .
>
> The House of Justice, however, according to the explicit text of the Law of God, is confined to men, this for a wisdom of the Lord God's, which will ere long be made manifest as clearly as the sun at high noon.
>
> As to you, O ye other handmaids who are enamoured of the heavenly fragrances, arrange ye holy gatherings, and found ye Spiritual Assemblies, for these are the basis for spreading the sweet savours of God, exalting His Word, uplifting the lamp of His grace, promulgating His religion and promoting His Teachings, and what bounty is there greater than this?[32]

Earlier, Corinne True along with Ella Nash had organized a ladies' auxiliary board which, after this letter, became known as the women's assembly of teaching. In practice this body functioned as a parallel institution to the Chicago house. It appears this body was able to maintain control of much of the funds of the Chicago Baha'i community, perhaps because the main contributors were women. The Chicago house frequently found itself without adequate financial support. At times their relations were anything but harmonious.

Thornton Chase, regarded as the first American Baha'i, strongly opposed the participation of women on Baha'i administrative bodies in communities where there were men available to serve. He believed women were much too emotional for these functions and that Baha'u'llah explicitly excluded their participation as "business controllers."[33] Abdu'l-Baha, however, did not seem to question women's abilities as planners and administrators. In 1903 the Chicago House of Spirituality determined to build a house of worship similar to one recently begun by Baha'is in Ishqabad, Russia. In 1906 Mrs. True visited Abdu'l-Baha in Palestine. At that time Abdu'l-Baha gave her specific instructions regarding the construction of the Chicago temple. Immediately afterward, Thornton Chase arrived in Palestine for his own pilgrimage. In response to Mr. Chase's questions regarding the temple, Abdu'l-Baha responded that he had given complete instructions to Mrs. True and that Chase should consult with her.[34]

When it became apparent that the construction of a house of worship constituted a more formidable task than the Chicago Baha'i community was then capable of undertaking. Corinne True urged the forming of a national Baha'i body for that purpose. With the approval of Abdu'l-Baha, delegates representing Baha'i communities throughout North America elected the Baha'i temple unity executive board in 1909. Of the nine members chosen, three were women, with Corinne True serving as financial secretary. Some of the Baha'i men objected to this "seeming open-handed kidnapping . . . of various institutions of the Cause by women." Others defended the women, insisting that at this stage the Baha'i faith required the kind of "mothering" that only women could provide.[35] By 1925 the executive board evolved into the National Spiritual Assembly of the Baha'is of the United States and Canada.

In 1909 Corinne True received a letter from Abdu'l-Baha in response to her insistent questioning on the issue of women serving on the Houses of Justice. It read:

> According to the ordinances of the Faith of God, women are the equals of men in all rights save only that of membership on the Universal House of Justice, for, as hath been stated in

the text of the Book, both the head and the members of the House of Justice are men. However, in all other bodies, such as the Temple Construction Committee, the Teaching Committee, the Spiritual Assembly, and in charitable and scientific associations, women share equally in all right with men.[36]

Unlike Abdu'l-Baha's previous correspondence, this letter seemed to exclude women's participation only on the, as yet, unformed international Baha'i body not on the local or national houses of justice.[37] At least this was the understanding of Corinne True, who again began to agitate for the election of women to the Chicago House of Spirituality. Not all Baha'is agreed with this interpretation, however, viewing it as a repetition of the Abdu'l-Baha's ruling in his earlier letter. Thornton Chase, irritated by True's activities, wrote in 1910:

> Several years ago, soon after the forming of the "House of Justice" . . . Mrs. True wrote to Abdu'l-Baha and asked if women should not be members of that House. He replied distinctly, that the House should be composed of men only, and told her that there was a wisdom in this. It was a difficult command for her to accept, and ever since (confidentially) there has been in that quarter and in those influenced by her a feeling of antagonism to the House of Spirituality, which has manifested itself in various forms. . . .
>
> Mrs. True received a Tablet, in which it was stated (in reply to her solicitation) that it was right for women to be members of all "Spiritual Gatherings" except the "Universal House of Justice," and she at once construed this to mean, that women were to be members of the House of Spirituality and the Council Boards, because in some of the Tablets for the House, it had been addressed as the "Spiritual Assembly" or "Spiritual Gathering."
>
> But the House of Spirituality could not so interpret the Master's meaning.[38]

Further investigation on the part of the Chicago House of Spirituality showed that elsewhere in the United States Abdu'l-Baha had authorized the election of both men and women to local bodies. They therefore concluded that "in organizing Spiritual Assemblies of Consultation *now*, it is deemed advisable by Abdu'l-Baha to have them composed of both men and women. The wisdom of this will become evident in due time, no doubt."[39] Apparently the members of this body expected that when local and national bodies became official "houses of justice" women would be removed from membership, but until then men would have to put up with the situation.[40] The all-male administrative bodies finally were completely dissolved by Abdu'l-Baha in his visit to America in 1912.

FROM WEST TO EAST

The introduction of the Baha'i faith to America had a profound effect on the position of Baha'i women in Iran. Western Baha'is began traveling to Iran, where they spoke to Baha'i gatherings. In the opening years of the twentieth century Iranian Baha'i women were still excluded from participation in Baha'i administrative institutions, had little access to education, and, in most cases, still wore the veil. Charles Mason Remey, who published a pamphlet relating his experiences in Iran in 1908, observed that many Persian Baha'i women expressed dissatisfaction with this state of affairs and began to agitate for change. He described one incident where he was speaking to a Baha'i gathering where men and women were separated by a curtain. Remey was asked by his hostess to describe the activities of Baha'i women in America. As he did, the hostess became more and more excited and finally drew back the curtain and urged the other women present to remove their veils and join the men. The men made room for the newcomers by withdrawing, somewhat uneasily, to the far side of the room. Bit by bit the men regained their composure, but then the women became rather embarrassed. Suddenly "all arose and like a flock of affrighted birds fluttered from the room."[41] Remey ended his account by suggesting that Western Baha'i women begin corresponding with their Eastern sisters. His hope was that eventually several would be able to settle in Iran as teachers and physicians.

The following year Dr. Susan Moody arrived from Chicago to join a small group of Iranian Baha'i doctors in establishing a hospital in Teheran. Over the next few years, Elizabeth Stewart, a nurse, Dr. Sarah Clock, and Lillian Kappes, a teacher, joined her. At this time a number of girls' schools were operated on an informal basis by Baha'i women. Since, with the assistance of American Baha'is, the community had maintained a highly reputed boys' school, Dr. Moody persuaded the executive committee of that school to adopt one of these girls' schools as a separate department. Eventually this school became one of the finest girls' college preparatory schools in Iran. In 1911 Godseah Ashraf became the first Iranian Baha'i woman to travel to America for the purpose of pursuing graduate work in educational psychology.[42] She then returned to Iran and taught in Baha'i schools.

During Abdu'l-Baha's travels to the West in 1911–1912, he made more explicit Baha'i teachings with regard to women's rights, stressing especially the need for women's education, the lack of which he viewed as the sole reason for the perceived inferiority of women. He deemed the education of mothers so essential to the proper upbringing of children that he held that the education of daughters should take precedence over that of sons. But Abdu'l-Baha did not restrict women's function in society to the home. He urged women to excel in all the arts and sciences and, further, expected their participation on an equal footing in the political sphere as well. He stated that women's political participation would be a prerequisite for peace. The only field (aside from membership on the Universal House of Justice) where Abdu'l-Baha did not extend full and equal participation was in military endeavors, since he regarded the taking of human life incompatible with women's role as mothers.

Copies of Abdu'l-Baha's talks were distributed throughout Iran, and these, along with the influence of American Baha'is residing in Iran, awakened Iranian Baha'i women to possibilities unthought of in previous generations. Apparently they began to advocate the immediate abolishment of the veil, as well as women's full participation in administrative affairs. Abdu'l-Baha was not entirely pleased with these developments, for, besides the stress and disunity these issues were creating within the Baha'i community itself, he felt that actions such as discarding the veil would bring on needless persecution in an already volatile situation. Abdu'l-Baha pleaded with the Iranian women not to do anything "contrary to wisdom."[43] Women's assemblages at this time should be confined to educational matters so that "differences will, day by day, be entirely wiped out, not that, God forbid, it will end in argumentation between men and women." Their efforts should be in the spiritual, not the political realm. Abdu'l-Baha would in time insure that they achieved full equality with men in all areas. In the meantime they ought not to agitate against the men for such changes. He chided the women for their impatience, saying "this newly born babe is traversing in one night the path that needeth a hundred years to tread."[44]

While women were allowed to vote within the Iranian Baha'i community, it was not until 1954 that they were permitted to serve on Baha'i institutions. As late as the 1970s one observer could only count two women delegates out of the more than one hundred attending the national Baha'i convention in Teheran.[45] Yet when the members of the National Spiritual Assembly of the Baha'is of Iran were arrested and executed in 1981, the chairperson was a woman, Zhinus Mahmudi.[46]

In recent years Baha'i institutions throughout the world have made a concerted efforts to insure equal participation of Baha'i women on them. Female membership in the higher institutions in the Americas and in Europe appears to be between 30 and 40 percent, while in Asia and Africa it remains at 10 to 20 percent. The numbers of women serving on national spiritual assemblies in the world has increased from 34 in 1953 to 354 in 1985.[47]

CONCLUSION

Perhaps no other religion offers a stronger scriptural basis for women's rights or a richer history for women to draw on than does the Baha'i faith. Yet cultural barriers, rigidity of certain administrative structures, conceptions of authority, and literalistic interpretations of scripture have at times militated against the ability of women to obtain full equality within the Baha'i community. Whereas all Baha'is in theory believe in the equality of men and women, there is no unanimity as to what that equality means. In many instances Baha'i conceptions of equality have distanced them from more radical forms of Western feminism. Whether or not Baha'i women will fully utilize the potentialities of Baha'i scriptures and history, or whether they will be relegated to "separate but equal spheres" that perpetuate structures of male dominance, remains to be seen. There exists no single theory of Baha'i feminism, but Baha'is, men and women alike, are agreed on one principle: hierarchical systems that place men above women in a divinely ordained order have no sanction within the Baha'i scriptures. In this respect the Baha'i faith is unique among revealed religions.

NOTES

INTRODUCTION

1 Though I have quoted liberally from the various chapters of the manuscript version of this volume, I alone am responsible for the general theories generated here. I hope that they do not do injustice to the scholarship of my colleagues.

2 Jordan Paper elaborates the following reasons for the incomplete historical record in his "Through the Earth Darkly: The Female Spirit in Native American Religions" in *Religion in Native North America*, edited by Christopher Vecsey (Moscow, Idaho: University of Idaho Press, 1990).

3 Ibid., 7.

4 Ibid., 17.

5 Sam D. Gill, *Mother Earth* (Chicago: University of Chicago Press, 1991).

6 Ibid., 5.

7 Ibid., 6, 14.

8 Ibid., 38.

9 Ibid., 21.

10 Ibid., 63–65.

11 Ibid., 66.

12 Quoted Ibid., 116.

13 Quoted Ibid., 118.

14 Dugan says that "perhaps it is inevitable that any people who work with the earth come to regard it as a mother-principle, and to speak of her identity and appearance in feminine terms." Earth as mother has

identity, personality, will, and emotions. Gill's analysis urges caution on this attribution. The symbolism is not always a personification of mother earth. More commonly, it is the idea that edible plants arise through the sacrifice of or gift by a goddess.

15 William Divale, *Matrilocal Residence in Pre-literate Society* (Ann Arbor, Michigan, UMI Research Press) 1984.

16 Divale notes the decline of the matriarchy theory in anthropology and observes that "matrilineal societies were at higher levels of cultural complexity than the patrilineal ones which they were supposed to have preceded, and that patrilineal societies were not the mirror image of matrilineal societies" (2). While much of Divale's theory is useful, he overstates the case. In this regard, he follows Alice Schlegel, *Male Dominance and Female Autonomy: Domestic Authority in Matrilineal Societies* (HRAF Press, 1972) who argues that authority is always in male hands in matrilocal and matrilineal societies. It is true that brothers and husbands wield considerable power in these societies but, at least in matrilocal ones, they experienced some marginalization and relative deprivation, which were projected into myths of matriarchy.

17 George R. Mead, *The Matrifocal Family: Transition, Economics, and Stress.* Museum of Anthropology, *Miscellaneous Series* no. 7, Colorado State College, 1968, 4.

18 Peggy Reeves Sanday, *Female Power and Male Dominance: On the Origins of Sexual Inequality* (Cambridge: Cambridge University Press, 1981) 117.

19 Ibid., 28.

20 Evan M. Zuesse, *Ritual Cosmos: The Sanctification of Life in African Religions* (Athens: Ohio University Press, 1979), 78.

21 Sanday, *Female Power,* 68.

22 Katherine K. Young, "Goddesses, Feminists, and Scholars," *The Annual Review of Women and World Religions* (SUNY Press, 1991). There is also evidence of dual sex symbolism and male deities.

23 This is also true of some hunting and gathering societies that have had cultural contact with horticulturalists or colonialists as in North America; the introduction of the horse and Western arms to such hunting societies, along with conflict over land rights, led to a warrior ethos.

24 They also appear among some groups of the Australian aborigines; this is likely due to culture contact with the horticultural societies of Melanesia. "Generally, myths of former female power are found in societies in which there is both male dominance and female power. . . . In all of these societies women have considerable autonomy. Naomi Quinn points out that male status among the Mundurucu is insecure and thus their ideology of dominance is defensive and uneasy. Myths of former female power provide men with a rationale for segregating themselves from women and a reason for dominating 'tyrannical' women. Wherever men perceive women in such terms, it is likely that women have considerable informal power. Thus, myths of former fe-

male power mirror the paradoxical relationship between the sexes that actually exists" (Sanday, *Female Power*, 181).

25 The Japanese do not identify themselves as Shintoists in the way that people think of themselves as Muslims, Buddhists, Christians, or Jews. The lives of women in Japan have been associated with Buddhism, Neo-confucianism (especially ancestor worship), and Shinto. While it is recognized that these religions may not be separable in Japanese experience, they may be distinguished in academic analysis. The fact that Shinto enjoys a chronological priority, notwithstanding the composite nature of Japanese culture, facilitates such an approach. In her essay for this volume, Yusa chooses to focus her essay not on the lives and roles of Japanese women today but rather on the ancient period of Japan when there were shamaness-queens. Accordingly, the essay is historical rather than anthropological in nature. It is extremely important, however, to demonstrate the thesis at hand.

26 Robert Ellwood, "Patriarchal Revolution in Ancient Japan: Episodes from the *Nihonshoki* Sujin Chronicle," *Journal of Feminist Studies in Religion*, 2:2 (1989).

27 Household deities and divination are very archaic religious phenomena in the history of religions. I would not attribute them to the changes proposed by Ellwood.

28 Sanday, *Female Power*, 28–29.

29 Some societies, however, may have retained feminine symbolism from an archaic kingdom that subsequently collapsed, though the cultural tradition continued at the village level.

30 The belief that women cannot be trusted also legitimates male secret societies.

31 Marion Kilson, "Women in African Traditional Religions" (*Journal of Religion in Africa*, vol. 8, facs. 2, 1976), 135–37.

32 Zuesse, *Cosmos*, 79.

33 By contrast, in hunting and gathering societies the onset of menses may be celebrated with initiation rituals performed by women. Among the Mbuti (a hunting and gathering tribe), "Menstrual blood in particular symbolizes life. . . . The blood that comes for the first time to the young girl comes as a gift, received with gratitude and rejoicing, because she is now a potential mother and can proudly take a husband. The girl enters seclusion taking with her all of her friends. Here they celebrate the happy event and are taught the arts and crafts of motherhood by an old and respected relative. They learn to live like adults and to sing songs of adult women. Pygmies from all around come to pay their respects, because for them this occasion is 'one of the happiest and most joyful occasions in their lives' " (Sanday, 24).

34 Lenora Greenbaum, "Societal Correlates of Possession Trance in Sub-Saharan Africa" in Bourguigon, ed., *Religion, Altered States of Consciousness and Social Change* (Columbus: Ohio State University Press, 1973), cited by Zuesse, *Cosmos*, 187.

35 Paper (n. 2, above), 16–17.

36 Mead, *Family*, 8

37 Ibid.

38 Young, "Goddesses," 137–42.

39 Katherine K. Young, "Introduction," *Women in World Religions* (Albany: SUNY Press, 1987), 21.

40 Considerable controversy surrounds the date of Zarathustra. According to Sven S. Hartman, *Parsism: The Religion of Zoroaster* (Leiden: E.J. Brill, 1980), the latest possible date is 600 B.C.E. since the name of the supreme god, Ahura Mazdāh, is post-Gāthic but pre-Achaemenid. "In the post-Gāthic Avesta the name is written in two words but in the Achaemenid inscriptions in one word (except for one single inscription). Since the writing in one word ought to be secondary in relation to the writing in two words, we may arrive at 600 B.C., at the latest, as the approximate dating of the post-gathic name—that is, a certain number of years before the Achaemenids. Zarathustra and the Gāthās must then belong to a still earlier time than about 600 B.C."(1). Hartman does not suggest how much earlier the prophet may have lived. Mary Boyce, in *Zoroastrians: Their Religious Beliefs and Practices* (London: Routledge and Kegan Paul, 1979) suggests that "Zoroastrianism was already old when it first enters recorded history" (1). On a basis of language (similar to the *Rgveda*) and religion (a reform of the ancient Indo-Iranian religion) described in the Gāthās (composed by Zarathustra), she suggests Zarathustra lived about 1400–1200 B.C.E. See *Textual Sources for the Study of Zoroastrianism* (Totowa, New Jersey: Barnes and Noble), 11. Others have suggested a date of about 1000 B.C.E.

41 The Avestan name of Zoroaster's father found in the *Vendidad*, however, contains the word for horse, *aspa*, as does the name of his patron (Vishtaspa). Curiously, Zoroaster does not mention bronze and the horse-drawn chariots; this may mean that his tribe had not begun to use the new technology, though these inventions were destabilizing the general region of the Russian steppes.

42 Originally, Ahura referred to Varuṇa when coupled with Mithra (as in the Vedic pair Mitra-Varuṇa) or was an epithet for Mithra and Apam Napāt (as in the Vedic *asura*). Mazdāh means "the Wise" (Hartman, *Parsism*, 2–3).

43 It is difficult to reconstruct the details of Zoroaster's life; the Gāthās mention his three marriages and one of the Gāthās (Y 53) refers to the marriage of his youngest daughter to the chief counselor of the tribal chief, Vishtaspa. According to the traditional biography, he left his own tribe when it refused to convert and went to the tribe of Vishtaspa who accepted the revelation of the prophet from God. In later conflicts with neighbouring tribes, Vishtaspa was victorious. These conquests along with proselytism and migrations may have helped to convert the tribes. It is very difficult, in the existing literature, to determine what ideas about women develop in which texts. Careful historical research has yet to be done.

44 Boyce, *Zoroastrians,* 39.

45 "Over the whole of the orderly and obsessively regulated vedic ritual there still hangs the dark cloud of a heroically violent world where gods and asuras are forever fighting each other in endlessly recurring rounds of conflict" (J. C. Heesterman, "Non-violence and Sacrifice" in *Indological Taurinensia,* vol. 12 [Torino: Edizioni Jollygrafica, 1984], 125]. The rise of kingdoms is almost always a time of warfare; India was no exception; the Kṣatriya warrior caste is prominent at this time and different religious groups begin to promote nonviolence as a reaction.

46 Katherine K. Young, "Hinduism," *Women in World Religions,* edited by Arvind Sharma (Albany: SUNY Press, 1987), 65.

47 Boyce, *Zoroastrians,* 94.

48 Ibid., 130

49 Pandurang Vaman Kane, *History of Dharmaśāstra* (Poona: Bhandarkar Oriental Research Institute, 1974), 2:594–95.

50 Young, "Hinduism," 76–79.

51 Padmanabh S. Jaini, *Gender and Salvation: Jain Debates on the Spiritual Liberation of Women* (Berkeley: University of California Press), 4.

52 Verne A. Dusenbery, "Punjabi Sikhs and Gora Sikhs: Conflicting Assertions of Sikh Identity in North America," *Sikh History and Religion in the Twentieth Century,* edited by Joseph T. O'Connell, Milton Israel, and Willard G. Oxtoby (Toronto: University of Toronto Press, 1988), 352–53.

53 Jaini, *Gender,* 25.

WOMEN IN AFRICAN RELIGIONS

The author would like to thank Miriam Levering, Rosalind Shaw, and Olabiyi Yai for their helpful comments on this paper and the Center for African Studies, University of Florida, for a research affiliate grant in the summer of 1989. This facilitated the research for and writing of this chapter. Invaluable bibliographic assistance was provided by Peter Malanchuk, the Africana bibliographer. A version of this paper was presented to the Institute for Cultural Studies at Ọbafẹmi Awolọwọ University on May 19, 1991. The author is grateful for the very valuable discussion, and in particular the suggestions of Mikelle Smith Omari and Miriam Travis.

1 An exception to this is the book by Theodora Foster Carroll, *Women, Religion and Development in the Third World* (New York: Praeger, 1983), although she does not, unfortunately, treat African or any other "tribal" religions.

2 There are at least two thousand ethnic groups in Africa, each with its own distinct religious traditions.

3 The concept of a "traditional"—timeless, ahistorical, and static—society is a Western invention, but the term is employed to denote the exclusion of more recent social contexts such as urban environments.

4   The edited work of Bennetta Jules-Rosette is extremely helpful in this regard, The New Religions of Africa (Norwood, N.J.: Ablex Publishing, 1979).

5   Smart has since revised this typology slightly in his The World's Religions (Englewood Cliffs, N.J.: Prentice Hall) by adding a seventh, the material dimension, which covers art and architectural expression. Preferring to retain the artistic images in proximity with particular ideas and rituals, I have opted for the earlier model.

6   I have been influenced in this regard by the work of art historians, notably the panel on "Ambiguity in African Sexual Metaphor" at the Eighth Triennial Symposium on African Art at the Museum of African Art, Washington, D.C., June 16, 1989.

7   Unless otherwise stated, the following account draws on the introduction to the book, Women and Class in Africa, eds. Robertson and Berger, 1986, 5f.

8   For information on the changes and choices faced by women regarding customary, civic, Christian, and Muslim marriages, see Pool 1972.

9   The following account of women's traditional roles draws on Women in Africa: Studies in Social and Economic Change, eds. Hafkin and Bay 1976, 7f.

10 This point requires more discussion than is possible here, but there are some who would argue that a word for "religion" exists, e.g., in Yoruba, esin, but that negative attitudes toward the indigenous religious cults have discouraged its use. This has led to the suggestion that the term only came into use with the advent of Christianity and Islam, as other have argued. I am grateful to Oyin Ogunba for this observation.

11 For comparative discussion on this topic, see Holden, Women's Religious Experience, 1983, 9.

13 Cited by Dime (1985, 40) from E. J. Alagoa, "IDU: Creator festival at Okpoma (Brass) in the Niger Delta," Africa 34,1 (January 1964):60.

14 The account of Mawu-Lisa is drawn chiefly from E. G. Parrinder, West African Religion (London: Epworth Press, 1961), pp. 17–18, and in African Ideas of God, ed. E. W. Smith (London: Edinburgh House Press, 1950), p. 226. The Fon, who live in the same region, also accept Mawu-Lisa as supreme, although the various vodu cults suggest that this is an androgynous being or two separate beings of the opposite sex, or even twins borne of Nanabukulu, a mother goddess; or another name for her; or the offspring of the parents of Gbade (another divinity). See M. J. Herskovits, Dahomey: An Ancient West African Kingdom (New York: Augustin, 1938), vol. 2, pp. 101–5.

15 This is evidenced by the cosmology and verses from the Ifa corpus, as well as myths and practices, such as the sacrificial use of a wooden knife rather than a metal one. This demonstrates the superiority and antecedence of Nana Buku over Ogun, the powerful god of iron, who attempted to usurp the authority of the former in earlier times. Olabiyi Yai, personal communication, August 8, 1989.

16 Here Odudua or Oduduwa is referred to as female, rather than the pre-
    vailing male conception. This sexual ambiguity of the progenitor of the
    Yoruba people is also apparent in the case of the farming deity, Orişa-
    Oko, and, to some extent, Olokun, a deity associated with Benin City
    and the sea.

17 This description of Nyame comes chiefly from Eva L.R. Meyerowitz,
    The Akan of Ghana (London: Faber and Faber 1958), pp. 131–33. Mey-
    erowitz pays much more attention to the female aspect of Nyame than
    other (male) writers on the Akan.

18 My information on Ala is taken from Arinze (1970) and Cole (1982).

19 S. O. Babayemi 1980. "The Fall and Rise of Qyǫ (ca. 1760–1905), a
    Study in Traditional Culture of an African Polity." Ph.D. thesis, Uni-
    versity of Birmingham, U.K., pp. 2–9 (cited by Armstrong 1982, 13.

20 The work of John S. Mbiti has been valuable in providing general, com-
    parative material on the various myths, beliefs, and practices of tradi-
    tional Africa. See his *Concepts of God in Africa* (London: SPCK, 1970)
    and *African Traditional Religions and Philosophy* (New York: Double-
    day, 1970). Here I am drawing in particular on a short piece entitled
    "Flowers in the Garden: The Role of Women in African Religion," *Af-
    rican Traditional Religions in Contemporary Society*, ed. J. K. Olupǫna.
    New York: Paragon House, 1991, pp. 59–72. Mbiti himself uses the
    work of Hermann Baumann, *Schöpfung und Urzeit des Menschen im
    Mythus der afrikanischer Völker* (Berlin: Reimer, 1964).

21 See previous note, Mbiti 1991, 61.

22 Ibid. 3.

23 All information on the Dinka is taken from Godfey Lienhardt, *Divinity
    and Experience* (Oxford: Clarendon Press, 1961), pp. 33–34, 198, 245.

24 The following account draws on Talbot 1968, 193–204.

25 Information is taken from E. J. Krige and J. D. Krige, *The Realm of a
    Rain Queen* (London: Oxford University Press, 1943), and J. D. Krige
    and E. J. Krige, "The Lovedu of the Transvaal" in *African Worlds*, ed.
    Forde, 1954, 55–82.

26 Qlabiyi Yai, personal communication, August 9, 1989.

27 For an account of the rituals involved in the initiation of a priestess
    into the Olokun cult of the Bini (Nigeria), see Joseph Nevadomsky with
    Norma Rosen, "The Initiation of a Priestess: Performance and Imagery
    in Olokun Ritual," *The Drama Review* 32,2 (T118) (summer 1988):
    186–207.

28 The phenomenon of spirit possession will be treated in the section on
    religious experience.

29 Qlabiyi Yai, personal communication, 14 August 1989.

30 Wande Abimbǫla, personal communication, 23 September, 1989.

31 For a rich and detailed account of such rituals among the Bantu in
    Tanzania, see Maria-Lisa Swantz, "The Religious and Magical Rites
    connected with the Life Cycle of the Woman in some Bantu Ethnic
    Groups of Tanzania," Ph.D. thesis, University of Dar-es-Salaam, Tan-
    zania, 1966.

32 For additional examples, see Turnbull's account of the *elima* premarital ritual among the Bambuti Pygmies (1962, 188–206) and Richards, Chisungu: A Girls' Initiation Ceremony among the Bemba of Northern Rhodesia, 1956.

33 The following account is based on Bonnie Weston's account of the northeastern Igbo in Cole and Aniakor 1984, 157–59.

34 There is also evidence of women masqueraders among the Bangwa of Cameroon (see R. Brain and A. Pollock, *Bangwa Funerary Art* (London: Duckworth, 1972, pp. 111–21) and among the Okpella, a northern Edo people of Nigeria (see J. Borgatti, "Dead Mothers of Okpella," *African Arts*, 13, 4 (1979):48–57). I am grateful to John R. Ojo for this information.

35 From a book on Ọṣun by Ademọla Onibonokuta and Tunji Beier, *The Okuta Percussion*, cited in an article on the Ọṣun festival, "She Reigns," in *Newswatch*, September 12, 1988.

WOMEN IN SHINTO

In this chapter, the number following an asterisk (*) signifies the order of the succession to the imperial throne.

After the manuscript has gone to press, Haruko Okano's *Die Stellung der Frau im Shintō* came to my attention. The work is highly recommended to anyone interested in the subject.

WOMEN IN SIKHISM

1 The eleven traditions being Udasi, Nirmala, Suthreshahi, Khalsa, Sangatshahi, Jitmali, Bakkatmali, Mihanshahi, Sahajdhari, Kuka, and Sarwaria.

2 The Ādi Granth or the Guru Granth Sahib, the primary scripture of the Sikhs, contains hymns attributed to Guru Nānak, followed by those of the third, fourth, fifth, and ninth gurus, and the verse of Kabīr, Farīd, Nāmdev, and Ravidās. The book is a collection of nearly six thousand hymns of the Sikh gurus (religious leaders) and various early and medieval saints of different religions and castes. The book was first compiled by the fifth Sikh guru, Arjun, at Amritsar in 1604 A.D. He included his own hymns and those of his predecessors, the gurus Nānak, Angad, Amardas, and Ramdas, and a selection of devotional songs of both Hindu and Islamic saints (notably Kabīr). In 1704 A.D. the tenth and last guru, Gobind Singh, added the hymns of his predecessor, Guru Tej Bahadur (the sixth, seventh, and eighth gurus did not write hymns), and enjoined that after his own death the Granth would take place of the gurus. The book opens with the Mūl Mantra (basic prayer), which is a declaration of the nature of God, followed by the Japjī (recital), the most

important Sikh scripture, written by the founder of the Sikh religion, Guru Nānak. The hymns are arranged according to the musical modes (*rāgas*) in which they are meant to be sung. The language is mostly Punjabi or Hindi, interspersed with Marathi, Persian, and Arabic words. After the death of Guru Gobind Singh his own hymns and other writings were compiled into a book known as the Dasam Granth.

3. The nine successors of Guru Nānak being gurus Angad, Amar Das, Ram Das, Arjan, Hargobind, Har Rai, Har Krishan, Tegh Bahadur, and Gobind Singh.

4. The literature (see bibliography) used, and people of the community (friends and total strangers) from across Canada and overseas, endorse the idea of equality between sexes.

5. The number indicates the page of the standard 1430-page printed original text of the Ādi Granth. It is to be noted that the quotations used in this study are from the English rendition of the Ādi Granth by Gurubachan Singh Talib more for reasons of convenience than choice. In fact, there is no adequate translation available in English. Much is lost in the process of translation mainly because certain concepts, words, and expressions remain unique to a given culture, and regardless of the quality of the translation, there are invariably portions that remain irreclaimable or misplaced. The task of translating the Ādi Granth continues to be demanding, as the hymns are arranged according to the Indian classical mode of music—that is to say, the sound as well the significance of the hymns are equally important. See *Sri Guru Granth Sahib* (4 vols.), translated by Gurubachan Singh Talib, Punjabi University, Patiala, 1987.

6. For a comprehensive description of the rites and procedures to be followed for the ceremonial, see Avtar Singh Vahira, *Khālsā Dharm Shāstar*, Amritsar, Sodhi Ram Narain Singh, 1914.

7. For extensive background on the ritual procedure, see Taihal Singh, *Gurmat Riti Anusār Vivāh Bidhi*, Lahore, 1903.

8. For a detailed description on Rāhat Maryādās, see the chapter in S. N. Mukherjee, ed., *Indian: History and Thought: Essays in Honour of A. L. Basham* (Calcutta: Subarnarekha, 1982).

9. There are four groups of Janam Sakhis, devotional biographies: the Puratan Janam-Sākhī, Miharban Janam-Sākhī, Bala Janam-Sākhī, and Gyan Ratnavali. For further details, see *Early Sikh Tradition: A Study of the Janamsākhīs* (Oxford: Clarendon Press, 1980).

WOMEN IN THE BAHA'I FAITH

Part of the research for this paper was made possible by a grant from the American Academy of Religion. I would like to thank Dr. Leslie Flemming, Mr. Anthony Lee, Mr. Richard Hollinger, Mr. Robert Stockman, and Rev. Paul Numrich for reading the earlier drafts and making helpful suggestions.

1 Abdu'l-Baha *The Promulgation of Universal Peace* (Wilmette: Baha'i Publishing Trust, 1982), 108.

2 Abdu'l-Baha cited in *Women* (Oakham: Baha'i Publishing Trust, 1986), 10.

3 Ibid., 29.

4 Ibid., Shoghi Effendi, entitled the Guardian served as head of the Baha'i community from 1921 to 1957.

5 Tahirih is not in the theological sense the most important woman in Babi-Baha'i history; that distinction belongs to Navvab, the wife of Baha'u'llah, and Bahiyih Khanum, his eldest daughter. Of the first figure, however, very little has been written in English, or to my knowledge in Persian. Bahiyyih Khanum is much better known, since she served as the de facto head of the Baha'i community several times. She has usually been depicted as playing a supportive role in relation to Abdu'l-Baha and Shoghi Effendi, although in the opinion of this writer she was much more of an independent actor. She has not attracted as much attention as Tahirih, about whom numerous (partly fictionalized) biographies exist. Tahirih is, in a word, a legend, and as such plays a much more important role among Baha'is as the paradigm of womanhood. Both in Iran and America, her name is probably the most popular Baha'i name given to girls.

6 Nineteen letters make up the Arabic phrase *Bismillah Ar-Rahman Ar-Rahim*, which introduces all but one of the *surihs* of the Quran. Hence the number nineteen has been endowed with great spiritual significance.

7 The Shaykhi school, founded by Shaykh Ahmad Ahsai (d. 1826) is a small sect within Twelver Shiism, which differs from the majority in that it denies the absolute authority of the *mujtahids* (ayatullahs) and holds to a less literal understanding of the resurrection. Nevertheless, they believed strongly in charismatic leadership and apparently, at this time, expected the eminent appearance of the Qa'im. Most of the early Babis were drawn from this sect. Tahirih had left Qazvin around 1843 in order to meet Siyyid Kazim Rashti, the Shaykhi head. He died shortly before her arrival. Supported by the widow of Rashti, Tahirih moved into his household where she taught classes and apparently assumed control of the more radical elements of the community there.

8 Abbas Amanat, *Resurrection and Renewal: The Making of the Babi Movement in Iran, 1844–1850* (Ithaca: Cornell University Press, 1989), 306–7.

9 The Bab's teachings certainly aimed at improving the condition of women by abolishing the temporary marriage allowable in Shi'ite Islam as well as instant divorce, but their position could hardly be regarded as equal.

10 Tahirih would, under normal circumstances, remain veiled. She removed it only when she had a particular point to make, no doubt because of its shock appeal.

11 Nabil-i-A'zam, *The Dawnbreakers: Nabil's Narrative of the Early Days of the Baha'i Revelation* (Baha'i Publishing Trust, Wilmette, 1979), 273–4.

12 After describing this incident, Abdu'l-Baha remarks: "These things would take place before the reality of this Cause was revealed and all was made plain. For in those days no one knew that the Manifestation of the Bab would culminate in the Manifestation of the Blessed Beauty (Baha'u'llah) and that the law of retaliation would be done away with, and the foundation-principle of the Law of God would be this, that "it is better for you to be killed that to kill;" that discord and contention would cease, and the rule of war and butchery would fall away. In those days, that sort of thing would happen" (*Memorials of the Faithful* Baha'i Publishing Trust, Wilmette, 1971), 198–99.)

13 Tahirih's father remained convinced of her innocence as well as her chastity, but the accusations caused him untold grief. At one point, the prayer leader at the Friday mosque or Qazvin read a verse mocking Mulla Salih: "No glory remains on that house/From which the hens crow like the cocks." Mulla Salih was said to have remained silent, as tears ran down his cheeks to his beard (Amanat, *Resurrection*, 322).

14 *Dawnbreakers*, 297.

15 H. Nugaba'i, *Tahirih* (Teheran: 128 Badi/1972 A.C.E.), 60.

16 Shoghi Effendi, *God Passes By* (Baha'i Publishing Committee, Wilmette), 32.

17 Ibid.

18 Baha'u'llah apparently proved instrumental in bringing about the reconciliation. His subsequent actions show that he himself, while advocating a total break with Islam, believed in nonviolent means for attaining the Babi aims.

19 Execution by strangulation was probably chosen to avoid the prohibition of shedding a woman's blood. Baha'i children were later executed in a similar manner.

20 *God Passes By*, 75.

21 Peter Smith, *The Babi and Baha'i Religions* (Cambridge, 1987), 92–93.

22 Research Department of the Universal House of Justice, *Women* (Oakham: Baha'i Publishing Trust, 1986), 2.

23 Ibid., 1.

24 The basic contents of the *Kitab-i Aqdas* can be found in *A Synopsis and Codification of the Kitab-i Aqdas* (Haifa: Universal House of Justice, 1973). This author made use of a manuscript copy of the Arabic text as well as several unpublished translations.

25 The independent investigation of truth is a paramount principle within the Baha'i faith and Baha'is are free and, indeed, enjoined to pursue their own understanding of the sacred text. Only Abdu'l-Baha (d. 1921) and after him, Shoghi Effendi (d. 1957) were authorized to make authoritative interpretations binding upon the body of believers. This is in di-

rect contrast to the Shi'ite practice of having a select group of clerics (*mujtahids*, now commonly known as *ayatullahs*) who alone are deemed capable of interpreting scripture. The laity must "imitate" (*taqlid*) one of these leaders in all matters of divine law. Baha'u'llah has forbidden both this form of interpretation and "blind imitation." Shoghi Effendi is regarded as infallible in his interpretations of the sacred text, and the Universal House of Justice is considered infallible in matters of legislation. This infallibility appears to me to be primarily an issue of moral immaculacy, since if the House of Justice makes a decision based on misinformation, it can be changed. Whether or not the accuracy of Shoghi Effendi's interpretations are likewise subject to his having had correct information regarding the context of the revealed scriptures, is an issue, which, to my knowledge, has never been addressed.

26 R. Jackson Armstrong-Ingram offers some valuable insights into these issues in *Dialogue*, vol. 2, no. 1, 19–25.

27 This argument is made by Linda and John Walbridge in "Baha'i Laws and the Status of Men" in *World Order*, Fall 1984. 25–36.

28 Responses to the Walbridge thesis can be found in "A Question of Gender: A Forum on the Status of Men in Baha'i Law," *Dialogue*, Fall 1987, vol. 2, no. 1, 14–34.

29 In this regard it should be noted that the inequality of women in Islam, as stated in the Quran, rests on economic grounds: "Men are the protectors and maintainers of women. Because God has given the one more than the other, and because they support them from their means. Therefore the righteous women are devoutly obedient, and guard in absence what God would have them guard." (Quran 33:35).

30 In 1902 Abdu'l-Baha urged the Chicago House of Justice to rename itself the house of spirituality in order to insure that no one should imagine its aims to be political. Later local and national bodies became known as spiritual assemblies and the term house of justice was reserved for the world administrative body: the Universal House of Justice. In the early part of the twentieth century the use of most of these terms was quite fluid. "Spiritual Assemblies," for instance, referred to nearly every sort of Baha'i gathering or body. In the future local and national bodies will be called houses of justice.

31 Cited in "The Service of Women on the Institutions of the Baha'i Faith" an unpublished paper by Anthony Lee, Peggy Caton, Richard Hollinger, Marjan Nirou, Nader Saiedi, Shahin Carrigan, Jackson Armstrong-Ingram, and Juan Cole (undated), 15–16. Much of what follows in this section has been derived from sources cited in this paper, although my interpretation of that material differs in that this paper argues that the 1909 letter did not necessarily refer to the Universal House of Justice as we now understand it. While it is true the word usage has sometimes changed within the Baha'i writings, I do not think

this is the case here. Abdu'l-Baha used that word in its present technical sense as early as 1903 when writing his will and testament.

32 *Selections from the Writings of Abdu'l-Baha* (Haifa: Baha'i World Centre, 1976), 79–80.

33 Chase to Scheffler, 5/10/10, Chase Papers, National Baha'i Archives.
Cited in Anthony Lee et al., "Service," 32. The same year Thornton
Chase wrote in a letter to Mason Remey: "women are emotional, uncertain, unsteady, unwise in business affairs, carried away by 'devotion,'
given to dreams and imaginations, and I am convinced that as long as
the Cause in this land is so largely in the hands of women, it CANNOT
PROSPER. . . . As long as the 'feminine element' dominates the movement, it cannot be carried on wisely and well" Chase to Remey January
19, 1910, National Baha'i Archives).

34 Bruce Whitmore, *The Dawning Place (Wilmette: Baha'i Publishing
Trust, 1984)*, 36.

35 Ibid., 23–24.

36 Cited in the May 31, 1988, letter of the universal house of justice to the
national spiritual assembly of the Baha'is of New Zealand.

37 The universal house of justice was first elected in 1963.

38 Chase to Remey, 1/19/10, Chase Papers, National Baha'i Archives.
Cited in Anthony Lee et al., "Service," 32.

39 House of Spirituality (Albert R. Windust, librarian to Board of Consultation, Kenosha, Wis., 7/23/10, House of Spirituality Papers, National
Baha'i Archives. Cited in Anthony Lee et al., "Service."

40 Shoghi Effendi, as well as the Universal House of Justice, have held that
references to male membership in the House of Justice refer specifically
to the Universal House of Justice and will never be applied to local and
national bodies. The Universal House of Justice seems to hold that
Abdu'l-Baha, in his 1909 letter, was merely clarifying the points in his
1902 letter, and that there was therefore no real change in policy. This
would presume that Abdu'l-Baha, in his first letter to Corinne True, did
not really understand the intent of her question and was ignorant of the
controversy in Chicago, which caused her to write to him. However,
Nathan Ruthstein, Corinne True's biographer insists, "Certainly
Abdu'l-Baha was aware of what was happening. The House of Spirituality sent Him weekly reports, and Mirza Asadu'llah was in contact
with Him" 32. The position of the Universal House of Justice is that
"the law regarding the membership of the Universal House of Justice is
embedded in the Text and has been merely restated by the divinely appointed interpreters. It is therefore neither amenable to change nor subject to speculation about some possible future condition." They go on
to say "the important fact to remember is that in the face of the categorical pronouncements in Baha'i Scripture establishing the equality of
men and women, the ineligibility of women for membership of the
Universal House of Justice does not constitute evidence of the superi-

ority of men over women" (May 31, 1988). From the standpoint of the Universal House of Justice this matter is immutable because of Baha'i positions with regard to authoritative interpretation and not because of any view of the status of women as such.

41. *Observations of a Bahai Traveller* (n.p., 1908), 76.

42. R. Jackson Armstrong-Ingram, "American Baha'i Women and the Education of Girls in Tehran, 1909–1934." *In Iran* (Los Angeles: Kalimat Press, 1986), 181–210.

43. Besides carrying the general meaning "wisdom" (*hikmat*) has a technical meaning in many of the Baha'i writings. To act according to wisdom generally infers behaving such a way as not to attract opposition toward the Baha'i faith in a situation where persecution or misunderstanding might otherwise result even when it is necessary to compromise some Baha'i principle to do so. Acts of providence which might otherwise be seen as negative are also described as having a "wisdom" if they benefit the progress of the religion in some unforseen way.

44. Portions of this letter are contained in *Women*. 5–6. Unfortunately no further information or even the date are provided regarding it, so I have been forced to be a little speculative regarding its context. The final line quoted is a well-known Persian proverb.

45. Peggy Caton, *Equal Circles*, xvi. (Los Angeles: Kalimat Press, 1987).

46. Mrs. Mahmudi had been a scientist of national prominence in Iran, where she served as president of the Iranian School of Meteorology. Unlike persecutions of the previous century, the Islamic republic of Iran has shown no reticence about executing female Baha'is. On June 18, 1983, ten Baha'i women were hanged in Shiraz. Since then all Baha'i institutions in Iran have been disbanded.

47. Statistics on the participation of women in Baha'i institutions can be found in *Dialogue*, Summer/Fall 1986, 31.

BIBLIOGRAPHY

INTRODUCTION

Boyce, Mary. 1979. *Zoroastrians: Their Religious Beliefs and Practices.* London: Routledge and Kegan Paul.

———. 1975. *Textual Sources for the Study of Zoroastrianism.* Totowa, New Jersey: Barnes and Noble.

Divale, William. 1984. *Matrilocal Residence in Pre-literate Society.* Ann Arbor, Michigan: UMI Research Press.

Dusenbery, Verne A. 1988. "Punjabi Sikhs and Gora Sikhs: Conflicting Assertions of Sikh Identity in North America." *Sikh History and Religion in the Twentieth Century.* Eds. Joseph T. O'Connell, Milton Israel, and Willard G. Oxtoby. Toronto: University of Toronto Press.

Ellwood, Robert. 1989. "Patriarchal Revolution in Ancient Japan: Episodes from the *Nihonshoki* Sujin Chronicle." *Journal of Feminist Studies in Religion,* 2:2.

Greenbaum, Lenora. 1973. "Societal Correlates of Possession Trance in Sub-Saharan Africa." *Religion, Altered States of Consciousness and Social Change.* Ed. Erika Bourguigon. Columbus: Ohio State University Press.

Gill, Sam D. 1991. *Mother Earth.* Chicago: University of Chicago Press.

Hartman, Sven S. 1980. *Parsism: The Religion of Zoroaster.* Leiden: E. J. Brill.

Hesterman, J. C. 1984. "Non-violence and Sacrifice." *Indological Taurinensia,* vol. 12. Torino: Edizioni Jollygrafica.

Jaini, Padmanabh S. 1991. *Gender and Salvation: Jain Debates on the Spiritual Liberation of Women.* Berkeley: University of California Press.

Kane, Pandurang Vaman. 1974. *History of Dharmaśāstra.* Poona: Bhandarkar Oriental Research Institute. 2:594–95.

Kilson, Marion. 1976. "Women in African Traditional Religions." *Journal of Religion in Africa.* Vol. 8, facs. 2, 135–37.

Mead, George R. 1968. *The Matrifocal Family: Transition, Economics, and Stress.* Museum of Anthropology, Miscellaneous Series no. 7, Colorado State College.

Paper, Jordan. 1990. "Through the Earth Darkly: The Female Spirit in Native American Religions." *Religion in Native North America.* Ed. Christopher Vecsey. Moscow, Idaho: University of Idaho Press.

Sanday, Peggy Reeves. 1981. *Female Power and Male Dominance: On the Origins of Sexual Inequality.* Cambridge: Cambridge University Press.

Young, Katherine K. 1981. "Goddesses, Feminists, and Scholars." *The Annual Review of Women and World Religions.* Eds. Arvind Sharma and Katherine K. Young. Albany: SUNY Press.

————. 1987. "Hinduism." *Women in World Religions.* Ed. Arvind Sharma. Albany: SUNY Press.

————. 1987. "Introduction." *Women in World Religions.* Ed. Arvind Sharma. Albany: SUNY Press.

Zuesse, Evan M. 1979. *Ritual Cosmos: The Sanctification of Life in African Religions.* Athens: Ohio University Press.

WOMEN IN NATIVE AMERICAN RELIGIOUS TRADITIONS

Allen, Paula Gunn. 1986. *The Sacred Hoop: Recovering the Feminine in American Indian Traditions.* Boston: Beacon Press.

Bataille, Gretchen M., and Kathleen Mullen Sands. 1984. *American Indian Women Telling Their Lives.* Lincoln: University of Nebraska Press.

Brown, Joseph, ed. and recorder. 1971. *The Sacred Pipe. Black Elk's Account of the Seven Rites of the Oglala Sioux.* New York: Penguin Books, 1985.

De Maillie, Raymond J., ed. 1984. *The Sixth Grandfather: Black Elk's Teachings Given to John G. Neihardt.* Lincoln: University of Nebraska Press.

Fletcher, Alice, and Frances La Flesche. 1972. *The Omaha Tribe,* vol. 2. Lincoln: University of Nebraska Press. 2 vols.

Grinnell, George Bird. *The Cheyenne Indians: Their History and Ways of Life.* 1923. 2 vols. Yale University Press.

Hungry Wolf, Beverly. *The Ways of My Grandmothers.* 1981. New York: William Morrow.

Landes, Ruth. 1969. *The Ojibwa Woman.* New York: AMS Press.

Medicine, Bea. 1978. *The Native American Woman.* Las Cruces: New Mexico State University.

Moon, Sheila. 1984. _Changing Woman and Her Sisters: Feminine Aspects of Selves and Duties._ San Francisco: Guild for Psychological Studies Publ. House.

Niethammer, Carolyn. 1977. _Daughters of the Earth._ New York: Macmillan.

Powell, Peter J. _Sweet Medicine._ 1979. Vol 2. Norman: University of Oklahoma Press. 2 vols.

Qoyawayma, Polingaysi. 1964. _No Turning Back._ As told to Vada F. Carlson. Albuquerque: University of New Mexico Press.

Reichard, Gladys. 1974. _Navajo Religion._ Princeton: Princeton University Press.

Shaw, Anna Moore. 1974. _A Pima Past._ Tucson: University of Arizona Press.

Steiger, Brad. 1984. _Indian Medicine Power._ West Chester, Pennsylvania: Schiffer Publishing.

Tsosie, Rebecca. 1988. "Changing Women: The Crosscurrents of American Indian Feminine Identity." _American Indian Culture and Research Journal_ 12:1, 1–37.

Walker, J. R. _The Sun Dance and Other Ceremonies of the Oglala Division of the Teton Dakota._ New York: AMS Press (reprint of 1917 ed.)

Wallace, Anthony F. C. 1970. _The Death and Rebirth of the Seneca._ New York: Knopf.

WOMEN IN AFRICAN RELIGIONS

Adams, Monni. 1986. "Women and Masks among the Western We of the Ivory Coast." _African Arts_ 19, 2 (February): 46–55.

Afonja, Simi. 1986. "Women, Power and Authority in Traditional Yoruba Society." _Visibility and Power: Essays on Women in Society and Development,_ eds. L. Dube, et al. Delhi: Indian University Press.

African-American Institute. 1976. _African Women/African Art: An Exhibition Illustrating the Different Roles of Women in African Society._ Guest curator, Roslyn A. Walker. New York: African-American Institute.

Amadiume, Ife. 1987. _Male Daughters, Female Husbands: Gender and Sex in an African Society._ London: Zed Press.

Ardener, E. 1975. "The 'Problem' Revisited." _Perceiving Women,_ ed. S. Ardener.

Ardener, S., ed. 1975. _Perceiving Women._ London: Dent Malaby.

Arinze, F. A. 1970. _Sacrifice in Igbo Religion._ Ibadan: Ibadan University Press.

Armstrong, R. G. 1982. "Is Earth Senior to God? An Old West African Theological Controversy." _African Notes_ 9, 1:7–21.

Barber, K. 1991. _I Could Speak Until Tomorrow: "Oriki", Women and the Past in a Yoruba Town._ Edinburgh: Edinburgh University Press for the International African Institute.

Beattie, J., and J. Middleton, eds. 1969. *Spirit Mediumship and Society in Africa*. London: Routledge, Kegan and Paul.

Berger, Iris. 1976. "Rebels or Status-Seekers? Women as Spirit Mediums." *Women in Africa*, eds. Hafkin and Bay, 157–82.

Binford, Martha. 1989. "Julia: An East African Diviner." *Unspoken Worlds: Women's Religious Lives*, eds. Falk and Gross, 3–14.

Boone, Sylvia A. 1986. *Radiance from the Waters: Ideals of Feminine Beauty in Mende Art*. New Haven: Yale University Press.

Boyd, Jean 1989. *The Caliph's Sister, Nana Asma'u, 1793–1865: Teacher, Poet and Islamic Leader*. London: Frank Cass.

Boyd, Jeann, and Murray Last. 1985. "The Role of Women as 'Agents Riligieux' in Sokoto." *Canadian Journal of African Studies* 19, 2: 283–300.

Brown, Karen McCarthy. 1989. "Mama Lola and the Ezilis: Themes of Mothering and Loving in Haitian Vodou." *Unspoken Worlds, Women's Religious Lives*, eds. Falk and Gross, 235–45.

———. 1991. *Mama Lola*. Los Angeles and Berkeley: University of California Press.

Calame-Griaule, Geneviève. 1965. *Ethnologie et Langage: la Parole chez les Dogon*. Paris: Gallimard.

Callaway, Helen. 1980. "Women in Yoruba Tradition and in the Cherubim and Seraphim Society." *The History of Christianity in West Africa*, ed. O. Kalu. London: Longman, 321–32.

Cole, Herbert M. 1982. *Mbari: Art and Life among the Owerri Igbo*. Bloomington: Indiana University Press.

Coulon, C. 1988. "Women, Islam and *Baraka*." *Charisma and Brotherhood in African Islam*, eds. D. B. Cruise O'Brien and C. Coulon. Oxford: Clarendon, 111–33.

Dime, C. A. 1985. "God: Male, Female or Asexual?" *Orita* 17,1:37–50.

Douglas, Mary. 1960. "The Lele of the Kasai." *African Worlds*, ed. Forde, 1–26.

Drewal, H. J. ed. 1988. "Object and Intellect: Interpretations of Meaning in African Art." *Art Journal* 47,2 (summer).

Drewal, Henry John, and Margaret Thompson Drewal. 1983. *Gelede: Art and Female Power among the Yoruba*. Bloomington: Indiana University Press.

Ezeanya, S. N. 1976. "Women in African Traditional Religion." *Journal of Religion in Africa* 10,2:105–21.

Falk, Nancy, and Rita Gross. 1989 (2nd ed.). *Unspoken Worlds: Women's Religious Lives*. Belmont, Calif.: Wadsworth.

Field, M. J. 1960. *Search for Security*. Evanston: Northwestern University Press.

———. 1937. *Religion and Medicine among the Gã People*. London.

Forde, Daryll, ed. 1954. *African Worlds*. London: Oxford University Press.

Gaba, Christian. 1987. "Women and Religious Experience among the Anlo of West Africa." *Women in the World's Religions*, ed. U. King, 177–98.

Glaze, Anita. 1986. "Dialectics of Gender: Senufo Masquerades." *African Arts* 19,3:30–39, 82.

———. 1975. "Woman Power and Art in a Senufo Village." *African Arts* 8,3:20–29, 64–68, 90.

Gleason, Judith. 1987. *Oya: In Praise of the Goddess.* Boston: Shambhala.

Hackett, Rosalind I. J. 1989. *Religion in Calabar: The Religious Life and History of a Nigerian Town.* Religion and Society, 26. Berlin: Mouton de Gruyter.

———, ed. 1987. *New Religious Movements in Nigeria.* Lewiston, N.Y.: Edwin Mellen Press.

———. 1985. "Sacred Paradoxes: Women and Religious Plurality in Nigeria." *Women, Religion and Social Change.* eds. Y. Haddad and E. Findly. Albany, N.Y.: SUNY Press, 247–70.

Hafkin, N. J., and Bay, E. G., eds. 1976. *Women in Africa: Studies in Social and Economic Change.* Stanford: Stanford University Press.

Hay, Margaret Jean, and Sharon Stichter, eds. 1984. *African Women South of the Sahara.* London: Longman.

Hoch-Smith, Judith, and Anita Spring, eds. 1978. *Women in Ritual and Symbolic Roles.* New York: Plenum Press.

Holden, Pat, ed. 1983. *Women's Religious Experience.* London: Croom Helm.

Horton, Robin. 1969. "Types of Spirit Possession in Kalabari Religion." *Spirit Mediumship and Society in Africa,* eds. Beattie and Middleton, 14–49.

Houlberg, Marilyn H. 1973. "Ibeji Images of the Yoruba." *African Arts* 7,1:202-27, 90–92.

Idowu, E. Bolaji. 1962. *Olodumare: God in Yoruba Belief.* London: Longman.

Isichei, Elizabeth. 1988. "On Masks and Audible Ghosts: Some Secret Male Cults in Central Nigeria." *Journal of Religion in Africa* 18, 1:42–70.

Janzen, John. 1977. "The Tradition of Renewal in Kongo Religion." *African Religions: A Symposium,* ed. N. Booth. New York: Nok.

Jules-Rosette, Bennetta. 1987. "Privilege Without Power: Women in African Cults and Churches." *Women in Africa and the African Diaspora,* eds. R. Terbory-Penn et al. Washington, D.C.: Howard University Press.

———. 1980. "Changing Aspects of Women's Initiation in Southern Africa." *Canadian Journal of African Studies* 13:1–16.

———, ed. 1979. *The New Religions of Africa.* Norwood, N.J.: Ablex.

Kiernan, J. P. 1982. "The 'Problem of Evil' in the Context of Ancestral Intervention in the Affairs of the Living in Africa." *Man* NS 17,2.

Kilson, Marion. 1972. "Ambivalence and Power: Mediums in Gā Traditional Religion." *Journal of Religion in Africa* 4,3:171–77.

———. 1975. "Ritual Portrait of a Ga Medium." *Journal of African Studies* 2,3:395–418.

————. 1976. "Women in African Traditional Religions." *Journal of Religion in Africa* 8,2:133–43.

King, Ursula, ed. 1987. *Women in the World's Religions, Past and Present.* New York: Paragon Press.

Lan, David. 1985. *Guns and Rain: Guerillas and Spirit Mediums in Zimbabwe.* London: James Currey.

Lawuyi, Olatunde B. 1988. "The Reality and Meaning of Being a Woman in the Yoruba Cosmogonic Myths, An Anthropologist's Contribution to O. Gbadegesin's 'Destiny, Personality and the Ultimate Reality and Meaning of Human Existence: A Yoruba Perspective' (*URAM* 7: 173–88)." *Ultimate Reality and Meaning,* 11,3:233–42.

Lawuyi, Olatunde B., and J. K. Olupọna. "Metaphoric Associations and the Concept of Death: Analysis of a Yoruba World View." *Journal of Religion in Africa,* 18, 1: 2–14.

Levine, R. A. 1963. "Witchcraft and Sorcery in a Gusii Community." *Witchcraft and Sorcery in East Africa,* eds. Middleton and Winter, 221–55.

Lewis, I. M. 1971. *Ecstatic Religion.* Harmondsworth, U.K.: Penguin Books.

MacCormack, Carol P. 1979. "Sande: The Public Face of a Secret Society." *The New Religions of Africa,* ed. Jules-Rosette, 27–37.

Marwick, M., ed. 1970. *Witchcraft and Sorcery.* Harmondsworth, U.K.: Penguin Books.

————. "Witchcraft as a Social Strain-Gauge." *Witchcraft and Sorcery,* ed. Marwick.

Mbon, Friday M. 1987. "Women in African Traditional Religions." *Women in the World Religions, Past and Present,* ed. Ursula King, 7–23.

McKenzie, P. R. 1976. "Yoruba *Orișa* Cults: Some Marginal Notes concerning their Cosmology and Concepts of Deity." *Journal of Religion in Africa* 8,3:189–207.

Mernissi, Fatima. 1977. "Women, Saints and Sanctuaries." *Signs* 3,1:101–12.

Meyerowitz, Eva L. 1958. *The Akan of Ghana.* London: Faber and Faber.

Middleton, J., and E. H. Winter, eds. 1963. *Witchcraft and Sorcery in East Africa.* London: Routledge and Kegal Paul.

Morton-Williams, Peter. 1964. "The Yoruba Ogboni Cult in Ọyọ." *Africa.* 30.

Morton-Williams, Peter. 1960. "An Outline of the Cosmology and Cult Organization of the Ọyọ Yoruba." *Africa* 34, 3.

Nadel, S. F. 1970. "Witchcraft in Four African Societies." *Witchcraft and Sorcery,* ed. Marwick.

Nevadomsky, J., with Norma Rosen. 1988. "The Initiation of a Priestess: Performance and Imagery in Olokun Ritual." *Drama Review,* 32,2 (T118) (summer).

Pool, Janet E. 1972. "A Cross-Comparative Study of Aspects of Conjugal Behavior among Women of Three West African Countries." *Canadian Journal of African Studies* 6,2:233–59.

Richards, Audrey I. 1956. *Chisungu: A Girls' Initiation Ceremony among Bemba of Northern Rhodesia.* London: Faber and Faber.

Robertson, Claire, and Iris Berger. eds. 1986. *Women and Class in Africa.* New York: Africana.

Salamone, Frank. 1986. "Religion and Repression Enforcing Feminine Inequality in an 'Egalitarian Society.' " *Anthropos* 81:517–28.

Schapera, I. 1970. "Sorcery and Witchcraft in Bechuanaland." *Witchcraft and Sorcery,* ed. Marwick.

Shaw, Rosalind. 1985. "Gender and the Structuring of Reality in Temne Divination: An Interactive Study." *Africa* 55, 3:286–303.

Shostak, Marjorie. 1981. *Nisa: The Life and Words of a !Kung Woman.* Cambridge: Harvard University Press.

Smart, Ninian. 1983. *Worldviews: Crosscultural Explorations of Human Beliefs.* New York: Scribner's.

Sojourner, Sabrina. 1982. "From the House of Yemanja: The Goddess Heritage of Black Women." *The Politics of Women's Spirituality: Essays on the Rise of Spiritual Power within the Feminist Movement,* ed. Charlene Spretnak. Garden City, N.Y.: Anchor Books, 56–63.

Spring, Anita. 1978. "Epidemiology of Spirit Possession among the Luvale of Zambia." *Women in Ritual and Symbolic Roles,* eds. Hoch-Smith and Spring.

Strobel, Margaret. 1984. "Women in Religion and in Secular Ideology." *African Women South of the Sahara,* eds. Hay and Stichter, 87–101.

Swantz, Maria-Liisa. 1966. "The Religious and Magical Rites connected with the Life Cycle of the Woman in some Bantu Ethnic Groups of Tanzania." Ph.D. thesis, University of Dar-es-Salaam, Tanzania.

Talbot, D. Amaury. 1968 [1915]. *Woman's Mysteries of a Primitive People.* London: Frank Cass.

Talbot, P. A. 1969 [1926]. *The Peoples of Southern Nigeria,* 2 vols. London: Frank Cass.

Tonkin, Elizabeth. 1982. "Women Excluded? Masking and Masquerading in West Africa." *Women's Religious Experience,* ed. Holden, 163–74.

Turnbull, Colin. 1962. *The Forest People: A Study of the Pygmies of the Congo.* New York: Doubleday.

Turner, Victor W. 1968. *The Drums of Affliction.* Oxford: Clarendon Press.

Wenger, Susanne, and Gert Chesi. 1983. *A Life with the Gods: In their Yoruba Homeland.* Worgl, Austria: Perlinger.

Whyte, Susan Reynolds. 1983. "Men, Women and Misfortune in Bunyole." *Women's Religious Experience,* ed. Holden, 175–92.

Wilson, P. J. 1967. "Status Ambiguity and Spirit Possession." *Man* N.S. 3:67–78.

Zahan, Dominique. 1979. *The Religion, Spirituality, and Thought of Traditional Africa.* Chicago: University of Chicago Press, 1979.

Zuesse, Evan. 1979. *Ritual Cosmos: The Ritual Sanctification of Life in African Religions.* Athens: Ohio University Press.

WOMEN IN SHINTO

Anzu Motohiko, and Umeda Yoshihiko, ed. 1968. *Shintō jiten.* Tokyo: Hori Shoten.

Asai Torao. 1985. *Nyokan tsūkai.* Tokyo: Kōdansha.

Aston, W. G. 1905. *Shinto (The Way of the Gods).* London, New York, and Bombay: Longmans, Green.

————. 1907. *Shinto, the Ancient Religion of Japan.* London: Archibald Constable.

————, tr. 1972. *Nihongi, Chronicles of Japan from the Earliest Times to A.D. 697.* Rutland: Charles Tuttle.

Baba Akiko. 1969. *Shikishi Naishinnō.* Tokyo: Kinokuniya.

Bock, Felicia G. tr. 1970. *Engi-Shiki, Procedures of the Engi Era,* vol. 1 (book I-V). Tokyo: Sophia University.

————. 1984. "Shito—As Seen Through Western Eyes." *Shintō-shi-ron sōsho (Takigawa Masajirō Sensei Beiju Kinen Ronbunshū).* Tokyo: Kokusho Kankō-kai, 1–23.

————. 1984. "Seiyōjin no me kara mita Shintō," tr. by Hirai Naofusa. *Shintō-shi-ron sōsho (Takigawa Masajirō Sensei Beiju Kinen Ronbunshū).* Tokyo: Kokusho Kankō-kai, 1073–87 (translation of the above article into Japanese).

Bowring, Richard, tr. 1982. *Murasaki Shikibu, Her Diary and Poetic Memoirs.* Princeton: Princeton University Press.

Chamberlain, Basil Hall, tr. 1981. *The Kojiki, Records of Ancient Matters.* Rutland: Charles Tuttle.

Ellwood, Robert. 1967. "The *Saigū:* Princess and Priestess." *History of Religions* (August 1967), 35–60.

————. 1986. "Patriarchal Revolution in Ancient Japan: Episodes from the *Nihonshoki* Sūjin Chronicle." *Journal of Feminist Studies in Religion,* 2.2 (Fall 1986), 23–37.

Fujitani Toshio, and Naoki Kōjirō, 1960. *Ise Jingū.* Tokyo: San-itsu Shobō.

Hagiwara Tatsuo, ed. 1985. *Ise shinkō: I.* Tokyo: Yūzankaku.

Holtom, D. C. 1928. *The Japanese Enthronement Ceremonies.* Tokyo: Kyōbunkan.

Hori Ichirō. 1968. *Folk Religion in Japan.* Chicago and London: University of Chicago Press.

Katō Genchi. 1971. *A Study of Shinto.* New York: Barnes and Noble.

Katō Genchi, and Hoshino Hikoshirō, tr. 1972. *Kogoshūi, Gleanings from Ancient Stories.* London: Curzon Press; New York: Barnes and Noble.

Keene, Donald, ed. 1970. *Twenty Plays of the No Theatre.* New York and London: Columbia University Press.

Kishimoto Yoshio. 1972. *Shintō nyūmon.* Tokyo: Kenpakusha.

Kondō Yoshihiro, ed. 1959. *Shintō-shū.* Tokyo: Kadokawa.

Kuroita Katsumi, et al., ed. 1965. *Engishiki (Shintei-zōho-Kokushi taikei),* v. 26. Tokyo: Yoshikawa Kōbunkan.

Makita Shigeru. 1981. *Kami to onna no minzokugaku.* Tokyo: Kōdansha.
Miyata Noboru. 1979. *Kami no minzokugaku.* Tokyo: Iwanami.
Murakami Shigeyoshi. 1977. *Tennō no saishi.* Tokyo: Iwanami.
Murakami Shigeyoshi, and Yasumaru Yoshio, eds. 1971. *Minshū shūkyō no shisō.* Tokyo: Iwanami.
Nishigaki Seiji. 1983. *Oisemairi.* Tokyo: Iwanami.
————, ed. 1984. *Ise shinkō: II.* Tokyo: Yūzankaku.
Ōbayashi Taryō. 1984. "Ise saigū no girei to shinwa," in his *Higashi Ajia no ōken shinwa,* Tokyo: Kōbundō, 70–76.
Okano, Haruko. 1976. *Die Stellung der Frau im Shintō.* Wiesbaden: Otto Harrassowitz.
Ōnishi Yoshiaki, ed. 1971. *Kagerō Nikki shinchūshaku.* Tokyo: Meiji Shoin.
Origuchi Shinobu. 1956. "Joteikō." *Origuchi Shinobu zenshū,* vol. 20. Tokyo: Chūōkōronsha, 1–23.
Otto, Rudolf. 1970. *The Idea of the Holy.* London: Oxford University Press.
Philippi, Donald L., tr. 1969. *Kojiki.* Tokyo: University of Tokyo Press.
Saigō Nobutsuna. 1967. *Kojiki no sekai.* Tokyo: Iwanami.
Taguchi Yōichi, ed. 1969. *Sarashina Nikki no kaishaku to kanshō.* Tokyo: Yūseidō.
Takatori Masao. 1979. *Shintō no seiritsu.* Tokyo: Heibonsha.
Tsunoda, Ryusaku, et al., ed. 1958. *Sources of Japanese Tradition.* New York and London: Columbia University Press.
Ueda Masaaki. 1970. *Nihon shinwa.* Tokyo: Iwanami.
————. 1973. *Nihon no jotei.* Tokyo: Kōdansha.
Umeda Yoshihiko. 1973. *Ise Jingū no shiteki kenkyū.* Tokyo: Yūzankaku.
Wakamori Tarō. 1964. *Onna no isshō.* Tokyo: Kawade Shōbō.
Watanabe Yasutada. 1964. *Ise to Izumo.* Tokyo: Heibonsha.
Yamakami Izumo. 1980. *Miko no rekishi.* Tokyo: Yūzankaku.
Yamakawa Uichi, ed. 1924. *Jingi jiten.* Tokyo: Heibonsha.
Yanagita Kunio. 1962. "Imōto no chikara." *Yanagita Kunio shū,* vol. 9. Tokyo: Chikuma Shobō, 1–219.

WOMEN IN JAINISM

Alsdorf, Ludwig. 1974. *Kleine Schriften,* herausgegeben von A. Wezler. Wiesbaden.
Babb, Lawrence A. 1988. "Giving and Giving up: The Eightfold Worship among Śvetāmbar Mūrtipūjak Jains." *Journal of Anthropological Research* 44, no. 1: 67–86.
Balbir, Nalini. 1983. "Observations sur la secte jaina des Terāpanthin." *Bulletin d'Etudes Indiennes* (Paris) 1:39–45.
Basham, Arthur L. 1951. *History and Doctrine of the Ājīvikas, A Vanished Indian Religion.* London.

Bhattacharya, Hari Satya. 1967. English translation and commentary of the *Pramāṇanayatattvālokālamkāra* of Vādidevasūri. Bombay: Jain Sahitya Vikas Mandal.

Cort, John. 1987. "Medieval Jaina Goddess Traditions." *Numen* 34, no. 2, December: 235–55.

Deo, Shantaram Bhalcandra. 1950. "Jaina Temples, Monks and Nuns in Poona." *The Jaina Antiquary* 16, no. 1: 17–33.

——. 1956. *History of Jaina Monachism from Inscriptions and Literature*. Poona.

Jaini, Padmanabh S. 1979. *The Jaina Path of Purification*. Delhi: Motilal Banarsidass.

——. 1986. "*Muktivicāra* of Bhāvasena: Text and Translation." *Indologica Taurinensia* 13:203–19.

——. 1991. *Gender and Salvation. Jaina Debates on the Spiritual Liberation of Women*. University of California Press.

Jambūvijaya Muni, ed. 1974. Śākaṭāyana, *Strīnirvāṇa-kevalibhuktiprakaraṇe*. Bhavnagar.

Leslie, I. Julia. 1989. *The Perfect Wife. The Orthodox Hindu Woman according to the Strīdharmapaddhati of Tryambakayajvan*. Delhi: Oxford University Press.

Mahias, Marie-Claude. 1985. *Délivrance et convivialité. Le système culinaire des Jaina*. Paris: Editions de la Maison des Sciences de l'Homme.

Misra, Rajalakshmi. 1972. "The Jains in an Urban Setting (The Ascetics and the Laity among the Jains of Mysore City)." *Bulletin of the Anthropological Survey of India* 21, nos. 1–2, January-June 1972: 1–68.

Mṛgāvatī, Sādhvī. 1989. "Sādhvī Sangh . . . ek vinatī." *Atma Vallabh Smarika*. Delhi: 51.

Radford Ruether, Rosemary. 1987. "Christianity." In *Women in World Religions*, ed. A. Sharma. Albany: SUNY Press, 207–33.

Reynell, Josephine. 1987. "Prestige, honour and the family: Laywomen's religiosity amongst the Śvetāmbar Mūrtipūjak Jains in Jaipur." *Bulletin d'Etudes Indiennes* 5: 313–59.

——. 1991. "Women and the Reproduction of the Jain Community." *The Assembly of Listeners. Jains in Society*. Eds. M. Carrithers and C. Humphrey. Cambridge University Press, 41–65.

Roth, Gustav. 1983. *Mallī-Jñāta. Das achte Kapitel des Nāyādhammakahāo im sechsten Aṅga des Śvetāmbara Jainakanons*. Wiesbaden: Franz Steiner Verlag.

Schubring, Walther. 1977. *Kleine Schriften*. Herausgegeben von K. Bruhn, Wiesbaden.

Schuster Barnes, Nancy. 1987. "Buddhism." *Women in World Religions*, ed. A. Sharma. Albany: SUNY Press, 105–33.

Shah, Umakant P. 1987. *Jaina-Rūpa-Maṇḍana* (Jaina iconography). Delhi: Abhinav Publications.

Shântâ, N. 1985. *La voie jaina. Histoire, spiritualité, vie des ascètes pèlerines de l'Inde*. Paris: O.E.I.L.

Stevenson, Margaret Sinclair. 1915. *The Heart of Jainism*. Delhi: Motilal Banarsidass, 1970, reprint.

Williams, R. 1963. *Jaina Yoga*. London (reprint 1983); Delhi: Motilal Banarsidass.

WOMEN IN ZOROASTRIANISM

Boyce, Mary. 1971. "The Zoroastrian House of Yazd." *Iran and Islam: In Memory of the Late Vladimir Minorsky*, ed. C. E. Bosworth, 125–47. Edinburgh: University Press.

────. 1975. *A History of Zoroastrianism*, vol 1. *Handbuch der Orientalistik*, ed. B. Spuler. Leiden: E. J. Brill.

────. 1977. *A Persian Stronghold of Zoroastrianism*. Oxford: Clarendon Press.

────. 1979. *Zoroastrians: Their Religious Beliefs and Practices*. London: Routledge and Kegan Paul.

────. 1982. *A History of Zoroastrianism*, vol. 2. *Handbuch der Orientalistik*, ed. B. Spuler. Leiden: E. J. Brill.

Buch, Maganlal A. 1919. *Zoroastrian Ethics. The Gaekwad Studies in Religion and Philosophy*, IV. Baroda: A. G. Widgery.

Carmody, Denise L. 1987. "Judaism." *Women in World Religions*, ed. Arvind Shama, 183–206. Albany: SUNY Press.

Census of India. 1883. *Census 1881: Bombay City and Island*. Bombay: Times of India Steam Press.

Census of India. 1984. *Census of India, 1981, Series 1—India, Paper 3 of 1984, Household Population by Religion of Head of Household*. Appendix A, p. 58. Delhi: Manager of Publications.

Choksy, Jamsheed K. 1988. "Women in the Zoroastrian Book of Primal Creation: Images and Functions Within a Religious Tradition." *Mankind Quarterly* 29, nos. 1–2, 73–83.

────. 1989. *Purity and Pollution in Zoroastrianism: Triumph Over Evil*. Austin: University of Texas Press.

Culpepper, Emily E. 1974. "Zoroastrian Menstruation Taboos: A Women's Studies Perspective." *Women and Religion*, eds. Judith Plaskow and Joan Arnold, 199–210. Missoula: Scholars Press.

Desai, Sapur Faredun. 1948. *A Community at the Cross-Road*. Bombay: New Book Company.

────. 1963. *The Parsi Panchayet and its Working: A Synoptic Survey*. Bombay: Trustees of the Parsi Punchayet Funds and Properties.

────. 1977. *History of the Bombay Parsi Punchayet 1860–1960*. Bombay: Trustees of the Parsi Punchayet Funds and Properties.

Dhalla, Maneckji Nusserwanji. 1922. *Zoroastrian Civilization: From the Earliest Times to the Downfall of the Last Zoroastrian Empire 651 A.D.* New York: Oxford University Press.

────. 1938. *History of Zoroastrianism*. New York: Oxford University Press.

Doctor, Adi F. 1988. "The State of Zoroastrian Orthodoxy." *Parsiana* 11, no. 2, 91–98.

Douglas, Mary. 1966. *Purity and Danger: An Analysis of the Concepts of Pollution and Taboo.* London: Routledge and Kegan Paul.

Fischer, Michael M. J. 1978. "On Changing the Conceptual Position of Persian Women." *Women in the Muslim World,* eds. Lois Beck and Nikki Keddie, 189–215. Cambridge: Harvard University Press.

Gae, Rustom S. 1977. "Adoption Marriage and Divorce." *Parsiana* 1, 18:40–47.

Gould, Ketayun H. 1972. "Parsis and Urban Demography: Some Research Possibilities." *Journal of Marriage and the Family* 34, no. 2, 345–52.

————. 1980 "Singling Out a Demographic Problem: The Never-Married Parsis." *Journal of Mithraic Studies* 3, nos. 1–2. 166–84.

————. 1982. "The Never-Married Parsis: A Demographic Dilemma." *Economic and Political Weekly* 17, no. 26, 1063–72.

————. 1983. "Sex Inequalities in the Dual System of Education: Parsis of Gujarat." *Economic and Political Weekly* 18, no. 39, 1668–76.

————. 1987. "An Aging, Dwindling Community." *Parsiana* 9, no. 9, 44–51.

————. 1988. "Parsi Demography: Biological or Sociocultural?" Paper presented at the South Asia Seminar, University of Texas at Austin, April 14, 1988.

————. In press. "A Perspective on the Parsis: The Minority-Majority." *Individuals and Ideas in Traditional India: Ten Interpretive Studies,* ed. Jagdish P. Shama. Jodhpur: Kusumanjali Prakashan.

Haug, Martin. 1878. *The Parsis: Essays on their Sacred Language, Writings and Religion.* Revised by K. W. West. New Delhi: Cosmo Publications, reprint, 1978.

Hays, H. R. 1964. *The Dangerous Sex: The Myth of Feminine Evil.* New York: Putnam's.

Hinnels, John R. 1978. "Parsis and the British." *Journal of the K. R. Cama Oriental Institute,* no. 46, 2–92.

————. 1981. *Zoroastrianism and the Parsis.* London: Ward Lock Educational.

————. 1985. "An Ancient Religion in Modern Exile: Contemporary Zoroastrianism Outside Iran." Paper presented at the 76th annual meeting of the American Academy of Religion, Anaheim, November 23–26. 19 pages.

Irani, Gustasp. 1990. "Our Faith is One." *Parsiana* 12, no. 7, 24–28.

Jessawalla, Dosebai Cowasjee. 1911. *The Story of My Life.* Bombay: Times Press.

Kaiser-E-Hind. 1902. "Parsi Chokrio Ane Angraji Kaluvni." Vol. 21, no. 1063, May 11:5 (in Gujarati).

Karkal, Malini. 1984. *Survey of Parsi Population of Greater Bombay.* Bombay: International Institute for Population Sciences and Trustees of the Parsi Punchayet Funds and Properties.

Katrak, Jamshid Cawasji. 1965. *Marriage in Ancient Iran.* Bombay: published by the author.

Khullar, Ava. 1990. "Demographic Despair." *Parsiana* 12, no. 7, 34–44.

Kulke, Eckehard. 1974. *The Parsees in India: A Minority as Agent of Social Change.* Delhi: Vikas Publishing House.

Lerner, Gerda. 1986. *The Creation of Patriarchy.* New York: Oxford University Press.

Lincoln, Bruce. 1981. *Emergency from the Chrysalis: Studies in Rituals of Women's Initiation.* Cambridge: Harvard University Press.

Malabari, Behramji M. 1884. *Gujarat and the Gujaratis: Picture of Men and Manners Taken from Life.* Bombay: Education Society's Press.

Masani, R. P. 1939. *Dadabhai Naoroji: The Grand Old Man of India.* London: George Allen and Unwin.

Mody, Jehangir, R. P. 1959. *Jamsetjee Jejeebhoy: The First Indian Knight and Baronet.* Bombay: published by the author.

Murzban, M. M. 1917. *The Parsis in India: Being an Enlarged and Copiously Annotated Up To Date English Edition of Mile. Delphine Menant's Les Parsis.* Bombay: published by the author, 2 vols.

O'Flaherty, Wendy Doniger. 1976. *The Origins of Evil in Hindu Mythology.* Berkeley: University of California Press.

Pangborn, Cyrus R. 1982. *Zoroastrianism: A Beleaguered Faith.* New Delhi: Vikas Publishing House.

Pavry, Jal Dastur Cursetji. 1929. *The Zoroastrian Doctrine of a Future Life: From Death to the Individual Judgement.* New York: Columbia Univeristy Press.

Paymaster, Rustom Burjorji. 1954. *Early History of the Parsees in India: From their Landing in Sanjan to 1700 A.D.* Bombay: Zartoshti Dharam Sambandhi Kelavni Apnari Ane Dnyan Felavnari Mandli.

Paymaster, Feroza, and Jeroo Gorimar. 1976. "Can Anyone Convert?" *Parsiana*, September, 32–35.

Power, Eileen. 1975. *Medieval Women*, ed. M. M. Postan. Cambridge: Cambridge University Press.

The Privy Council Judgement: Saklat vs Bella-1." 1991. *Parsiana* 12, no. 10:28–30.

"Readers' Forum." 1990. *Parsiana* 12, no. 12, 3–6.

Rudolph, Lloyd, and Susanne Hoeber Rudolph. 1967. *The Modernity of Tradition.* Berkeley: University of California Press.

Sahiar, Gooloo H. 1955. "Social Change with Particular Reference to the Parsi Community." Doctoral dissertation, School of Economics and Sociology, University of Bombay.

Sanjana, Darab Dastur Peshotan. 1892. *The Position of Zoroastrian Women in Remote Antiquity.* Bombay: Education Society Steam Press.

———. 1932. *Collected Works of the Late Dastur Darab Peshotan Sanjana.* Bombay: British India Press.

Shahzadi, Ervad Rustam. 1990. "Adopting to Future Possibilities." *Parsiana* 12, no. 9, 37–40.

Simmons, H. Michael. 1987. "The Spandarmad/Jeh Syzygy." Paper presented at the annual meeting of the Middle East Studies Association, Baltimore. 7 pages.

Swidler, Leonard. 1974. "Is Sexism a Sign of Decadence in Religion?" Women and Religion, eds. Judith Plaskow and Joan Arnold, 167–75. Missoula: Scholars Press.

Toddywalla, Parinaz. 1987a. "Obstacles to a Novjote." Parsiana 9, no. 8, 1–6.

———. 1987b. "The Federation Debates Equal Rights." Parsiana 10, no. 5, 24–29.

Tong, Paul K. K. 1977. "A Cross-Cultural Approach to Women's Liberation Theology." Beyond Androcentrism: New Essays on Women and Religion, ed. Rita M. Gross, 335–347. Missoula: Scholars Press.

Vacha, P. B. 1950. Firdousi and the Shahnama. Bombay: New Book Company.

Visaria, Leela. 1972. "Religious and Regional Differences in Mortality and Fertilitly in the Indian Subcontinent." Doctoral dissertation, Princeton University.

———. 1974. "Demographic Transition among Parsis: 1881–1971, III-Fertility Trends." Economic and Political Weekly 9, no. 43, 1828–32.

Young, Katherine K. 1987. "Introduction." Women in World Religions, ed. Arvind Sharma. 1–36. Albany: SUNY Press.

Zaehner, R. C. 1955. Zurvan: A Zoroastrian Dilemma. Oxford: Clarendon Press.

———. 1956. The Teachings of the Magi: A Compendium of Zoroastrian Beliefs. London: George Allen and Unwin.

———. 1961. The Dawn and Twilight of Zoroastrianism. London: Weidenfeld and Nicolson.

WOMEN IN SIKHISM

Akbar, M. J. 1985. India: The Seige Within. New Delhi: Penguin.

Gross, Rita M. 1987. Tribal Religions: Aboriginal Australia. Arvind Sharma, ed., Women in World Religions. Albany, N.Y.: SUNY Press.

Honigberger, J. M. 1952. Fifty-Five Years in the Past. London: H. Bailliere.

Ibbetson, D. C. 1883. The Religion of the Punjab. Calcutta: Government Printing Press.

Kinsley, David. 1986. Hindu Goddesses. Berkeley: University of California Press.

Kishwar, Madhu. 1988. Nature of Women's Mobilization. Economic and Political Weekly, Dec. 24–31.

Macauliffe, M. A. 1909. The Sikh Religion. Oxford: Oxford University Press, vol. 1.

Manushi 1987, no. 40.

McLeod, W. H. 1989. *The Sikhs: History, Religion and Society.* New York: Columbia University Press.

———. 1984. *Textual Sources for the Study of Sikhism.* Manchester, Manchester University Press.

———. 1980. *Early Sikh Tradition: A Study of the Janamsākhīs.* Oxford: Clarendon Press.

Oberoi, Harjot Singh. 1988. "From Ritual to Counter Ritual." J. T. O'Connell, M. Israel and W. G. Oxtoby, eds., *Sikh History and Religion in the Twentieth Century.* Toronto: Centre for South Asian Studies, University of Toronto.

———. 1987. "A World Reconstructed: Religion, Ritual and the Community among the Sikhs." Ph.d. dissertation, Canberra, Australia, Faculty of Asian Studies, Australian National University.

Singh, Khuswant. 1966. *A History of the Sikhs.* Delhi: Oxford University Press, vols. 1 and 2.

Singh. Ranbir. 1965. *Glimpses of the Divine Masters.* New Delhi: International Trade Corporation.

Smith, W. C. 1962. *The Meaning and End of Religion.* New York: Macmillan.

Trotter, L. J. 1880. *Life of Lord Lawrence.* Oxford: Oxford University Press, vol. 1.

Young, Katherine K. 1987. *Hinduism.* Arvind Sharma, ed., *Women in World Religions.* Albany, N.Y.: SUNY Press.

WOMEN IN THE BAHA'I FAITH

Abdu'l-Baha. 1971. *Memorials of the Faithful.* Wilmette: Baha'i Publishing Trust.

———. 1976. *Selections from the Writings of Abdu'l-Baha.* Haifa: Baha'i World Centre.

———. 1982. *The Promulgation of Universal Peace.* Wilmette: Baha'i Publishing Trust.

Amanat, Abbas. 1989. *Resurrection and Renewal: The Making of the Babi Movement in Iran, 1844–1850.* Ithaca: Cornell University Press.

Armstrong-Ingram, R. Jackson. 1986. "American Baha'i Women and the Education of Girls in Tehran, 1909–1934." *In Iran: Studies in Babi and Baha'i History,* vol. 3, ed. Peter Smith, 181–210. Los Angeles: Kalimat Press.

Baha'u'llah. 1973. *Synopsis and Codification of the Kitab-i Aqdas.* Haifa: Universal House of Justice.

Caton, Peggy. 1987. *Equal Circles: Women and Men in the Baha'i Community.* Los Angeles: Kalimat Press.

Effendi, Shoghi. 1944 *God Passes By.* Wilmette: Baha'i Publishing Committee.

Maneck, Susan Stiles, et al. 1987. "A Question of Gender: A Forum on the Status of Men in Baha'i Law." *Dialogue*, 2, no. 1, 14–34.

———. 1989. "Tahirih: A Religious Paradigm of Womanhood," in *The Journal of Bahai Studies* 2, no. 2, 39–54.

Nabil-i-A'zam. 1979. *The Dawnbreakers: Nabil's Narrative of the Early Days of the Baha'i Revelation*. Wilmette: Baha'i Publishing Trust.

Nugaba'i, H. 1972. *Tahirih*. Tehran: n.p.

Remey, Charles Mason. 1908. *Observations of a Baha'i Traveler*. n.p.

Research Department of the Universal House of Justice, eds. 1986. *Women*. Okham: Baha'i Publishing Trust of the United Kingdom.

Smith, Peter. 1987. *The Babi and Baha'i Religions*. Cambridge: Cambridge University Press.

Walbridge, Linda and John. 1984. "Baha'i Laws and the Status of Men." *World Order*, 18, no. 1, 25–36.

Whitmore, Bruce. 1984. *The Dawning Place*. Wilmette: Baha'i Publishing Trust.

CONTRIBUTORS

NALINI BALBIR (PhD. 1980, DLitt. 1986, Paris) is professor at the University of Paris-3 (Sorbonne Nouvelle) since 1988 where she teaches Sanskrit, Middle-Indian languages, and Hindi, and member of the research group UA 1058 (CNRS). She is specialized in Middle-Indian and Jaina studies. Her publications include translations and study of Jain narrative and religious literature as well as research on modern Jainism (places of pilgrimage, festivals). Besides several articles (in French and English), she is the author of three books: *Dānâṣṭakakathā* (Paris, 1982); *Récits jaina: le corpus āvaśyakéen*, vol. 1 (Alt- und Neu-Indische Studien, Hamburg; in press); *La Défaite d'Amour*. Poème allégorique jaina de Nāgadeva (in collaboration with J.-P. Osier. Paris: Ed. du Cerf; in press). She is also the editor of the *Bulletin d'Etudes Indiennes* (Paris).

KATHLEEN DUGAN is a professor of Theological and Religious studies at the University of San Diego. In her career there she has taught broadly in the field of religious studies, centering her research and teaching on contemporary Catholic theology and its dialogue with the world's religious traditions. Focus on the spiritual center of each tradition led to inquiry concerning the central ritual of vision questing guiding the Native American Indian religious traditions, and many years of research into the vibrant presence of the primal traditions in our world. Growing interest in the diverse ways of perception and knowledge among the sexes, as well as in diverse cultures, led to the present article.

KETAYUN H. GOULD is professor emerita in the school of Social Work, University of Illinois at Urbana-Champaign. She is a partner in Independent Scholars Associated, and now lives in Stafford, Virginia. She received her Ph.D. from the University of Pittsburgh in 1966 in social work. She has taught at the University of Illinois at Urbana-Champaign from 1968 to 1990, when she elected the early retirement option to pursue her research and scholarship. She has done research in India, the United States, and England. Her writings have dealt with two main areas: feminist theory, models, and practice frameworks in the area of women and ethnic minority concerns in social work, and historical and demographic studies of the Parsi Zoroastrian community in India. She has written extensively on topics related to these issues. Currently she is authoring a book on the historical and demographic decline of the Parsi Zoroastrian community in the rural and urban areas of Gujarat, India. From the early 1970s, she has also been very active in serving on university and national committees and commissions in social work and Asian studies to improve the status of women and/or minorities in academia and the professions. She is a member of the Parsi Zoroastrian community, and considers her dual scholarly interests as an extension of her own dual identity and cultural experiences.

ROSALIND I. J. HACKETT is associate professor of religious studies at the University of Tennessee, Knoxville. She received her Ph.D. from the University of Aberdeen, Scotland, in 1986 and has taught and conducted research in West Africa at the Universities of Ibadan and Calabar from 1975 to 1983, and again in 1991 at Obafemi Awolowo University, Ile-Ife, and the University of Ghana, Legon. She has published two books, *New Religious Movements in Nigeria* (ed.) (1987) and *Religion in Calabar: the Religious Life and History of a Nigerian Town* (1989). She has also published many articles on religion and social change in Nigeria and is currently focusing on Christian revivalist and charismatic movements in Africa, and bringing to completion a manuscript *Art and Religion in Africa*.

SUSAN STILES MANECK received her A.B. in religious studies from the University of California at Santa Cruz, her M.A. in oriental studies from the University of Arizona, and is currently completing her Ph.D. in history from the University of Arizona. She has taught at Northern Arizona University, the University of the South, and Franklin and Marshall College. She presently teaches Middle East history at Murray State University in Kentucky. Her publications include: "The Conversion of Religious Minorities to the Baha'i Faith in Iran" (*The Journal of Baha'i Studies* 3, no. 3 [1991], 33–48); "Tahirih: A Religious Paradigm of Womanhood" (*Journal of Baha'i Studies,* 2, no. 2 [1990], 39–54); "The Presbyterians and the Parsis" *Fides et Historia,* 21, no. 2 [1989], 51–60); "The Conversion of Zoroastrians to the Baha'i Faith in Yazd, Iran" (*From Iran East and West,* ed. Juan Cole, Los Angeles: Kalimat Press, 1984, pp. 67–93).

RAJKUMARI SHANKER received her M.A. from the University of Rajasthan, Jaipur, India, and Ph.D. from the University of Sorbonne, Paris, France. She has been teaching at the University of Ottawa in the Department of Religious Studies since 1976. She also works as a freelance development consultant for the Canadian International Development Agency (CIDA), especially on issues pertaining to women in development.

ARVIND SHARMA (B.A., Allahabad 1958; M.A., Syracuse 1970; M.T.S., Harvard Divinity School 1974; Ph.D., Harvard University 1978) is professor of comparative religion in the faculty of religious studies at McGill University, Montreal, Canada. He has published several papers and monographs on the position of women in Indian religions. He is the editor of *Women in World Religions* (SUNY Press, 1987) and co-editor of the journals *The Annual Review of Women in World Religions* and *Gender in World Religions.*

KATHERINE K. YOUNG is associate professor, history of religions, McGill University. She publishes in the areas of South Indian religions, gender and religion, and comparative ethics. She has co-authored with H. C. Coward and Julius J. Lipner *Hindu Ethics: Purity, Abortion, and Euthanasia* (State University of New York Press) and has edited *Hermeneutical Paths to the Sacred Worlds of India* (Scholar's Press). She has a forthcoming book entitled *New Perspectives on Women in Hinduism.* Along with being the general editor of a series with State University of New York Press called McGill Studies in the History of Religions: A Series Devoted to International Scholarship, she is one of the editors of *The Annual Review of Women in World Religions* (State University of New York Press) and *Gender in World Religions* (McGill).

MICHIKO YUSA (Ph.D., department of religious studies, University of California, Santa Barbara) is associate professor of Japanese and East Asian studies at Western Washington University. Her training is cross-cultural and interdisciplinary, and she is currently working in the areas of modern Japanese philosophy, philosophy of Zen Buddhism, and medieval Japanese aesthetics. Her publications include *Basic Kanji* (Tokyo: Taishūkan, 1989); an English translation of Nishida Kitarō's final essay, "The Logic of *Topos* and the Religious Worldview," *Eastern Buddhist*, 19.2 (1986) and 20.1 (1987); "*Riken no ken:* Zeami's Theory of Acting and Theatrical Appreciation," *Monumenta Nipponica*, 42.3 (1987); "Nishida and the Question of Nationalism," *Monumenta Nipponica* 46.2 (1991). She is writing an intellectual biography of the founding figure of modern Japanese philosophy, Nishida Kitarō.

INDEX OF NAMES

INDEX OF TERMS

SUBJECT INDEX